# Transforming Vocation

# Australian College of Theology Monograph Series

SERIES EDITOR GRAEME R. CHATFIELD

The ACT Monograph Series, generously supported by the Board of Directors of the Australian College of Theology, provides a forum for publishing quality research theses and studies by its graduates and affiliated college staff in the broad fields of Biblical Studies, Christian Thought and History, and Practical Theology with Wipf and Stock Publishers of Eugene, Oregon. The ACT selects the best of its doctoral and research masters theses as well as monographs that offer the academic community, scholars, church leaders and the wider community uniquely Australian and New Zealand perspectives on significant research topics and topics of current debate. The ACT also provides opportunity for contributors beyond its graduates and affiliated college staff to publish monographs which support the mission and values of the ACT.

Rev. Dr. Graeme Chatfield
Series Editor and Associate Dean

# Transforming Vocation

Connecting Theology, Church, and the
Workplace for a Flourishing World

Edited by
DAVID BENSON,
KARA MARTIN,
and
ANDREW SLOANE

WIPF & STOCK · Eugene, Oregon

TRANSFORMING VOCATION
Connecting Theology, Church, and the Workplace for a Flourishing World

Australian College of Theology Monograph Series

Copyright © 2021 Wipf and Stock Publishers. All rights reserved. Except for brief quotations in critical publications or reviews, no part of this book may be reproduced in any manner without prior written permission from the publisher. Write: Permissions, Wipf and Stock Publishers, 199 W. 8th Ave., Suite 3, Eugene, OR 97401.

Wipf & Stock
An Imprint of Wipf and Stock Publishers
199 W. 8th Ave., Suite 3
Eugene, OR 97401

www.wipfandstock.com

PAPERBACK ISBN: 978-1-6667-0156-2
HARDCOVER ISBN: 978-1-6667-0157-9
EBOOK ISBN: 978-1-6667-0158-6

04/27/21

# Contents

*List of Contributors* | vii

*Preface* | xiii

*Acknowledgements* | xxv

1   Introduction: A Brief Overview of the Faith and Work Movement | 1
    —KARA MARTIN AND ANDREW SLOANE

   Part 1: Workplace

2   How Do We Shape Christians for the Workplace? | 17
    —KARA MARTIN

3   Educating for the Kingdom: A Participatory Model of Character Development | 37
    —JAMES PIETSCH

4   Exploring the Connections between Authentic Leadership and Evangelical Christian Leadership: Framing Practice to Achieve Authenticity in Leadership | 54
    —PETER WHITE

5   Christian Values and Economic Knowledge: The Implications of Wolterstorff's Epistemology for a Christian Perspective on Economics | 71
    —PETER DOCHERTY

6   Rehumanizing Precarious Work: Vocation in Location Versus a New Priesthood of Cosmopolitan Techno-Creatives | 88
    —GORDON PREECE

### Part 2: Church and Pastoral Ministry

7   Sustainability and Preventing Dropout in the Human Services Industry: A Study of Pastors in the Australian Context | 111
    —KEITH MITCHELL

8   Church as Formative Ecology: The Youth Work Vocation in Secular Settings | 125
    —DAVID FAGG

9   The Attitude of Queensland Baptist Pastors to the "Whole-Life Discipleship" and "Faith and Work Integration" Movements: Where Are We and What Do We Need to Do? | 145
    —IAN HUSSEY AND DAVID BENSON

### Part 3: Theology of Work

10  Exploring Sabbath as a Response to the Liturgy of the Workplace in Light of the Work of James K. A. Smith | 175
    —COLIN NOBLE

11  A Fine Line Between Pleasure and Pain: The Perspective of Labor from the Book of Ecclesiastes | 193
    —ANDREW W. G. MATTHEWS

12  Hegel and Vocation: Beyond a Sacred–Secular Divide | 207
    —SARAH BACALLER

13  Encountering Subjectivity: Terry Eagleton and the Tax Collector's Embodied Vocation | 220
    —SAM CURKPATRICK

14  Theology of Work: Eschatology, Co-Creativity and the Pneumatological Impetus | 234
    —MARGUERITE KAPPELHOFF

15  Conclusion: Where to From Here? | 246
    —KARA MARTIN

# Contributors

## Sarah Bacaller

Stirling Theological College

Sarah is a PhD student, university tutor, and audiobook narrator from Melbourne, Australia. Research interests include the history and identity of Churches of Christ in Australia, particularly the writings of Gordon Stirling, with a focus on language and the philosophy of Christian thought. Her current research brings the work of G. W. F. Hegel into dialogue with attachment theory in relation to the formation of the self, exploring the implications for theological ethics and method. She has also been co-editor of the Stirling Theological College open access online student journal, *Reo: a journal of theology and ministry*.

## David Benson

The London Institute for Contemporary Christianity

Dave is passionate about commending Christ and his kingdom in Australia's post-Christendom culture. He has lectured part-time at Malyon College since 2009 in the areas of evangelism, apologetics, worldviews, faith and work integration, and practical theology. This parallels Dave's work as director of Malyon Traverse (the center for bridging church and culture), consultation work in the Christian schooling sector, and with his wife, Nikki, leading the house church, *Christ's Pieces*. Dave now works as director of Culture and Discipleship, with the London Institute for Contemporary Christianity (licc.org.uk).

## Sam Curkpatrick

Sam is a music performance honors graduate (Monash), with further training at the Australian National Academy of Music, and has a doctorate in ethnomusicology (ANU, Canberra). Sam is the inaugural curator of the Hindmarsh Research Centre, which gives focus to the memory, identity, mission, and ministry of Churches of Christ; he is the Vic-Tas Partnership Coordinator with GMP. Sam is an online tutor in the discipline of Christian Theology at Stirling and an accredited University of Divinity lecturer for the theology unit *Culture and Country: Engaging Faith in Contemporary Australian Society*.

## Peter Docherty

University of Technology Sydney

Economics Group, UTS Business School, University of Technology, Sydney

Peter has a PhD in monetary economics and the history of economic thought from the University of Sydney, and a BTh (Hons) from the Australian College of Theology. He is the author of *Money and Employment: A Study of the Theoretical Implications of Endogenous Money* and has published articles in a range of academic journals including the *History of Economics Review*, *Journal of Financial Stability*, and the *Review of Political Economy*. Peter's ongoing research interests include the development of macroeconomic models and their application to understanding financial crises and policy responses to such crises. He also works on Australian monetary and banking history, and has a strong interest in ethical perspectives on economics and how Christian faith should shape our understanding of the economic world. He is also actively involved in his local Anglican church.

## David Fagg

Deakin University

David is a doctoral student at Deakin University, in Melbourne, Australia. His interests are the sociology of youth work, youth, and religion. With qualifications in education, theology, and youth work, David has twenty years of experience in youth work, and youth worker education. He lives in Bendigo, a regional town in Victoria, Australia, and works as a community and youth worker at St. Matthew's Church.

## Mark Greene

London Institute for Contemporary Christianity

Mark joined the London Institute for Contemporary Christianity as executive director in 1999, and in twenty years has spoken on all God's people empowered to live their whole lives in fruitful relationship with Christ in the UK, Continental Europe, and the US. His published works include *Thank God It's Monday*, *Supporting Christians at Work*, *Pocket Prayers for Work*, and *Fruitfulness on the Frontline*. Most recently, Mark has written *The One About . . .*, a collection of true stories about God at work in our everyday lives. Mark has degrees in Hebrew from Cambridge, theology from London School of Theology (LST), and communications and media from Edinburgh (he worked as an advertising executive for ten years). He was formerly vice principal at LST.

## Ian Hussey

Malyon Theological College

After working as a high school teacher for three years, Ian moved into pastoral ministry. From 1993 to 2010 he was the solo then senior pastor of Nundah/North-East Baptist Church, during which time the church grew from thirty-five to five hundred people. Ian teaches and researches in the areas of pastoral leadership, preaching, and research methods. He also oversees the development of postgraduate research at Malyon.

## Marguerite Kappelhoff

University of Divinity

Maggie holds a PhD in systematic theology from Charles Sturt University and St. Marks National Theological Centre in Canberra (2015). Her PhD entitled: *The Marks of the Church as "Gift" and "Task": A Paradigm for the Twenty-First-Century Church*, considers the transcendent and dynamic nature of the four creedal marks of the church: "one, holy, catholic, and apostolic" and their relevance for ecumenical dialogue. A related book chapter of the same name was published in 2015 in *Hope in the Ecumenical Future: Pathways for Ecumenical and Interreligious Dialogue*, edited by Mark D. Chapman. Maggie's qualifications, training, and experience are primarily in social work, theology, and higher education and she currently works as the dean of academic programs at the *University of Divinity*.

### Kara Martin

Mary Andrews College

Kara has authored *Workship: How to Use Your Work to Worship God*, and *Workship 2: How to Flourish at Work*. She lectures at Mary Andrews College and Alphacrucis College, and has worked in media and communications, human resources, business analysis, and policy development. Kara is undertaking a PhD, researching how to effectively equip workplace Christians, and has had three chapters published in peer-reviewed books.

### Andrew Matthews

Andrew is a PhD candidate at Christ College, Sydney, working on a doctorate on the book of Ecclesiastes entitled, *The Worth of Work in a World of Vanity: Qohelet's Vocational Dialectic*. Andrew has published two works on Christian discipleship: *Christian CoreStrength*, and *Christian Jump Start*. Andrew is an ordained minister in the Presbyterian Church of Australia and lives in the Wollongong region.

### Keith Mitchell

Morling Theological College

Keith is an adult educator who teaches pastoral and practical theological studies at Morling Theological College, Sydney. His doctoral studies were in the area of developing leadership sustainability so as to reduce vocational dropout amongst pastors. Besides enabling people to become reflective practitioners, Keith has a focus on ensuring awareness and insight are developed in people for effective living and service of Jesus. He lives on the Central Coast, north of Sydney, and is married to a beautiful wife with four wonderful children.

### Colin Noble

Colin is a PhD candidate at Morling College and chaplain at William Clarke College, a Christ-centred educational community of nearly two thousand people. He is the author of *Working for God*, an exploration of what it means to live all of life as if God were the boss. He blogs occasionally at https://noblethoughtsdotblog.wordpress.com/, thinks Sabbath is important, and spends lots of time alone on bush tracks near his home in Sydney.

## James Pietsch

Inaburra School

James is the principal of Inaburra School in Sydney's Sutherland Shire. He has previously worked at New College, UNSW, and completed his PhD in education at the University of Sydney. James has worked in a number of different schools, both government and nongovernment, as well as lecturing and tutoring at the University of Sydney and the University of Ballarat.

## Gordon Preece

Ethos

Rev. Dr. Gordon Preece is the director of Ethos: Evangelical Alliance Centre for Christianity and Society, facilitator of the Religion and Social Policy Network at the University of Divinity, and chair and executive of the Social Responsibilities Committee of the Anglican Diocese of Melbourne. Gordon has international leadership roles on the board of the Theology of Work Project and with the Lausanne Movement's Marketplace Ministry and Workplace Networks. He is author/editor of thirteen books, about half on ethics and half on work. Gordon is married to Susan and has three adult children and three spirited grandsons.

## Andrew Sloane

Morling College

Andrew is director of research and senior lecturer in Old Testament and Christian Thought at Morling College, Sydney. He teaches in the areas of OT exegesis and interpretation, integration of faith and work, philosophy of religion, and bioethics. Andrew qualified in medicine and practiced briefly as a doctor before going into Baptist ministry. He has published in Old Testament and hermeneutics, ethics, philosophy, and theology. His most recent book is *Vulnerability and Care: Christian Reflections on the Philosophy of Medicine* (London: Bloomsbury T. & T. Clark, 2016). Andrew is married to Alison, and they have three adult daughters.

## Peter White

Anglican EdComm

Peter has worked in education and ministry contexts for almost twenty-five years, having trained as both a primary and secondary teacher. He holds a bachelor of arts, bachelor of teaching, masters in educational leadership, and a diploma of biblical studies. He has worked on church ministry teams, taught in primary, secondary, and tertiary educational institutions, and held various leadership positions in that time. Peter is currently an education consultant at the Anglican Education Commission (Anglican EdComm) and is passionate about educational ministries. He is married to Karen and together they have four children.

# Preface

## Theological Education and Disciple-making Church Leaders

When I was invited to speak at the 2019 Transforming Vocation conference in Sydney—out of which this book emerged—I was delighted.[1] This only increased as I looked at the breadth of papers, and realized that that we would probably not at that time have been able to hold a conference with such scope in the United Kingdom.

It was a joy to be in a room with so many people with the liberation of all God's people on their hearts. A joy for there to be academic research being done in this vital overall subject area. A joy for there to be such a range of topics being explored. A joy for there to be theological educators and church leaders and workplace practitioners all involved together. And a joy for there to be some of the movement's global pioneers present with us, torchbearers who had not only blazed a trail for whole-life disciplemaking and fruitful workplace mission but showed others the way.

In this preface, I want to highlight some of the main questions that we have sought to explore in our work at the London Institute for Contemporary Christianity. Specifically, what helps church leaders shift the historic culture of their churches? What actually liberates people for Monday to Sunday

---

1. Eds.—Mark Greene's contribution and international perspective at the inaugural *Transforming Vocation* conference was invaluable. His reflections framed each of the three conference streams and subsequent sections comprising this book—workplace, church and pastoral ministry, and theology of work, alongside their synergy—which were interacted with by each presenter, captured in the chapters which follow.

mission? What are the implications for theological education? What might best practice look like in theological education?

Of course, they are all connected. As one church leader we worked with asked himself:

*What kind of disciples does Jesus want to send out into the world?*

*And what kind of church will help to make those kinds of disciples?*

One definition of disciple we've found helpful is "someone learning the way of Jesus in their context at this time." A disciple then is not someone merely acquiring general information about Jesus, but someone who is learning to walk in the way of Jesus in the particular places they find themselves day-by-day at this particular point in their lives.

Does the student in the university, the parent at the school gate, the cleaner in the hotel, the laborer at the port, the executive in an office, have a rich vision for the way of Jesus in their context? Are they going into their everyday contexts actively seeking God's best for the work they do, the people they meet, and the organizations they're involved with, seeking and offering wisdom from above, praying for physical protection, witnessing clearly, and seeking to take prayerful and practical action for the physical, emotional, spiritual welfare of those around them?

Is this the vision of the disciple-in-mission that fuels our teaching as theological educators, pastors, mentors, disciplers, Bible study leaders?

## The Terrible Impact of the Sacred–Secular Divide

The central challenge to this vision is well-documented: it is the sacred–secular divide (SSD) and its many spawn. SSD shrinks our ecclesiology, putting more focus and value on the gathered church than the sent church. It shrinks our pneumatology, inadvertently limiting our expectation of the action of the Spirit to particular places and particular kinds of tasks. It shrinks our soteriology, focusing on individual conversion rather than on whole-life disciplemaking and the *missio Dei*. And SSD shrivels people's theological imagination for how the creator and redeemer God of all things might work in and through them in all of life.

The reality is that SSD makes lay Christians think they are second-class Christians. It diminishes the value of their daily work, it blinds them to the fruit that God may be producing right where they are, it dulls their alertness to God's action in their ordinary daily lives, and so it cuts them off from accessing prayer, wisdom, and the support of the body for their everyday contexts. And it blinds them to recognizing how the Bible addresses all of life. In sum, SSD shrinks the very scope of the gospel itself.

Further, SSD has a hugely damaging impact on global mission, precisely because in the majority of Christian minority 10/40 window countries you cannot get a resident's visa as a missionary or a reverend, but you can as an electrician or a nurse or a midwife or a cleaner or a teacher or an accountant or a business developer. In today's world, global mission agencies need people who know how to be effective for Christ in workplace cultures, because that is not only how people can gain access to a country, it's a place where relationships of trust can be built, and the gospel lived and shared.

However, there is even more to this issue of SSD.

At the first Lausanne Conference in 1974, Samuel Escobar, René Padilla, Billy Graham, and John Stott made the case that the followers of Christ were not only commanded to proclaim the gospel but also to work out the social, economic, political implications of the gospel for their contexts, and in particular to seek to address poverty. The holistic mission movement that Lausanne birthed has, however, often not been as holistic as its founders intended. It has been much more energized about poverty alleviation than poverty prevention, more energized about wealth distribution than wealth generation. This can mean that many of the Christian social action networks can brilliantly create schemes that give people skills for jobs but not foster the skills to enable Christians to create jobs for them to do. Or, can brilliantly create jobs that lift people out of poverty but not give people the theology of vocation and work and of the *missio Dei* that enables them to see the value to God of the work they do in his mission in the world.

The result is that in some countries many Christians are not economically ambitious. Their operational theology of vocation and work contribute to keeping them at lower economic levels than they otherwise might be, and their pastors' emphasis on church commitment serves to prioritize church meeting attendance over, for example, working the extra hour that would enable their children to have electric light to do their homework by.

Further, a thin theology of vocation weakens the ministry of the local church in its own community and neighborhood, leading it to be ignorant of the skills and aptitudes present in the congregation that might be deployed to strengthen local initiatives, or it leads them to ignore forms of ministry that are already going on in the neighborhood. So, for example, at the annual general meeting of one church in Manchester, a team reported on the church's outreach into a poor estate close to the church. At the end of the meeting a doctor asked why they had not asked her for a report, since her practice was on the estate and she spent forty hours a week ministering in that context, and had therefore a rather accurate sense of the emotional, mental, physical, and spiritual needs of the community.

## Offering a Partial Gospel

Back in the 1940s the great British writer, apologist, and evangelistic broadcaster Dorothy Sayers bemoaned the church's failure to engage with the world of work:

> In nothing has the Church so lost Her hold on reality as Her failure to understand and respect the secular vocation. She has allowed work and religion to become separate departments, and is astonished to find that, as a result, the secular work of the world is turned to purely selfish and destructive ends, and that the greater part of the world's intelligent workers have become irreligious or at least uninterested in religion. But is it astonishing? How can anyone remain interested in a religion which seems to have no concern with nine-tenths of his life?[2]

Her point was not just about work—her point was about the gospel, and how it applies today. The failure to teach work and vocation well is part of a wider failure to offer a whole-life gospel to believers and a failure to offer a whole-life gospel to nonbelievers. No wonder people are not gripped by the gospel, when the gospel we present rarely includes any compelling vision for the transformation of ordinary daily life. Who indeed would be interested in a religion that ignores nine-tenths of their lives?

Indeed, across the Western world, we wonder why young people aren't gripped by the gospel. Maybe it's because the gospel we have shared with them is just too small? Colossians 1:15–20 tells us that Jesus is the co-creator of all things, visible and invisible, in heaven and on earth. It tells us that God the Father sent God the Son to reconcile all things, in heaven and on earth, to make shalom through his blood shed on the cross.

All things, not some things.

God invites people to come to know his Son, not only so that they may spend eternity in his presence, but so that they might live out the good

---

2. Sayers, *Why Work?* Note: This was an Address delivered at Eastbourne, UK, April 23rd, 1942. She continues, "The official Church wastes time and energy and moreover, commits sacrilege, in demanding that secular workers should neglect their proper vocation in order to do Christian work—by which She means ecclesiastical work. The only Christian work is good work well done. Let the Church see to it that the workers are Christian people and do their work well, as to God: then all the work will be Christian work, whether it is church embroidery, or sewage farming. As Jacques Maritain says: 'If you want to produce Christian work, be a Christian, and try to make a work of beauty into which you have put your heart; do not adopt a Christian pose.' He is right. And let the Church remember that the beauty of the work will be judged by its own, and not by ecclesiastical standards."

purposes he has for them in every area of life, to pursue their daily role in his mission in all of life.

## The Importance of Context

Yet it goes still further than this. One of the implications of a thin theology of vocation is to limit the scope of our disciplemaking, that is, not to take account of the contexts God's people are called to, day by day. It is one thing to have a robust theology of work, to know how work is an instrument that God uses to create human flourishing, to know how one's particular work might align with God's work in bringing order, making provision, generating joy, creating beauty, and releasing potential in people and materials; but, it is another to envision and equip and empower someone for the challenges, for example, of working sixty hours a week in a relentlessly demanding financial services environment, or indeed any environment at all.

Let me illustrate this with a conversation I had with Alan, a senior city banker in a global bank. He described it as a toxic place. He'd been longing to leave and had been praying for a way out for a while. In fact, he couldn't understand why God had him there at all.

Alan was brought into a team being led by a much younger man who needed an older head to help him steady the ship. There were 130 in the team, profitability was plummeting, and their employee engagement numbers were plummeting faster than their profitability.

Alan was asked to restructure the whole team and to ensure that he "restructured out" one particular individual, Keith, for unnamed reasons.

"What am I doing in a place like this? Where's God in this?" Alan wondered.

About a month into his new role Alan offered everyone in his subteam half an hour of his time. They could talk about anything—career, family, hopes, ambition, God. Alan's "half-hour" opened the floodgates for genuine communication.

Alan told me about Keith, the man his boss wanted to "restructure" out. "I knew Keith had applied for my job and been rejected. And he told me that he was divorced. He was in tears. I could see he was a man of substance, so I told him that we would look at why he hadn't got my job and figure out how he could work towards the next promotion."

Then he told me that Keith was the only person in his team of thirty who was client-facing, that is, he had all the relationships. "If we 'restructured' Keith out, he'd go to another bank and take our clients with him, at a potential future loss of £185 million."

A few months later, Alan told me, "Last week my team did five deals. That is outstanding, by any measure. Outstanding!" And the employee engagement numbers in his team of forty-five are soaring. Human Resources can't understand it. He told them, "I talk to people." HR still couldn't understand it.

I told him he sounded like Boaz to me—Boaz who praises Ruth's good qualities, protects her from sexual harassment, gives her lunch, ensures she goes home with plenty of food, and prays for her (Ruth 2:12). Similarly, Alan has an eye and a heart for the vulnerable, praising his people appropriately, protecting them, providing for them, and praying for them.

At that point, Alan began to realize why God has him in that big bank: he is there to embody the kingdom, which is what he has been doing. Is it still a toxic place to work? Yes. Does he still want out? As it happens, yes. But does he know why God has placed him there? Yes.

## Our Role: To Help People Live Out Their Vocation

So, my contention is that the task of theological education is to ensure that graduates have the biblical frameworks, spiritual disciplines, and practical skills, to live out their vocation fruitfully, and to enable others to do so. As such the question is:

*What kind of seminary is required to train a church leader to create a church community that can envision and support the Alans and Elenas for their ministry out in God's world?*

At LICC, when we began looking at how to shift the culture of the church, our analysis identified two major barriers to the empowering of all God's people for everyday faith:

1. A theological barrier: the sacred–secular divide.
2. A methodological barrier: the dearth of disciplemaking.

If we are going to see God's people live out their vocation, we need to do more than help them grasp the theology of it; we need to help them discern the way of Jesus for their context. They need to be discipled and strengthened in a community of prayer and encouragement.

## Overcoming SSD in Theological Education

In 2016 we began work with the Langham Partnership on a project called "Overcoming the Sacred–Secular Divide through Theological Education."

One of the Langham Partnership emphases has been the identification and training of majority world scholars for theological education in majority world contexts, and they've trained over 370 to PhD level and beyond.

Our thesis was this: most of these scholars had been trained in Western theological institutions which were deeply affected by the sacred–secular divide. As such, it was likely that they would inadvertently continue to reinforce SSD in their home institutions. Langham Partnership and LICC tested this thesis in two consultations in Oxford and Cambridge.

The participant feedback confirmed the hypothesis: SSD was alive and well in theological education across the globe. The reality is that most Christians are in SSD churches, most of our students come from SSD churches, and on the whole, they go back into SSD churches.

So, the challenge for our theological colleges is to ask: Is my institution's culture affected by SSD? Are our courses affected by SSD? Is my teaching affected by SSD? Am I affected by SSD? How can we teach and train our students in such a way that they are able to excise the SSD in themselves and then go on to create genuinely whole-life disciplemaking communities where everyone understands their role in God's rich purposes?

The aim of our research was not to work out how we might crowbar modules or lectures on work, or vocation, or disciplemaking into the curricula of theological colleges. Of course, there is nothing wrong with that. And it might need to start there. However, the overall aim of our research was to work out how to help theological educators shift the core culture of their institutions from one shaped by SSD to one shaped theologically by the whole-life gospel, and methodologically by the command to make disciples.

## Changing Theological Education to Change Church Culture

What is required is a concerted effort to change the core culture of theological education. This requires more than the inclusion of faith, work, and vocation into the curriculum; more than the integration of faith, work, and vocation into various subject areas; it requires the eradication of SSD from the presentation of every subject and the reorientation of every subject area round the whole-life gospel and Jesus's missional disciplemaking priority. Vitally, this will also entail a radical shift in the way we read and teach Scripture and doctrine, because both these core disciplines have been deeply affected by SSD. And that is why global church culture is so deeply affected by it.

## The Challenge of Changing Culture

"Culture is the way we do things round here," said Archbishop Derek Worlock.[3] And the way we do things around here often seems obvious to us, entirely rational, completely benign, optimal even. What is clear is that behind the things that people do lie a set of beliefs—conscious or unconscious. Those beliefs direct behavior, and tend to shape every aspect of that culture: the stories we tell, the people we celebrate, the structures we put in place, the priorities for our use of time, of money, of resources, and so on. Our core values affect everything we do. Our ethos shapes our praxis.

In the case of the seminary, we need to ask: *Is the way we do things round here likely to help people become whole-life disciples, and enable them to equip whole-life disciples?*

To answer that, we need to consider who are the heroes in your seminary and what stories are told. In my former seminary, one of the "heroes" was Sir John Laing (1879–1978). There was a building named after him and an annual lecture endowed in his name. Every year, at the annual lecture in his name, we would be reminded that he was a Carlisle builder who had created one of the largest construction companies in the UK and that he had been critical to the founding of the college and to its capacity to move to its new location. The focus was on his financial generosity, and our gratitude for it. The impression given was that what mattered about him was the money he gave.

However, Sir John Laing was not only a gifted, successful, and generous businessperson; he was an extraordinary disciple of Christ and a man who changed his industry. He pioneered higher standards of health and safety for his employees and offered sick pay, bad weather pay, and holiday pay long before these became statutory requirements. He created employee savings schemes for school fees and holidays at a time when most workers didn't even have a bank account. He demanded commitment but gave loyalty. Discovering through a manager that a former employee was destitute and seriously ill, he sent a telegram: "Relieve immediate distress and report—further instructions will follow."

In fact, it is hard to think of any graduate of my seminary who has directly impacted the wellbeing of more people in mainstream society than Sir John Laing. Furthermore, he conducted his business in conscious partnership with Christ from the moment when, as a young man of twenty-eight, he invited God to be the senior partner in his business.

---

3. Derek Worlock, Roman Catholic Archbishop of Liverpool (1976–1994), quoted in Gallagher, *Clashing Symbols*, 12.

Everyone at my former college knew that Sir John Laing was a generous donor; very few knew how remarkable a whole-life disciple he was. The stories we tell reflect what is most important to us; and so do the emphases we choose in curriculum design, module descriptors, assessments, and our own lectures.

## Bringing about Change

In LICC's work, we have found a simple model that helps clarify the key requirements for initiating significant change: the Beckhard-Harris Model.[4] It is based on this formula:

$D \ x \ V \ x \ F > R.$

Dissatisfaction x Vision x First Steps needs to be greater than the Resistance to change.

As such, to generate change, to overcome resistance to change, you need three things.

### 1. You Need Some Level of Dissatisfaction

Your seminary may be recruiting enough students, your students may be performing well academically, the feedback on your own teaching may be very positive, and the reports from receiving churches may be positive. In such a situation, there is not much incentive to change.

However, if you are dissatisfied with the impact your students are having in the churches they serve, if you are frustrated by the thinness of Christian impact in your nation, then you might be open to doing the hard work of getting a radical change to your curriculum approved.

### 2. The "V" for Vision Has to Be Compelling

If there's no compelling alternative to the current situation, there's no incentive to change.

Do we want to see the church make whole-life disciples or not?

Do we want to see Christians in our nation making more of an impact or not?

Do we have a vision for a college that's committed to serving the church scattered as well as the church gathered?

---

4. For more information, see Warrilow, "Beckhard Change Equation."

Curricula in most colleges is often determined by what the existing faculty can teach, or want to teach, but I remember when I was at the London School of Theology and the faculty developed a new, alternative three-year-degree program, which contained components that no one could teach when it was first devised. It was like that because they began with the question: "What is it that Christians need in order to be fruitful for Christ in the emerging culture?"

## 3. There Need to Be Some Doable First Steps

If I can't see how to begin, I won't begin.

One of my very favorite doable first steps came from Dr. Edwin Tay, historical theologian, and now the vice-principal of Trinity Theological College in Singapore who hosted our consultation. When a new administrator joined his office, as part of her induction, he asked her to read three articles from Robert Banks and Paul Stevens's *The Complete Book of Everyday Christianity*. One on "Vocation," one on the "Theology of Work," and one on "Ministry at Work." Then, each week they discussed one of those articles for half an hour. As it happened, it transformed his administrator's vision for her role, enabling her to go beyond brilliantly efficient task fulfillment to creating a warm, relational, service-oriented culture and atmosphere.

I love that example because it reflects the reality that Edwin realized if a seminary is to change, he had to change his bit of the seminary; and each educator in the organization has to change their part of the seminary. It also reflects the reality that the administrative and support staff need a biblical view of work and vocation which shapes the way they do their work. Finally, it reflects a determination that if we are sending people out in the world to disciple people who work in organizations, it would be helpful if we could model to them what a good organization might look like. In Dr. Tay's case, it reflected his conviction that if he was going to create a whole-life disciplemaking culture in the seminary it needed to begin in his office.

Now in this formula, it's important to note the "multiply" sign. Just as in mathematics, any number multiplied by zero creates a total of zero, so here if any of the elements are missing, the result will be zero. You need all three to be operational, which means it's not enough to communicate dissatisfaction and offer a compelling vision; you also have to show someone how they can begin.

And we at LICC and the educators we have worked with have discovered many ways to begin. But it all stems ultimately from a grasp of the grandeur and glory of God and the beauty of his purposes. Indeed, the more deeply we grasp God's love for the world he has created, his purposes for it, and for his people in it, and the more deeply we appreciate the texture of people's lives and the opportunities and challenges they have, the more likely it is that we will be able to teach and train the church leaders of the future to do what the master disciplemaker commanded them to do: liberate all God's people to live their everyday in the strengthening knowledge of his rich and fruitful purposes for their ministry in his world. To his glory.

As we seek to survey the Faith and Work Movement, and delve into the details of how God is active in the workplace, church and pastoral ministry, and our theological frames of reference, may this book offer a significant step in the direction of life abundant.

Mark Greene
London Institute for Contemporary Christianity

## Bibliography

Gallagher, Michael Paul. *Clashing Symbols: An Introduction to Faith and Culture*. Rev. ed. New York: Paulist, 2004.

Sayers, Dorothy L. *Why Work? Discovering Real Purpose, Peace, and Fulfillment at Work: A Christian Perspective*. CreateSpace Independent Publishing Platform, 2014.

Warrilow, Stephen. "Beckhard Change Equation." *Strategies for Managing Change*. http://www.strategies-for-managing-change.com/beckhard.html.

# Acknowledgements

THE EDITORS WOULD LIKE to acknowledge the following for their assistance in this project and the Transforming Vocation conference from which it emerged:

The *Australian College of Theology*, Australia's largest theological provider with eighteen colleges, twenty-nine courses, and over one thousand subjects of study. The ACT's chief purpose is to collaborate with its affiliated colleges to equip people to faithfully serve God's church and God's world primarily by the provision of quality-assured courses in theology and ministry. The Transforming Vocation conference was ACT's way of encouraging colleges to enable students to faithfully serve God's world. As part of their support they funded a consortium-wide audit of faith–work activities, the conference, publication of this book, and preparation of the Transforming Vocation website. Special thanks to Megan Powell du Toit for her assistance in preparing this publication.

The mission of *Reventure* is to be the catalyst, collaborator, and encourager for new thinking and renewal that transforms the way people, organizations, and churches view the purpose, value, and meaning of work. Their strategy to see work transformed in Australia is to work in two key areas—engaging believers and engaging the world of work. Their ongoing support of the Transforming Vocation conference is greatly appreciated.

This publication flows from the Transforming Vocation conference held in July 2019, at *Morling College* in Sydney, and we would like to thank the following groups involved in the conference:

- Katherine Lawless, and others in the Morling College team, who wonderfully managed the conference;

- Those speakers who agreed to allow their work to become part of this volume, and who spent considerable extra effort refining their writing;
- Those speakers who were part of the conference's success but whose work was unable to be included in this publication. The additional material is available on the Transforming Vocation website (https://transformingvocation.org/).

We are also indebted to *Mark Greene* from the *London Institute for Contemporary Christianity* for agreeing to speak at the conference, delivering four exhilarating addresses, and also contributing the preface to this volume. We also want to thank Lindsay McMillan and Murray Wright who facilitated the Mark Greene *Putting your Faith to Work* tour.

Finally, the editors have thoroughly enjoyed working together in preparing this volume, and have experienced unity in the Spirit, as we did this work in the name of the Lord Jesus, with thanks to God.

# I

# Introduction

## A Brief Overview of the Faith and Work Movement

### Kara Martin

Mary Andrews College and
Alphacrucis College

### Andrew Sloane

Morling College (Australian College
of Theology; University of Divinity)

When Pete Hammond, Paul Stevens, and Todd Sanoe published their *Marketplace Annotated Bibliography* in 2002, it marked a critical juncture in David Miller's third wave of the faith and work movement: the faith at work era (ca. 1985–present).[1] Until that point, it was possible to comfortably name the main influencers in the movement. Since then there has been an explosion of interest, research, and publishing. However, generally there has been a lack of research within vocations, and insufficient recogni-

---

1. Miller, *God at Work*.

tion and integration of three perspectives: the church, the workplace, and biblical/theological study; hence the need for the Transforming Vocation research conference from which this volume emerges. This introduction aims to provide a context for the contributions that follow. To that end, we will briefly rehearse the background to the conference and its rationale, before identifying its context in the growing literature on the integration of Christian faith and work and the particular contribution this volume and the conference from which it emerged make.

Along with many others, we have been thinking and working in this space for a number of years. We have been delighted to see growing awareness of the neglect of matters of the integration of faith and work amongst evangelical pastors, theologians, and practitioners, and have celebrated moves to address it. Nonetheless, a number of things troubled us. While people from across the globe have contributed to this developing conversation (including notable examples from Australia such as Robert Banks), it has largely been focused on, even captive to, the interests of North Americans. Not only do the issues that need to be addressed vary from place to place, but each of these contexts has an important contribution to make to the discussion. We thought it time to bring Australian voices into the conversation. However, we were also aware that in some respects Australia is lagging behind our sisters and brothers in other parts of the world—especially in the attention given in theological colleges to the integration of faith and work (and the formation of workers). Perhaps, we thought, that may in part be due to economies of scale and the lack of a critical mass that can sustain programs and appointments in individual colleges. Perhaps. But perhaps it might also be due to distortions in the operational theologies of our institutions and networks. Distortions of neglect, of emphasis, even explicitly an espoused theology that values pastoral ministry and, perhaps, mission-as-evangelism (be that traditional cross-cultural mission or more locally oriented) as *true* (gospel) ministry, and sees personal evangelism, and financial support of pastors and missionaries as the only real contribution that "ordinary" workers make to the mission of God. In light of that, and an awareness of the general nature of much of the literature in the field, we thought it might be time to foster serious research from an antipodean perspective into the nature of work in the contemporary workplace, the role of churches in the formation of workers, and the contribution that particular theological disciplines might make to our understanding and practice of kingdom-oriented work in the world as we now find it. We think this is warranted in light of the work that has been done in this area so far; thus, we turn to a brief survey of the current literature.

We begin with a brief overview of work in the Bible and Christian history, then look at the historical development of theologies of work. The focus will turn to key developments in the areas of a faith and work movement, theology of work, and a broader excursion into religion and the workplace. We will consider the intensifying spotlight on spiritual formation for work, and touch on the assessment techniques for formation which are currently being used in the workplace and churches.

## Brief Overview of Work in the Bible and Christian History

While faith and work theology and practice may be considered a new discipline of study, it has deep biblical roots and is consistently evident at key moments in Christian history. This is evident as early as Genesis 1—2, the narrative of the creation of the world. It is there that we see the linguistic link between the work of our hands and worship in the temple, through the Hebrew verb roots *avad* and *shamar*, particularly in Genesis 2:15.[2] This holistic view of worship and work is exemplified by God, who describes himself in terms related to work and workers: composer (Ps 33:3) and performer (Ps 147:1), metalworker (Ps 12:6), and potter (Jer 18:1–6), garment maker (Isa 61:10), gardener (Amos 9:14), farmer (2 Cor 9:10), shepherd (Ps 23), tentmaker (Exod 25:9), and builder (Ps 127:1).[3]

We may be tempted to see Jesus and Paul only as spiritual teachers, however there is evidence that they worked hard, not seeing such work as separate from their teaching and worship of God. Jesus worked as a builder (*tekton*, is often mistranslated as "carpenter"[4]) for at least twenty years before he began what is often termed his "public ministry." He was recognized as a builder as he preached, taught, healed, prayed, and conversed.[5]

In Mark 6:1–3 we read:

> Jesus left there and went to his hometown, accompanied by his disciples. When the Sabbath came, he began to teach in the synagogue, and many who heard him were amazed. "Where did this man get these things?" they asked. "What's this wisdom that

---

2. Bergsma, "Creation Narratives." Bergsma says, "It is difficult to accept as purely coincidental that the juxtaposition of the verbal roots 'work' and 'guard' occur together in the Pentateuch only in Genesis 2:15 and . . . texts in Numbers concerning the tasks of the Levites and priests in the Tabernacle" (16).

3. Banks, *God the Worker*.

4. Mounce, "Τέκτων."

5. Matt 13:55.

> has been given him? What are these remarkable miracles he is performing? Isn't this the carpenter (sic)? Isn't this Mary's son and the brother of James, Joseph, Judas and Simon? Aren't his sisters here with us?" And they took offence at him.

The reason for the sarcasm and offence is that the Greco-Roman culture saw manual work as evidence of a lack of philosophical/teaching ability.[6] Jesus, by choosing to work in his father's trade until the appointed time, grants such manual labour dignity.

Paul also did manual labour, working as a tentmaker, as well as being recognized as a highly educated philosopher/teacher.[7] He continued to do manual work to support his own preaching and teaching to ensure his message was received freely.[8] He was also highly critical of the Thessalonians who chose to stop work, and await the coming Jesus. He taught them the importance of working to support family, to be generous to others, and to ensure we are not idle or troublesome.[9] John Taylor argues:

> Paul celebrates the work, labour, and endurance of the Thessalonians as the proper products, and therefore evidence of their faith, love and hope in Jesus. Working to support themselves, and refusing to burden others, as Paul had set an example, is an act of love and faith, and an expression of eschatological hope.[10]

The Christian history of approaches to work show these holistic patterns in Christian understanding. One example is Augustine, who is supportive of the good of work before the fall, but also aware of the impact post-fall, following the judgment on Adam's work. He values monastic and church roles, but equally values manual labor and various professions and artistry as having capacity to "produce things which can be used to enjoy God or express love for God."[11] Benedict utilized this holistic view of work and worship in the development of his Rule for monastic communities, which combines both aspects seamlessly. In fact, the motto of the Benedictine movement is *ora et labora* (pray and work).

In spite of this promising beginning, the rise of Christendom centralized power in the world of the sacred until Martin Luther questioned the

---

6. See Leshem, "Retrospectives," 228: "Such antagonism to the marketplace reflected an opposition to the social classes who were selling goods and labor in the market."

7. He clearly states his Jewish educational credentials (Acts 26:5) and was recognized by the established philosophical schools in Athens (Acts 17:16–34).

8. Acts 20:33–35.

9. 2 Thess 3:6–11.

10. Taylor, "Labour of Love," 64.

11. Kidwell, "Labour in Augustine's Thought," 779.

separation of sacred and secular. He articulated what emerged as the Protestant view of work when he paraphrased Job 5:6–7 "as to the birds to flying, so is man born unto labour,"[12] thereby suggesting that humankind is created to work. Zapf and Seele identify the key thoughts of Luther's interpretation of work as: a social activity; being equal in every vocation and an instrument of divine mercy; and the means of integrating the inner spiritual life, and the outer physical life.[13]

Max Weber credits Luther and the emergence of the Protestant work ethic with the rise of capitalism,[14] and this is to an extent verified by the rise of religious industrialists, particularly in England. Donkin makes a study of Quaker businesses which were established in metalworking, smithing, chemicals, and confectionary, as well as establishment of enabling financial institutions such as the Lloyds and Barclays banks. Quakers particularly saw the advantages of eating chocolate, and Fry & Sons, Cadbury, and Rowntree all owed their origins to Quaker development.[15]

Along with the rise of industrialization, came the rise of exploitation, and the competing activities of wealthy Christian industrialists committed to the wellbeing of their employees and their families. Miller and others write about the Pullman and Hershey families where employers "constructed entire communities, designed recreational public spaces, and operated stores to provide for the needs of employees and their families."[16] They also point to chaplaincy as a mid-twentieth-century strategy for engagement between religious institutions and workplaces. "Through the British Industrial Mission, the Church of England introduced industrial chaplains to serve as arbiters of class struggle between labour and capital, between employees and their employers." Another expression of this social justice approach were the French worker-priests who took positions as ordinary employees within companies to reconnect the church with the working class.[17]

## Key Developments in the Faith and Work Movement

The concept of developing a theology of work is a relatively recent phenomenon and is not on a simple upward trajectory. For instance, despite

12. As quoted in Zapf and Seele, "As to the Birds Flying," 103.
13. Zapf and Seele, "As to the Birds Flying," 104–6.
14. Weber and Tawney, *Protestant Ethic*.
15. Donkin, *History of Work*, 53–55.
16. Miller et al., "Caring for Employees," 135.
17. Miller et al., "Caring for Employees," 135–36.

initial enthusiasm, the era of opening of centers of research for "marketplace theology" or "faith and work" or "workplace theology" in Australian theological colleges has now seemingly passed.[18] A brief survey will help locate the work of this volume.

The faith and work movement, as it is most widely known, is a recognition of the dualism which has emerged, rooted in Platonic thought, and impacted by the industrial revolution when work became separated from the home.[19] Yale theologian, David W. Miller, has carefully chronicled the rise of the modern faith and work movement in the West (particularly the United States), with its goal of integration of work and worship. In *God at Work* he chronicles three periods: the social gospel era (ca.1890s–1945); the ministry of the laity era (ca. 1946–1985); and the faith at work era (ca. 1985–present).[20]

The era of social gospel emphasized Christianity's response to the social needs around an "expectation of bringing in the kingdom of God on earth."[21] The key figure of this era was New York pastor Walter Rauschenbusch who influenced three generations of social justice action (his best-known work, *A Theology for the Social Gospel*, was published in 1917). His preaching and active work paralleled the impact of Pope Leo XIII's social encyclical *Rerum Novarum* (*The Condition of Labor*) in 1891.[22]

In the ministry of the laity era, Miller tracks the rise of special purpose groups exemplified by Sam Shoemaker, credited with establishing Alcoholics Anonymous and Faith and Work magazine (1956), as well as the International Christian Leadership group, hosting prayer breakfasts with business leaders around the world.[23] William Diehl was representative of a business leader who saw his work as part of God's design, and wrote books to help people explore the application of their faith to work, such as the bestselling *The Monday Connection: On Being an Authentic Christian in a Weekday World* (1991).[24] Miller suggests several reasons for the ending of the laity

---

18. I am most familiar with the Australian College of Theology consortium, which includes eighteen colleges. The most generous resourcing includes Malyon Workplace which opened in 2013 (since October 2019 has no active director), and the Ridley Marketplace Institute in 2013 (since December 2018 has no active dean).

19. Preece, "Work," 1140–41.

20. Miller, *God at Work*.

21. Miller, *God at Work*, 25.

22. Miller also makes mention of Charles Sheldon's book *In His Steps: What Would Jesus Do?*, which emphasized the workplace as a context for transformation as a result of Christian social action.

23. Miller, *God at Work*, 50–51.

24. Miller, *God at Work*, 54.

movement: rapid societal changes in the 1960s and 70s, which took the focus of church off the lay movement; the church utilized lay energy within the church rather than equipping the laity for their public lives; lay people were never included in authority structures; and the theological academy focused on ordination. Additionally, Miller comments on the way that the rise of liberation theology defined wealth and business as negatives, and the continued separation of the spiritual and material in church teaching.[25]

Miller sees the faith and work era in the US as arising from the re-engagement of conservative religious forces in political conversations, and increased religious expression in the workplace.[26] In the 1980s and 90s, the rise of "greed" as a philosophy, and the ongoing tumultuous changes during that time led to articles featuring businesspeople describing themselves as feeling spiritually empty because of their compartmentalized lives, leading to a search for greater meaning.[27] This quest for integration has resulted in an explosion of books (key authors include Robert Banks, R. Paul Stevens, and more recently Tim Keller), groups (such as New York Redeemer's Faith and Work Center) and tools for analysis, including David Miller's development of "The Integration Box."[28] From 2015, the Theology of Work Project, co-ordinated by Will Messenger, has provided an online resource for scholars, pastors, and workplace Christians, describing itself as the "deepest, largest, and most trusted source of biblical, theological, and pastoral material related to work."[29] Key authors in Australia include theologians Robert Banks (*Faith Goes to Work* and *God the Worker*) and Gordon Preece (*Changing Work Values*), and popular authors Andrew Laird (*Under Pressure*), Kara Martin (*Workship*), and Mark Bilton (*Monday Matters*).

## Theology of Work

There is no consensus as to what constitutes a theology of work. Even so, Regent College's R. Paul Stevens has provided a helpful typology of approaches[30] with their most recognized adherents. The table below outlines them, with two additions in light of recent developments.

---

25. Miller, *God at Work*, 58–61.
26. Miller, *God at Work*, 66–67.
27. Miller, *God at Work*, 71.
28. Miller and Ewest, "Integration Box."
29. "About/Theology of Work," *Theology of Work Project*.
30. Stevens, *Work Matters*, 2–4.

Table 1

| Theology of Work Types | Sample Authors |
|---|---|
| • Trinitarian theologies: that our work flows from our triune God | • Robert Banks, Gordon Preece |
| • Creation theologies: focusing on the creation mandate and our work as God's vice-regents | • *Laborems Exercens* by John Paul II, Doug Sherman and William Hendricks |
| • Image of God theologies: that we are made in the image of a God who works | • Dennis Bakke |
| • Curse theologies: our work is impacted by the curse | • David Jensen |
| • New creation theologies: work is done in anticipation of the new creation | • Tim Keller and Katherine Leary Alsdorf |
| • Vocation theologies: all work is done in response to a calling from God | • Stephen Garber, Gene Veith, Alistair Mackenzie |
| • Spirit theologies: work as an expression of the Spirit's gifting for the world | • Miroslav Volf |
| • Kingdom theologies: work is a means of bringing shalom to the world | • Ben Witherington III, Amy Sherman |
| • Heaven and end-times theologies: our work has eternal significance | • Darrell Cosden |
| • Mission theologies: that our work can be an expression of the church's mission in the world | • Christopher Wright |
| • Formational theologies: that work is the place and means of our discipleship | • Denise Daniels and Shannon Vanderwarker, David Kinnaman, Sutrisna Harjanto |

# Religion and the Workplace and Spiritual Formation for Work

While seminaries have focused on developing theologies of work, there is a wider conversation about the relationship between religion and the workplace, also captured by terms such as "workplace spirituality," "spirit at work," "faith at work," and "workplace ministry." In summarizing the movement, Judith Neal explains that scholarship is located primarily in the field of management but overlaps with scholars from all major religious traditions. It has grown as management scholarship has turned more to an "increasingly holistic view of the relationship between the human being and the workplace."[31] Related to this, there is a new emphasis on spiritual formation theology in the faith and work movement. Over the years there has been the development of a variety of measurement tools in a desire to understand the range and depth and impact of spiritual/religious beliefs in the workplace. Generally, their shortfall is that they are self-assessment tools, impacted by the issues relating to conceptual confusion and validation of measurement mentioned.[32] Additionally, many are designed to be used in the workplace for the sake of employee wellbeing and to maximize the "spiritual capital" of organizations identified.[33] Finally, many are broad in their interpretation of spirituality and assessment, seeking to be palatable to a variety of religious traditions.

As such, while it is clear that there is a rich and growing body of literature in this area, a number of gaps have become apparent. Much of the work is general in nature, either in its broad-brush treatment of "work" as a single generic entity, or in its treatment of "religion" or "spirituality" as generic phenomena. We need the particular, as well as the generic. We need to theologically reflect on particular features of work, and the particularities of specific kinds of work or workplaces. This is the task of the first section of the book. The workplace is, we believe, the best place to start, both to ensure that we don't allow the abstract, general nature of (much, but not all) evangelical theology to control the discussion, but also to signal that our primary concern is to enrich reflection on, and so the actual practice of, the phenomena of work on cultures such as ours. But if our concern is with the formation of workers, we need to think about how churches—as a primary vehicle for the formation of individual Christians and the shapers of their theological and cultural imaginations—are doing that job and how they might do it better. This is the focus of the second section of the book. There is also a need to bring the particularities of specific (evangelical, Protestant) Christian theological disciplines to bear on work—and rest—and our experience of life in the workplace. And that is the task of the third, and final section of the book.

---

31. Neal, *Handbook of Faith*, 4–5.

32. See Hill and Dik, *Psychology of Religion*, 4.

33. See, for instance, Malloch, *Spiritual Enterprise*, and the Discipleship Dynamics Assessment.

Let me give a brief overview of how this plays out in the rest of the volume.[34]

In the first chapter in the *Workplace* section, Kara Martin asks the question: "How do we shape Christians for the workplace?" Using the repertory grid technique, she reports on a pilot study into the formation of Christians for the workplace. She examines the cognitive, behavioral, and affective factors that contribute to narratives that effectively shape Christians towards the *telos* of being faithful workers. James Pietsch takes this focus on formation into the school context in his chapter, "Educating for the Kingdom: A Participatory Model of Character Development." He argues that Christian education involves more than simply speaking *about* the kingdom (but not less than that); it is preparing students to *participate in* the kingdom, initially here on earth in whatever occupation they choose to pursue, as well as in the new creation to come. Educating for the kingdom represents a particular approach to education in which the character traits of the new creation—such as grace, humility, compassion, and kindness—are promoted, modelled, practiced, and experienced. Peter White's contribution, "Exploring the Connections between Authentic Leadership and Evangelical Christian Leadership: Framing Practice to Achieve Authenticity in Leadership," continues this focus on education, albeit with a shift to questions of leadership. Having critically reviewed the relevant literature, he proposes that a *Christian* approach to authentic leadership entails consideration of: (1) personal identity and the transformational work of the Holy Spirit in leading us from the "old" and to a "new" identity in Christ; (2) belief as it impacts (particularly moral) behavior; (3) how personal identity and an ethical framework shape the leadership of others and the wider community to serve the common good under Christ.

Peter Docherty's chapter pivots away from the school environment to the world of economics, particularly economic theory. In "Christian Values and Economic Knowledge: The Implications of Wolterstorff's Epistemology for a Christian Perspective on Economics," he demonstrates that, contrary to its own dominant self-understanding, economics is far from a value-free enterprise. Drawing on the work of Nicholas Wolterstorff, he argues that in light of the failure of modernist foundationalism, it is entirely proper for Christians to allow their Christian beliefs and values to inform their economic theory, reshaping the discipline in light of grace, justice, and

---

34. I should note at this point that the individual papers we have compiled are instances of a much richer conversation evident at the conference which, regrettably, cannot be captured in this book. Glimpses of that can be seen in the conference program which is available at http://bit.ly/TVProgram2019; more can be found at the *Transforming Vocation* website: https://transformingvocation.org/.

righteousness, as well as a recognition of God's abundant material provision. The final chapter in this section from veteran Australian workplace theologian Gordon Preece, "Rehumanizing Precarious Work: Vocation in Location Versus a New Priesthood of Cosmopolitan Techno-Creatives," sheds light on important features of the contemporary marketplace. He shows how increasing monopolization of Liquid Modernity's sense of vocation by celebrity techno-creatives displaces, divides, dehumanizes, and destabilizes true vocation. The increasingly disruptive and inhumane technological pace of change requires contemporary and classical theological resources to rehumanize it. These include the priority of the general calling to and by Christ and his people over particular callings and individual choices of vocation, the priority of justification by faith—not justification by one's job—and the symbiotic relationship of vocation and location within a creation/new creation and Trinitarian framework.

The opening chapter in the second section, *Church and Pastoral Ministry*, picks up on this concern for the well-being of workers. In "Sustainability and Preventing Dropout in the Human Services Industry: A Study of Pastors in the Australian Context," Keith Mitchell turns his attention to a phenomenological study of experiences in burnout in pastoral ministry. While his research demonstrates both convergence and divergence in various features surrounding social support, emotionality, conflict, spiritual expression, and spousal relationships, he proposes that the key to sustainability and preventing dropout in pastors is the development of emotional intelligence. David Fagg's chapter, "Church as Formative Ecology: The Youth Work Vocation in Secular Settings," attends to how churches form workers for "secular" youth work contexts. Drawing on extensive interviews with youth workers, he suggests that their vocation is formed through the participatory community of the church, but that many leave a church-based context as a result of discontent with the "safe" nature of church-based youth. He notes that there is a problematic divide between Christians in secular youth work, and leaders in church-based youth ministry, and argues that churches need to better their formative role in this vocation, and ministry leaders need to engage in constructive dialogue with Christian youth workers. This matter of formation is taken up in Ian Hussey and David Benson's final chapter in this section, "The Attitude of Queensland Baptist Pastors to the 'Whole-Life Discipleship' and 'Faith and Work Integration' Movements: Where Are We and What Do We Need to Do?" In the first research of its kind in Australia, Hussey and Benson respond to Tom Nelson's famous pastoral "apology" to his church, seeking to determine whether such "pastoral malpractice" is evident amongst Queensland Baptist pastors, and what implications this might have for the work of training institutions such as Malyon Theological College. While finding encouraging signs of acceptance of key concepts and terms, they argue that colleges need to develop clearer institutional alignment in curricula, learning, and assessment, stronger connections with other organizations involved in this movement, a more robust theology of persons, and a clearer focus on *shalom* as the center and goal of God's mission in the world. As a side note, it is puzzling and not a little disturbing to realize that this was the section of the conference with the fewest offerings. This is not reflected in the quality of the papers (either at the conference or in this volume). There is a richness of insight into effective practice (and potential barriers to it) from which we can learn much. But this area of practical theology needs more focused attention—from which we would be rewarded. The same could be said about research into the practice of theological colleges and their role in shaping people for ministry (including, but not restricted to, pastoral ministry). This relates of course to the final section of the book.

The final section on *Theology of Work* opens perhaps ironically, perhaps fortuitously, with a piece on *rest* rather than *work*. In "Exploring Sabbath as a Response to the Liturgy of the Workplace in Light of the Work of James K. A. Smith," Colin Noble extends Smith's work on "cultural liturgies" and ecclesial counter-formation in two areas that his work neglects: the workplace as a context in which liturgical practices occur, and Sabbath keeping as a genuine form of Christian counter-liturgy. In particular, he argues that Sabbath keeping has liberating potential, reshaping anthropology to challenge the culture of ubiquitous availability, enhance the formative function of church-oriented liturgical practices, and provide a prophetic critique of deformational aspects of workplace culture. Andrew Matthews brings an important, and frequently misunderstood, book to bear on questions of work. His chapter, "A Fine Line Between Pleasure and Pain: The Perspective of Labor from the Book of Ecclesiastes," notes the way that the book is often read as a despairing reflection on work as little more than painful toil. He argues that this is a distortion of its message. While Qoheleth is both enigmatic and aware of the enigmas and ambiguities of life and work, he acknowledges the real gains that work can bring, as well as the frustrations of this, as with all aspects of human life. While both sin and finitude are sources of frustration in our labor, the sovereign God gives us joy in our labor, which we can accept with gratitude.

Sarah Bacaller's chapter, "Hegel and Vocation: Beyond a Sacred–Secular Divide," turns from biblical studies to bring continental philosophy to bear on the theology of work. She identifies resources from Hegel that both challenge and remediate the "oppositional" structures of much of our thinking and practice in relation to work. She argues that Hegel's contributions in relation to understanding identity in light of demarcation and distinction, Christ as both fulfillment and end of the law, and notions of objective right, help overcome the oppositions, legitimize the role of the secular in human life, and integrate vocation into our fostering of human flourishing. Sam Curkpatrick brings insights from philosopher and social critic Terry Eagleton to bear on one of Jesus's more confronting parables in "Encountering Subjectivity: Terry Eagleton and the Tax Collector's Embodied Vocation." Using Eagleton's categories of the *imaginary*, the *symbolic*, and the *real*, he shows how Luke's parable of the pharisee and tax collector (Luke 18:9–14) illustrates contrasting trajectories of vocation. Self-woven narratives of vocation do not provide satisfactory or enduring resolution to the anxieties and dislocations of human existence. The surrender of self-assured narratives of vocation provide a radical alternative. Seen in this light, Luke's ironic parable inverts expectations regarding secular and profane occupation, while encouraging humility in discovering God's possibilities for life. Eschatology fittingly closes the section on theology of work. Maggie Kappelhoff's chapter, "Theology of Work: Eschatology, Co-Creativity, and the Pneumatological Impetus," draws on the work of Miroslav Volf, in particular the nexus he establishes between the person and work of the Spirit (pneumatology) and the Christian hope (eschatology). She suggests that the theme of humans as co-creators with God deserves further exploration, enriching our understanding of the Spirit's work in our work, and the way that work (and we as workers) can be reframed and revalidated in light of the eschatological significance of workers and their work.

But enough of the preliminaries. We trust that we've whetted your appetite for some thought-provoking reflections on how vocation can be best understood and embraced in the overlapping contexts of workplace, church, and the theological academy.

## Bibliography

"About/Theology of Work." *Theology of Work Project.* https://www.theologyofwork.org/about.

Banks, Robert. *God the Worker: Journeys into The Mind, Heart, and Imagination of God.* vEugene, OR: Wipf & Stock, 2008.

Bergsma, John. "The Creation Narratives and the Original Unity of Work and Worship in the Human Vocation." In *Work: Theological Foundations and Practical Implications*, edited by R. Keith Loftin and Trey Dimsdale, 11–29. London: SCM, 2018.

Cawley, Brian D., and Peter J. Snyder. "People as Workers in the Image of God: Opportunities to Promote Flourishing." *Journal of Markets and Morality* 18, no.

    1 (July 15, 2015) 163–87. https://www.marketsandmorality.com/index.php/mandm/article/view/1063.

Discipleship Dynamics. "What Is the Discipleship Dynamics Assessment?" https://discipleshipdynamics.com/.

Donkin, Richard. *The History of Work*. New York: Palgrave Macmillan, 2010.

Hill, Peter C., and Bryan J. Dik, eds. *Psychology of Religion and Workplace Spirituality*. Charlotte: Information Age, 2012.

International Bible Society. *NIV Popular Bible: New International Version*. London: Hodder & Stoughton, 1996.

Kidwell, Jeremy H. "Labour in Augustine's Thought." In *The Oxford Guide to the Historical Reception of Augustine*, edited by Karla Pollmann and Willemien Otten, 779–84. Oxford: Oxford University Press, 2014.

Leshem, Dotan. "Retrospectives: What Did the Ancient Greeks Mean by *Oikonomia*?" *Journal of Economic Perspectives* 30, no. 1 (February 2016) 225–38. https://doi.org/10.1257/jep.30.1.225.

Malloch, Theodore Roosevelt. *Spiritual Enterprise: Doing Virtual Business*. New York: Encounter, 2008.

Miller, David W. *God at Work: The History and Promise of the Faith at Work Movement*. Oxford: Oxford University Press, 2007.

Miller, David W., and Timothy Ewest. "The Integration Box." In *Handbook of Faith and Spirituality in the Workplace: Emerging Research and Practice*, edited by Judi Neal, 403–18. New York: Springer-Verlag, 2013.

Miller, David W., Faith W. Ngunjiri, and James D. LoRusso. "Caring for Employees." In *Faith and Work: Christian Perspectives, Research and Insights into the Movement*, edited by Timothy Ewest, 131–50. Charlotte: Information Age, 2018.

Mounce, Bill. "Τέκτων." https://www.billmounce.com/greek-dictionary/tekton.

Neal, Judi, ed. *Handbook of Faith and Spirituality in the Workplace: Emerging Research and Practice*. New York: Springer-Verlag, 2013. https://www.springer.com/gp/book/9781461452324.

Preece, Gordon. "Work." In *The Complete Book of Everyday Christianity*, edited by Robert Banks and R. Paul Stevens, 1140–41. Singapore: Graceworks, 2011.

Stevens, R. Paul. *Work Matters: Lessons from Scripture*. Grand Rapids: Eerdmans, 2012.

Taylor, John. "Labour of Love: The Theology of Work in First and Second Thessalonians." In *Work: Theological Foundations and Practical Implications*, edited by R. Keith Loftin and Trey Dimsdale, 49–68. London: SCM, 2018.

Weber, Max, and R. H. Tawney. *The Protestant Ethic and the Spirit of Capitalism*. Translated by Talcott Parsons. Mineola: Dover, 2003.

Zapf, Lucas, and Peter Seele. "As to the Birds Flying, So Is Man Born Unto Work." In *Faith and Work: Christian Perspectives, Research and Insights into the Movement*, edited by Timothy Ewest, 97–114. Charlotte: Information Age, 2018.

# PART I

# Workplace

# 2

# How Do We Shape Christians for the Workplace?

### Kara Martin

*Mary Andrews College and Alphacrucis College*

### Abstract

WHILE THERE ARE TOOLS for assessing spiritual values in the workplace, there has been little research into how to spiritually form Christians for the workplace. What are the priorities of learning knowledge (cognition), skills (behaviors), and values (affections) that should be prioritized for a Christian to effectively navigate the modern workplace? These questions of spiritual formation are critical to Christian schools, theological colleges, Christian higher education providers, professional Christian organizations, and university groups seeking to prepare workplace Christians who will be able to influence society and culture. What, then, is the shape of the *telos* of faithful workplace Christians, and how can they be formed?

This research contributes to this conversation by employing the repertory grid technique (RGT)—a structured interview research method—allowing the discovery of individuals' personal constructs that influence their behavior, leading to a better understanding of the connection between faith and work. Interviewees are encouraged to tell the story of their spiritual formation. These narratives are subsequently analyzed for integration of formation techniques with personal constructs. This chapter includes findings from a pilot study of six Christian doctors, and recommendations for educators and individual workers. It will lay the groundwork for future research into the faithful worker in the contemporary workplace.

## Introduction

In 2015 I was asked to spend some time mentoring and teaching young Christian doctors who were involved in the Christian Medical and Dental Fellowship Australia (CMDFA), a professional Christian organization with a long history around the world. It was difficult to know where to begin, so I started with some material I had been teaching in theological colleges on Jesus-shaped leadership and mentoring. My efforts were extremely well-received; in fact, there was a great hunger for any sort of Christian teaching that applied to the work that was taking such an enormous amount of their time and energy.

However, part of me was frustrated that I really had no idea about the endpoint of what I was doing; I was trying out some concepts, but the reality was that I had no idea what should be in the curriculum that equips Christians for their workplaces.

## Organizations in the Faith–Work Space

This is the struggle that a lot of organizations face in this space, and there are many players:

- *Professional Christian organizations* such as the CMDFA, Nurses Christian Fellowship, and Lawyers Christian Fellowship;
- *Parachurch workplace organizations* such as City Bible Forum, Kingdom Business, and Business as Mission;
- *University Christian groups* preparing graduates for the workplace, such as International Fellowship of Evangelical Students, Cru/Power to Change, and Navigators;
- *Local churches* seeking to equip members for where 98 percent of their congregations spend 95 percent of their time (that is, outside church gatherings);
- *Theological colleges or seminaries*, many of which rely on students with no intention of going into paid Christian work (church, parachurch or mission) to help subsidize those who do; and
- *Christian vocational higher education providers* seeking to help their students integrate their faith into their other studies.

These organizations attempt to provide coherent material, and examples are included in the table below.

Table 1

| | |
|---|---|
| Professional Christian organizations | • Focus on character |
| | • Ethical issues particular to the vocation |
| | • Concepts of calling to a particular vocation |
| | • Evangelism in the workplace |
| | • Bible study material pertinent to the vocation |
| | • Issues of stress or work-life balance[1] |
| Parachurch workplace organizations | • Workplace evangelism |
| | • Apologetics |
| | • Work issues such as dealing with ambition or work idolatry |
| | • Working with excellence[2] |
| University Christian groups | • Personal spiritual disciplines (Bible reading and prayer) |
| | • Evangelism |
| | • Importance of Christian character[3] |

1. The Christian Medical and Dental Fellowship Australia website "Resource" links refer to Ethics, Bible Study material pertinent to the vocation, and Luke's Journal, which regularly prints articles on calling (e.g. "Bringing Spirituality into Clinical Practice," 22, no. 2 [Sep 2017]), evangelism (e.g. "Sharing Comfort through Christ," 23, no. 1 [Jan 2018]), character (e.g. "Compassionate Christian Healthcare," 23, no. 2 [June 2018]). See http://www.cmdfa.org.au/Resources/resources. As another example, the Lawyers Christian Fellowship (headquartered in the United Kingdom) has resources under the categories of evangelism, biblical legal principles, life as a lawyer-to-be, and vocational specific issues such as business and family law. See "Library," https://lawcf.org/resources/library.

2. City Bible Forum covers topics on apologetics (such as other religions, Jesus, Christianity, science, and faith), and work issues (work-life balance, money, and wealth). See "Resource Library/City Bible Forum," https://citybibleforum.org/library. Business as Mission has global reports that cover topics such as biblical foundations and church planting. The four pillars of equipping are described as personal character, biblical foundations, business excellence, and best practice. See "Get Started—Business as Mission," http://businessasmission.com/get-started/#tab-id-4.

3. International Fellowship of Evangelical Students describes its programs as focused on evangelism and leadership development which includes spiritual disciplines and a Christian witness on key issues. See "Our Work," https://www.ifesworld.org/en/our-work. Navigators describe their role thus: "Our emphasis is on training and supporting students to help them grow their relationship with Jesus and their ability to lead

| Local churches | - A basic theology of work |
| --- | --- |
| | - Importance of good (godly) character |
| | - Priority of evangelism |
| | - Importance of balancing church and work[4] |
| Theological colleges or seminaries | - An introduction to a theology of work |
| | - Pastoral care issues for workplace Christians |
| | - Ethical issues for workplace Christians |
| | - Examination of different worldviews |
| | - Theology for everyday life[5] |
| Christian vocational higher education providers | - Biblical overview with vocational application |
| | - Examination of different worldviews |
| | - Ethics for particular vocations[6] |

their friends and classmates towards Christ. Each campus group regularly spend time reading and studying the Bible, praying, and volunteering in the local community." See "Student," https://navigators.org.au/community/student/.

4. This list comes from requests for me to preach and my own surveys of churches in Australia. A review of Sermon Central reveals 4,312 sermons (although only the fiftieth most viewed sermon dealt directly with a work topic: ambition), the majority of which focus on a basic theology of work ("Faith at work"), character ("Integrity"), being a witness for the Lord ("God Working Attitude"), and focusing on God's work not ours ("Work Worth Doing"). See "Sermons about Work—SermonCentral.Com."

5. My focus is on Australian theological colleges which are the same as seminaries in the US. The Australian College of Theology is a consortium of eighteen colleges around Australia and has five distinct units dealing with faith and work: A Biblical Theology of Work; Introduction to Workplace Ministry; Mentoring and Pastoral Care of Workers; Putting Faith to Work; and Finding your Vocation (aka Principles of Vocational Stewardship). Workplace ethical issues may be considered as a subset of units on ethics. There are five units on worldview and apologetics, and one unit on theology for everyday life. See "Our Units—Australian College of Theology," https://www.actheology.edu.au/our-units/.

6. One college in Australia (Excelsia) teaches worldview, ethics, biblical studies, and vocation. See "Integrative Studies/Christian College/Excelsia College," https://excelsia.edu.au/courses/integrative-studies/. Alphacrucis College includes units on Christian Worldview and Christian Ethics as core. As a sample, see "Bachelor of Business," https://www.ac.edu.au/awards/bachelor-business/. Christian Heritage College has three units covering Christian worldview including an explanation of Christian doctrine, aspects of a Christian worldview using the unifying theme of the kingdom of God, and comparison with other religions and worldviews. See "CHC/Bachelor of Business," https://www.chc.edu.au/courses/business/bachelor-of-business/.

## Issues With What Is Offered

On first glance, this is an impressive list of faith-work materials. However, for a range of reasons explored below, it is possible to *attend these organizations* and not encounter any vocational teaching at all, particularly when provided by churches and theological colleges. Further, while all this material may be provided, many workplace Christians are unaware of its existence or relevance, having neatly divided their Sundays from their Mondays.

*For leaders of organizations*, there is rarely a concept of a coherent curriculum of teaching that would assist Christians to rediscover how integral faith is to work. There is a smorgasbord of material made available, and members or students are expected to work their way through it.

*For churches*, the availability and depth of material is dependent on the willingness of church leadership to prioritize an area which is not core to church programs. While I would argue that it is the role of the church to equip every church member for expression of their faith in every aspect of life, the focus of many churches is on resourcing and implementing their internal programs.

*In theological colleges*, the material is usually available as electives, and often not identified as part of recommended learning pathways.[7]

*In Christian vocational colleges* the units are usually compulsory, but this tends to mean they are generalist in application, and many of the vocational applications are left up to the students to make. An example of this was a college I taught in where units included overviews of the Old Testament and New Testament with no direct application to the other study areas of the students. Assessments were exegetical essays, rather than opportunities to thoughtfully explore connections between the text and their own area of study.[8]

## The Integration Gap

There are some basic distinctions and borderline dualistic divisions in this material that cause issues for anyone wanting to genuinely integrate their faith with their work:

---

7. In the Australian College of Theology, none of the units identified in footnote 5 are core units; all are electives. None of those electives are identified in the description for the key vocational course of Master of Divinity. See "Course—Australian College of Theology," https://www.actheology.edu.au/course/MDIV02/.

8. This was a college which now offers a broader range of options as a direct result of me applying a unit vocationally, with resulting positive feedback from students both non-Christian and Christian.

Table 2

| | |
|---|---|
| Internal (example: character) | External (example: worldviews) |
| Sacred (example: Bible studies) | Secular (example: ethics) |
| Ministry (example: evangelism) | Work (example: calling) |
| Knowledge (example: biblical narrative) | Skills (example: apologetical conversations) |
| Foundation (example: spiritual disciplines) | Expression (example: church–work balance) |
| Being (example: theology of work) | Doing (example: working excellently) |

These binaries mean that individuals have to forge the connection between the lists on the left and the lists on the right. To make the issue more difficult for the individual workplace Christian, the list on the left is often prioritized and valued more highly than the list on the right.[9]

My contention is that, typically, workplace Christians are not asked what they want to learn or need to learn. There is a tendency in Christian organizations for the content to be developed by those in leadership, then delivered without enquiry or feedback from the congregation, members, or students in their care.[10]

One counter to this might be that students/clients/members of Christian organizations are not the best people to be consulted in terms of their learning needs. Metaphorically, this is equivalent to a patient self-diagnosing versus a doctor advising. However, there is a growing body of evidence of the need for patient consultation in diagnosis, with the conclusion that, "Making sense of illness can be enhanced by inviting and recognizing the patient's story."[11] In education in Australia, there is a growing move toward inquiry-based pedagogy which is student-centered and motivated, and builds on prior student experience;[12] and in a recent study this was expanded

---

9. This preference is illustrated through what units are core at theological colleges and in university groups (see footnotes 3, 5, and 7).

10. This is an assertion by observation following years of being involved in leadership of theological colleges, on faculty, as an adjunct, in academic committees, and on the boards of colleges; working in and with university groups, professional Christian groups, and parachurch organizations; and being an Elder with a church while preaching and speaking at churches across the Protestant denominational spectrum in the US, Singapore, Malaysia, and Australia: Anglican, Baptist, Methodist, Presbyterian, Uniting, Pentecostal, Churches of Christ.

11. Undeland and Malterud, "Diagnostic Interaction."

12. "Lutheran-Education-Queensland-Inquiry-Based-Learning.Pdf." In this explainer

to preserve teacher training with "increased engagement and enhanced learning outcomes."[13]

This research is about consultation with mature faith–work integrators (all recommended by professional Christian organizations) and gaining value from their extensive experience in application of faith in workplace settings.

## What Is Needed

In thirty years on the frontline of the nexus between faith and work, this growing awareness of the gaps drove me to desire more consultation with workplace Christians, leading to the development of coherent curricular concepts for organizations equipping workplace Christians. While a survey of workplace Christians was a useful starting place, what was required was a tool that would go deeper.

I am very grateful to Professor Felix Tan, of Excelsia College, who introduced me to the repertory grid technique.[14] This tool was originally developed by George Kelly (1955/1991) to investigate his personal construct theory, but has now been applied in organizational settings, including job design where it is used to interrogate the usual wish list of characteristics required for roles.

The technique involves an interviewee thinking of three work colleagues in a particular role, and when offered a particular role variable (construct), describe narratives of two colleagues who demonstrate the variable positively, and one who demonstrates the variable negatively. In applying the technique to the role of being a workplace Christian, I have been able to identify priorities of learning knowledge (cognition), skills (behaviors), and values (affections), as well as gathering a wealth of examples of what good expression looks like.

There were several difficulties with applying the technique:

- I could only survey those vocations where Christians observed other Christians in the workplace. For this reason, I decided to focus on doctors.

---

for schools overseen by Lutheran Education in Queensland, a range of benefits of student-centered inquiry-based learning are explored.

13. Preston et al., "Inquiry-Based Learning."

14. Felix Tan has pioneered the use of the repertory grid technique in Information Systems in identifying IS Manager constructs. See Tan and Hunter, "Repertory Grid Technique."

- I had to formulate a list of constructs (cognitive, behavioral, and affective) since early interviews revealed that interviewees struggled to offer these spontaneously when considering integration of faith and work (as contrasted with thinking of the essential qualities for paid work roles). This reveals the lack of language that Christians have to articulate how faith is integral to work.

However, the technique overcomes one of the challenges of capturing information about integration, often done through surveys[15] or narratives;[16] that is, many Christians downplay their own abilities in areas (a false idea of humility).

## What Has Emerged

### Knowledge

What would we imagine we would need to *know* to be effective as Christians in integrating our faith at work? Interviewees were asked to choose a first and second priority from the following list:[17]

- The sacred/secular dichotomy
- The biblical narrative
- A basic theology of work
- A history of work
- Worldviews and how to engage with them
- Spiritual disciplines that deepen intimacy with God
- Ethical framework for decision-making
- A basic understanding of people, groups and organizations.

The most frequently chosen construct was "Spiritual disciplines that deepen intimacy with God."

Spiritual disciplines are those practices that deepen our personal relationship with God. They usually include practices of daily Bible reading

---

15. The best known of these is developed by Miller and Ewest, "The Integration Box (TIB)."

16. One of the latest examples is Harjanto, *The Development of Vocational Stewardship*—a series of interviews and narratives among Indonesian Christian Professionals.

17. Development of the list of constructs resulted from studies of what is taught at various theological colleges, Christian higher education providers, and Christian organizations.

and prayer, but they can also include a range of practices such as: the inward disciplines of prayer, fasting, meditation, and study in the Christian life; the outward disciplines of simplicity, solitude, submission, and service; and the corporate disciplines of confession, worship, guidance, and celebration.[18] One interviewee commented that such disciplines are essential "for keeping grounded, especially when faith is under attack."

Interviewees were then asked to tell some stories of those who demonstrate this construct.[19]

> You can tell Anne has a deep foundation with God because of her speech and the way she carries herself. It shows in the way that she prays, and everything she says and does. You can even see it in the things she asks prayer for, such as building God's kingdom and her consideration for others.
>
> Brenda reads verses and reflects on them deeply. You can sense in her a deep understanding of God. At work you will see her buying chocolate for the young workers to encourage them.
>
> Carl naturally talks about faith in a way that is compelling because he has a genuine relationship with God. His faith underpins everything he does, and you can see that it is fundamental to who he is and what he does.
>
> Darren talks about Jesus with every patient because he sees faith as fundamental to humanity. He explains how spiritual brokenness contributes to their disease. He is a prayerful person. He knows how to deal with the tough situations: people with addiction, who are experiencing terrible consequences from their choices. He holds on to a sense of hope, and gives others hope that there is an opportunity for restoration, that there is something worthwhile they can look forward to.
>
> Elaine prays frequently and asks others for prayer. She is grateful to God for answered prayer.

Interviewees were also asked to identify stories that demonstrate when this construct is negatively demonstrated, to further describe what this looks like by contrast:

> You cannot see as much evidence in Felicity's life that she is a person of faith. She comes across as a very detached and logical person.

---

18. Foster, *Celebration of Discipline*.

19. Note that names have been given to help us identify with respondents but are changed from the original.

> George does not reveal much about his personal circumstances. I work closely with him, yet he hardly ever talks about faith and work. When I've brought it up, it has been awkward.
>
> Harold is not committed to a Christian community and is not supporting his family in going to church. When he does show up, it seems he is only going to church for show.

"A basic theology of work" was seen by a couple of interviewees as very important. This would cover a biblical view of work in the bigger story of what God is doing in the world. Typical basic theologies cover the four-point gospel outline that work is good, working is cursed, work can be redeemed, and there will be work in the new creation. The narratives of when this construct is demonstrated positively include:

> Ian understands that work is not everything; he knows that family is important, and that rest is important. He knows that when he works, he is committed to work.
>
> John treats people well, he doesn't gossip or participate in gossip. He understands God's intention for work.
>
> Katie demonstrates a very balanced theology of work, and knows her boundaries, practicing good self-care.
>
> Lynne enjoys her work, and she works really hard, often going beyond what is required. She is widely recognized as reliable.

Then, interviewees related stories of when there is no understanding of a basic theology of work.

> Max places too much importance on work, and he drags his family around because of his work. He talks himself up, elevates himself as a doctor, enjoys the privileges and perks.
>
> Nancy is a workaholic and does not have good boundaries.

This commentary on what good theology does is interesting. Having a good biblical understanding of work should ensure that work is in its right place compared to other demands on our time and our heart. Both examples of poor understanding of a theology of work were directed at those who work too hard, neglecting family and other priorities. It also means that work is having a poor impact on one's character.

## Skill

In the preparation for faith–work integration, churches and theological colleges and professional Christian groups have almost exclusively focused on cognition: improved knowledge. Even when teaching about prayer we have tended to do biblical studies on prayer rather than demonstrating how to pray. Mostly, we hope workplace disciples will pick up the skills they need through osmosis. I have found the same in some colleges where teaching on biblical exegesis has not actually seen exegesis as a skill rather than as something you mysteriously learn by reading lots of exegetical examples!

What *skills* would be useful to learn as a workplace Christian? This was the longest list of the three considered. (The second longest was *values*, while the shortest list was *knowledge*.) Interviewees were asked to choose from the following:

- Build authentic relationships
- Demonstrate excellent competency for the job
- Understand systems so that one can engage with them for the common good
- Engage with the popular and work culture
- Understand and respond to suffering
- Imagine and innovate
- Counter suspicion and hostility with hospitality
- Pray deeply
- Exegete the Bible with application in work context
- Influence others through servant leadership
- Theologically reflect on current issues and situations
- Connect biblical material with work
- Synthesize a biblical worldview with work
- Transform working, working relationships, the workplace, and work recipients through gospel renewal.

In the initial interviews conducted for the research, "Building authentic relationships" emerged a top priority. This was fascinating considering no one in society is taught how to form relationships beyond "how to be a good friend" classes in kindergarten, and marriage preparation classes. It is a complex skill to form adult relationships with people we might not agree with, and sometimes do not even like, so that we can effectively work with them, and build a platform for sharing meaning.

A clear selection from this group of interviewees was "Influence others through servant leadership." Servant leadership is a distinctive Christian practice.[20] In the workplaces which most of the interviewees inhabit, the dominant leadership style is the "hero" leader: autocratic, privileged, and used to being worshipped.[21] Jesus introduced an idea of leadership marked by humility, with a desire to serve rather than to be served.[22] These characteristics are brought out in the stories shared by interviewees of those who demonstrate this construct:

> Aaron is approachable for problems and requests. He is a senior leader, and he does not put himself on a pedestal, but works alongside others, always looking to help those around him improve.
>
> Beatrice works in a Christian hospital, and she worships at the Cathedral. She has a cell group which is very Bible-based and evangelical. She knows a lot of Bible. She joins the mission teams and she is the most active in doing things whenever there is a need, helping and serving others. Recently there was a doctor from Sydney who needed upskilling in medical skills for preventative medicine. She took up the servant-leadership role and coordinated his upskilling through a number of hospitals, so he could observe and learn. She took initiative. She is very effective at getting others to do things. She ignores the personal cost for the sake of others and advancing God's kingdom.
>
> Colin thinks ahead and anticipates needs of others. He does the messy, smelly dirty stuff that most leaders avoid, or think is "beneath him." He is eager to learn, asking lots of questions. He has tissues ready for patients receiving bad news.
>
> Dana loves buying chocolate and coffee for others; she is very generous, nurturing and supportive of all her work colleagues. She is also generous with her time, and her words.
>
> When there was a time of severe bullying, Eric stepped in when he didn't have to and spoke up for justice, and defended those who resigned. As a consequence, he was criticized by management.
>
> Francis takes responsibility for things, checking to see how others are, and puts others before himself.
>
> Georgina makes sure people feel included. She shows people that they are loved through simple gestures such as baking food for them.

---

20. See Roach, *Servant-Leadership Style*.
21. See Fulop and Day, "Leader to Leadership."
22. See "Jesus-Shaped Leadership" in Martin, *Workship 2*.

Interviewees were also asked to identify stories of where it is not done well, to further describe what this looks like by contrast.

> Henry lords it over others and put himself on a pedestal. His office door is always closed; he is never available. He considered what he was doing as always more important than the person in front of him.
>
> Ivor lacks humility and is always putting himself first. When it is a busy time we take turns taking breaks, but he is the first person out the door rather than checking with others.
>
> Jenny runs her area as if she is a dictator in charge of a small kingdom. She does not seem to notice what a massive ego she has.

The second area chosen was the skill of "Transforming working, working relationships, the workplace and work recipients through gospel renewal." As one interviewee commented: "the gospel is at the center of transforming us and then flows through to everything. It also involves building authentic relationships: not to get something out of them but because I want to work with them." Another commented that this goes "beyond the spiritual; applying faith to every part of the work."

The narratives of when this construct is demonstrated positively include:

> Ken builds authentic relationships, mentoring and encouraging them, and going deeper with people. People see him as a friend rather than a threat. The sense of respect and care he offers permeates the workplace.
>
> The gospel informs Len's whole life, his behavior, and his choice of career. He is not as ambitious as others because he prioritizes service, faith, and family. He stands out from those around him because he is not obsessed with promotion, money, or success. Len's work doesn't identify who he is; he focuses on relationships instead.
>
> Matt is a surgeon, and is busy with a young family. He should be stressed out but he is a beautiful gentle person all the time. He is consistently kind, generous with his time, friendly and pleasant, and happy to teach. He does the small things that make him stand out in terms of colleagues and patients. Most of his fellow leaders act like jerks. Matt doesn't get into office politics; he changes the team atmosphere to be positive.
>
> Neridah does the simple things like showing kindness and patience, which aren't common in the workplace. She speaks

well of other people. She is also really skilled and interacts well with people.

Oliver is at the forefront of working with difficult people, and his work is intense. He has this knack for being grounded and diplomatic. He doesn't set people off, even in a stressful environment. He is very considerate. He would never put someone down, in spite of the crap he faces. He is always working to affirm others. He makes it a point to pay someone a formal compliment rather than a formal complaint. He could complain about doctors who are difficult. There was one colleague, a surgeon, who was particularly obliging, and he made it a point to inform his department heads how this doctor made it easy for Oliver to get some work done. The department heads talked, and the compliment became communicated on and articulated the sort of behavior that should occur in the workplace. Oliver transforms the workplace by highlighting the positive.

Penny is great at encouraging people and thanking them for their hard work. She is genuine in relating to people. She tries to make the workplace better through encouragement.

Queenie is always sharing food. She makes people feel included, and part of the team. She is different by not complaining all the time. She tries to make the workplace better rather than bitter.

Interviewees then shared stories of workplace Christians who lack skills in transforming the workplace.

Rick actively avoids the opportunity to share his faith or integrate because he does not see the gospel as having a place in the workplace. He acts as if relationships are not as important as the work that needs to be done. He has no desire to transform the workplace.

Sue is rude and brief with people, and difficult to distinguish from others. She complains about things and swears at work. Sue perpetuates the poor culture rather than transforming and renewing it in positive ways.

I saw Tanya dismissive of a request from a nurse, thereby highlighting the stratification, rather than seeking to break down barriers.

## Values

As Christians, our character is our best promotion of Christ, and lack of character is the worst detraction from the name of Christ.[23] While many would agree that *values* are important, we do not know how to grow those values in people. Identifying the behavior that reveals the values is part of the way forward, and this is what is revealed in the interviews.

Interviewees were asked to choose from the following values:

- Intimacy with God as the basis for relationship with others and the world
- Working in all its variety and aspects
- Faithful working
- Godly (good) character
- Serving people and the organization
- The church gathered as support for the church scattered
- Continuous learning and personal spiritual formation
- Human flourishing
- Community flourishing
- Work as a means of worship
- Humility as a corrective to the drivenness of modern working
- Seeking justice for others
- A felt call to a place of working.

A clear selection among this group of interviewees was "godly character." This is not surprising, since it is the broadest description of the set of values that might be expected to be revealed. As one interviewee said: "competence in the job is important to a certain level, but godly character is not covered by good competence." Thus, godly character is the way the competent Christian doctor stands out.

Interviewees revealed the following stories of when godly character is revealed:

> The way Adam treats others reveals his character. There is genuine care and it is clear that he wants the best for others. He never puts down or bad-mouths others.

---

23. See this blog piece by a pastor and commentator hosted by Christianity Today: Vaters, "Question Of Character."

> If he makes a mistake, Ben admits it. If something hasn't been done right, he will learn from it. Ben doesn't try to hide or excuse mistakes, he learns and improves for next time.
>
> Caitlyn doesn't complain through a tough situation. She was asked to do something extra in an environment that was not ideal, with equipment that failed, yet the joy of the work before her meant she kept going. She saw any discomfort as momentary. She expressed a joy and peace in spite of circumstances.
>
> Delia is exemplary. She brings a lot of positive energy and fosters a nurturing environment in the workplace. As an educator as well as a clinician, she influences a lot of people, and inspires a lot of people. She is a good role model. She lives out the values: helping others to flourish and a community to flourish. Out of her good character everything else flows.
>
> Given the intensity of Edward's work, he always does it with excellence. He is never lazy. He puts his heart and soul into his work. His colleagues like him. He gets such positive comments on his 360 [performance review], from nurses, allied health, pharmacists, as well as doctor colleagues. If you have good character you are valued in the workplace. He is light in the workplace.
>
> Felicity demonstrates compassion, integrity, kindness, and sacrificial and unconditional love. One way she does this is speaking up against injustice.

Interviewees were also asked to identify stories of where it is not done well, to further describe what this looks like by contrast:

> Gary insists on getting his own way. His intention is to get ahead. He is always competing, looking out for himself. You know he always has an agenda.
>
> Whenever Helen faces a difficulty, she will blow it out of proportion and become the center of attention, so that she attracts care and concern. The irony is that godly character would minimize the difficulty. She thinks the worst of every situation and every person.
>
> Isaiah doesn't have much integrity. He goes to big conferences and stays in fancy hotels sponsored by drug companies. He never considers the ethical implications. To be a good example to colleagues, one's integrity is so important.

The second value chosen was "Valuing intimacy with God as the basis for relationship with others and the world." As one interviewee commented:

"the closer we get to God, the more we are aware of our own failings and need for God."

The narratives of when this construct is demonstrated positively include:

> Jill prays all the time, and you can tell she is deep with God because of the things that concern her, such as other Christians being persecuted. She is aware of the bigger picture of the spiritual reality.
>
> Kim is active in the hospital, showing individual care and concern. She does little acts of kindness and develops close relationships with others.
>
> Leo has a strong understanding of who God is and that affects the way he engages with people professionally and personally. His intimacy with God flows out into all his words and actions.
>
> Michael is a godly guy: respectful, encouraging of others, letting people see his relationship with God. He is respected because of his values that flow from his intimate relationship with God.

In contrast, consider this story of when someone does not operate from this value of intimacy with God:

> Pride and arrogance can emerge if you are not close to God. Ned is also willing to go the way of the world, and respect of peers is more important to him than a faithful relationship with God.[24]

## Conclusions

This pilot study has demonstrated both the effectiveness of the research method, and the value of the data obtained. It has contradicted some of the assumptions applied by organizations, and also has elicited a wealth of stories with the potential to form and inspire workplace Christians.

This research has the potential to benefit a range of Christian organizations operating in the intersection of faith and work to clarify the skills, knowledge, and values that would best equip Christians to be integral in the workplace. The knowledge, skills, and values already identified are not those which typically are addressed in offerings from those organizations, as can be seen by reference to Table 1.

---

24. Note that this was one area where interviewees found it difficult to comment on, that is, how do we measure someone's intimacy with God?

Further, the stories that illustrate what those variables look like in practice, enable contextualization beyond the medical workplaces investigated. The power of story as a means of describing and changing complex behavior is well documented. Bruner was among the first to identify that narrative is the primary way that humans construct reality.[25] The particular features that he highlights are the fact that it is outside time, particular to a person, invites awareness of emotional state, allows meaning-making, demonstrates exception to conventional expectations, bears witness to reality, is recognizable, establishes new norms, can be translated into other contexts, and is able to be absorbed into other stories.

Advancing Bruner's work, Drumm has established how storytelling can be used to develop skills and shape systems. She suggests this is possible because stories center on people, they enrich understanding, develop empathy, allow for reflection, are not limited to one objective truth, represent both individual and communal reality, as well as aiding learning and development.[26]

In Australia there is considerable debate about the public expression of faith, including in the workplace (as the sacking of Israel Folau by Rugby Australia, the retaliatory legal action, and the ongoing media speculation has aptly demonstrated[27]). What is needed is a coordinated and focused application of precious resources on developing the particular variables that are most likely to form workplace Christians who commend Jesus and the gospel, that is, the "good news" of the reconciling work of Christ and the inauguration of the kingdom of God.

## Future Research

These pilot interviews were conducted with six doctors selected by the Christian Medical and Dental Fellowship of Australia. However, more interviews would confirm the validity of the responses.

Another question is whether there are vocational differences for Christians integrating their faith in other areas of work. These results need to be compared and contrasted with interviews with other groups. Teachers are another vocational group where the interaction with other Christians in the workplace would allow the RGT to be applied.

Finally, it would be good to compare the results with Christians outside the "helping" professions, particularly Christians operating at a

---

25. Bruner, "Narrative Construction," 4.
26. Drumm, "Personal Storytelling," 4–6.
27. As a sample, see "ABC Search."

different educational level, and in a different work culture. It is intended that interviews be conducted with tradespeople.

## Bibliography

"ABC Search." https://search-beta.abc.net.au/#/?query=Israel%20Folau&page=1&configure%5BgetRankingInfo%5D=true&configure%5BclickAnalytics%5D=true&configure%5Banalytics%5D=true&refinementList%5Bsite.title%5D%5B0%5D=ABC%20News.

"Bachelor of Business." https://www.ac.edu.au/awards/bachelor-business/.

Bruner, Jerome. "The Narrative Construction of Reality." *Critical Inquiry* 18, no. 1 (1991) 1–21.

"CHC/Bachelor of Business." https://www.chc.edu.au/courses/business/bachelor-of-business/.

"Course—Australian College of Theology." https://www.actheology.edu.au/course/MDIV02/.

Drumm, Michelle. "The Role of Personal Storytelling in Practice." *Insight, IRISS* 23 (November 28, 2013). https://www.iriss.org.uk/sites/default/files/iriss-insight-23.pdf.

Foster, Richard. *Celebration of Discipline*. London: Hodder & Stoughton Ltd, 2008.

Fulop, Liz, and Gary E. Day. "From Leader to Leadership: Clinician Managers and Where to Next?" *Australian Health Review* 34, no. 3 (2010) 344–51. https://doi.org/10.1071/AH09763.

"Get Started—Business as Mission." http://businessasmission.com/get-started/#tab-id-4.

"Integrative Studies/Christian College/Excelsia College." https://excelsia.edu.au/courses/integrative-studies/.

International Fellowship of Evangelical Students. "Our Work" (April 29, 2014). https://www.ifesworld.org/en/our-work.

Lawyers' Christian Fellowship. "Library." https://lawcf.org/resources/library.

"Lutheran-Education-Queensland-Inquiry-Based-Learning.Pdf." https://www.australiancurriculum.edu.au/media/1360/lutheran-education-queensland-inquiry-based-learning.pdf.

Martin, Kara. *Workshop 2: How to Flourish at Work*. Singapore: Graceworks, 2018.

"Our Units—Australian College of Theology." https://www.actheology.edu.au/our-units/.

Preston, Lou, Kate Harvie, and Heather Wallace. "Inquiry-Based Learning in Teacher Education: A Primary Humanities Example." *Australian Journal of Teacher Education* 40, no. 12 (January 1, 2015). https://doi.org/10.14221/ajte.2015v40n12.6.

"Resource Library/City Bible Forum." https://citybibleforum.org/library.

Roach, Dale. *The Servant-Leadership Style of Jesus: A Biblical Strategy for Leadership Development*. Grand Rapids, MI: WestBow, 2016.

"Sermons about Work—SermonCentral.Com." https://www.sermoncentral.com/sermons/sermons-about-work/?page=1&sortBy=Relevance&keyword=work&contributorId=&rewrittenurltype=&searchResultSort=Relevance&CheckedScriptu

reBookId=&minRating=&maxAge=365&denominationFreeText=&searchPhrase=work.

The Australian Navigators. "Student." https://navigators.org.au/community/student/.

Tan, Felix B., and M. Gordon Hunter. "The Repertory Grid Technique: A Method for the Study of Cognition in Information Systems." *MIS Quarterly* 26, no. 1 (March 2002) 39–57. https://doi.org/10.2307/4132340.

Undeland, Merete, and Kirsti Malterud. "Diagnostic Interaction: The Patient as a Source of Knowledge?" *Scandinavian Journal of Primary Health Care* 26, no. 4 (2008) 222–27. https://doi.org/10.1080/02813430802325086.

Vaters, Karl. "A Question of Character: Getting Unstuck Is Not the Church's Biggest Problem." Pivot/A Blog by Karl Vaters. https://www.christianitytoday.com/karl-vaters/2019/march/question-of-character-getting-unstuck.html.

# 3

# Educating for the Kingdom

*A Participatory Model of
Character Development*

JAMES PIETSCH

*Inaburra School*

## Abstract

TODAY, MORE THAN EVER before, it is Christian faith-based schools where most people come into contact with Christianity. How, then, do Christian teachers approach the task of educating young people in these schools? This chapter describes how educating for the kingdom includes, but is not limited to, specific conversations about who God is and how he has established his kingdom through the death and resurrection of Jesus. Educating for the kingdom also focuses our attention on the development of character rather than just knowledge and skills. It is more than simply speaking *about* the kingdom; it is preparing students to *participate in* the kingdom—preparing students to participate initially here on earth in whatever occupation they choose to pursue, as well as in the new creation to come.

In this manner, students are encouraged to put on the virtues of the new creation in the same way that the early Christians were encouraged to do so by Paul. The writers of the New Testament commend their readers to *be who they are becoming*—to put on the character traits of the new creation today. The process of character development, according to the writers of the New Testament, begins with habit formation, through the conscious choice to act in a certain manner time and time again until, one day, such habits become dispositions to act in a certain way without conscious thought or attention. Finally, clusters of associated dispositions associated with specific virtues become evidence of a person's maturing and developing character. Educating for the kingdom, therefore, represents a particular approach to education in which the character traits of the new creation such as grace, humility, compassion, and kindness are promoted, modelled, practiced, and experienced.

## Introduction

Research in education continues to contribute to our understanding of how students learn and how schools can be more effective places of learning for both teachers and students. However, much research pertaining to education and learning is yet to find its way into classrooms where the practices established in the nineteenth century for educating the working classes remain. This is despite the clear case for reforming our educational practice given the significant societal, cultural, and technological changes that we have experienced over the past two hundred years.

Any case for change rests on assumptions and attitudes regarding the purpose of education. Only once the question of purpose has been answered can we then turn our attention to evaluating different strategies for achieving our goals as educators. In *What's the Point of School*,[1] Claxton challenges the idea that the purpose of schools is to transmit knowledge and information to students. Instead, he argues that schools should be places that teach students how to learn. Schools should teach students about how to deal with uncertainty, building resilient learners, encouraging students to be resourceful, reflective, and developing amongst students the capacity to learn with others. This emphasis on teaching students how to learn, Claxton argues, should be evident in each classroom as students learn about Shakespeare, the periodic table, and quadratic equations.

This represents a significant challenge for schools whose activities have been framed by programs focused on delivering content rather than developing learning dispositions. Furthermore, it represents an additional challenge for Christian schools who have not only understood their purpose as teaching content but have also placed particular emphasis on teaching content associated with the gospel. If the purpose of schooling is

1. Claxton, *What's the Point*, 45.

not the transferal of knowledge from teachers to students, but rather the development of students' capacity to learn, then what would this look like in a Christian school?

The purpose of this chapter is to outline a theoretical framework that can support a model for Christian education that is focused on the development of *learning character*.[2] Educating for the kingdom is more than the presentation of propositions which constitute the *evangelion*. Educating for the kingdom engages students in learning activities in which they have opportunities to "put on" (Col 3:12) the character traits of redeemed humanity.[3] Moreover, they are given opportunities to experience a kingdom-of-God-shaped learning community—a community characterized by faith, hope, love, forgiveness, grace, compassion, and humility. They are given an opportunity to experience a uniquely Christian perspective on human flourishing that is based on serving others rather than individual self-actualization.

Drawing on educational research from many different theoretical perspectives, this approach identifies a range of dispositions associated with powerful learning and situates learning activity within a larger purpose for education—that of character formation, drawing on the specifically Christian vision of human flourishing found in the New Testament.

## Routines, Habits, Dispositions, and Virtues

Almost all vision statements developed by schools include the identification of desirable character traits (or virtues) which the school hopes its students will have at the conclusion of their formal schooling. So the concept of virtue is not a foreign one in education. But the process by which virtues are formed through educational activity and the connection between virtues and the outcomes typically associated with educational activity, such as the development of understanding and the capacity to learn, have received little attention in educational research.

According to Tom Wright in his book *Virtue Reborn*,[4] virtues grow out of the habits that we form over a long period of time. They become part of our character, imprinted within and evident in our spontaneous action. They

---

2. Note that the development of learning character is a goal for students from multiple faith backgrounds. It provides all students with the opportunity to reflect on the Christian anthropology of human becoming which informs a particular approach to teaching and learning.

3. Pietsch, *Character Reborn*. See also Cooling et al., "What If Learning," http://www.whatiflearning.com/.

4. Wright, *Virtue Reborn*.

are ways of thinking and acting which become grounded in our brains and bodies so that we can perform certain tasks "intuitively." They are the *second* nature that we take on rather than the nature into which we are born. Character formation begins with establishing habits of action, habits of mind, and, in the context of this discussion, learning dispositions.[5]

Certain categories of habits, however, become indicative of different character traits. People who have developed a collection of associated habits may be described as having a certain disposition. For example, a fastidious person regarding their appearance (a disposition) may be known by a range of habits which identify them as such—routinely brushing their hair, checking the length of their nails each week, flossing every couple of days, and so on. The disposition of being fastidious about one's appearance describes a person who displays this collection of associated habits.

Habits, therefore, refer to specific actions, while dispositions refer to a general approach which is characterized by certain habits. This distinction is evident when comparing Art Costa's "Habits of Mind" approach[6] and Claxton's "Building Learning Power."[7]

Art Costa's approach uses the language of "habits," although he defines such habits as being associated with multiple behaviors that could be regarded as "dispositions." He identifies sixteen "habits" of mind that teachers can promote amongst their students, each of which describe a category of behaviors (some may be conscious; some may eventually become automatic). For example, one habit is "Creating, Imagining, and Innovating." Within this habit, there are a number of different behaviors teachers encourage their students to adopt—trying a different strategy when they get stuck, generating new ideas, developing fluency of thought, and seeking ways to promote originality. Students who are strong in creativity are more likely to generate new ideas automatically when faced with problems, rather than having to remind themselves of the need to do this.

In parallel with Costa's *Habits of Mind*, Guy Claxton describes dispositions of powerful learners. One such disposition is *imagining*. But the definition proposed by Claxton and how he describes what this disposition entails sounds quite different to the set of behaviors outlined by Costa. Imagining, according to Claxton, refers to being able to let your mind explore and play with different possibilities, rehearse things in your mind, ask "what if?" questions, and using your imagination to think of new experiences. This

---

5. For an outline of the theory of character development, see James Smith's *Desiring the Kingdom* and Alasdair McIntyre's *After Virtue*, both of which have their genesis in Aristotle's *Nicomachean Ethics*.

6. Costa and Kallick, *Habits of Mind*.

7. Claxton, *Building Learning Power*.

definition refers to tendencies and characteristics of thinking rather than specific activities. While there are many behaviors associated with *imagining* identified by Costa and others, Claxton suggests that the goal of education should be more than simply providing strategies and techniques: rather, the goal should be the development of dispositions—ways of acting that emerge from a deeper transformation of learning character.

We might represent the relationship between these different ways of thinking using a framework drawn from Peterson and Seligman.[8] They argue that virtues are formed from different character strengths; these in turn are built up by *situational themes*—"specific habits that lead people to manifest given character strengths in given situations." Situational themes in schools emerge from the traditional curriculum through which students are encouraged to develop ways of thinking and doing. Drawing together these different models, we can develop the following diagram through which these different aspects of learning character can be connected.

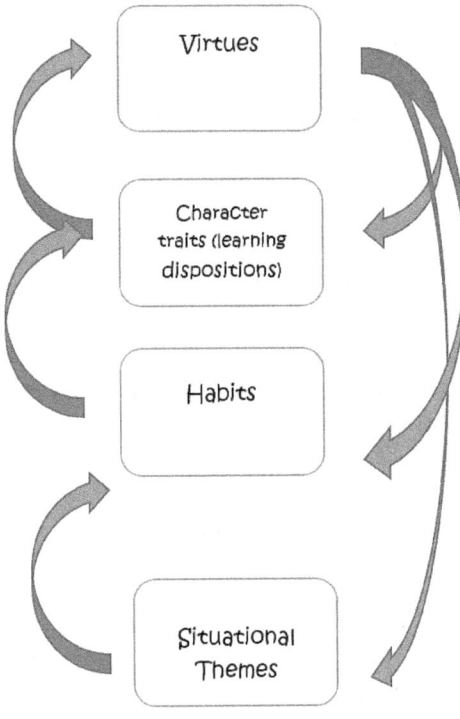

Figure 1

---

8. Peterson and Seligman, *Character Strengths and Virtues*.

By engaging with situational themes emerging from our study of English, Mathematics, Science, and other subjects in school, we identify various strategies, routines, and techniques which support our understanding of these different subjects. The regular use of these different strategies, routines, and techniques leads to the development of a smaller number of habits. In turn, these habits contribute to the development of a smaller number of character strengths or learning dispositions (Peterson and Seligman identify twenty-four character strengths, Claxton identifies seventeen dispositions, and Costa identifies sixteen "habits of mind"—many of which can be located at this level). These, in turn, support the development of a smaller number of virtues.

This describes the left-hand side of the diagram whereby each level informs the next level. However, virtues also inform each of these different aspects of learning character. They are the fundamental grounds of our character and our humanness and, therefore, also provide a foundation from which learning character grows. People of compassion and grace will become learners who are focused on teaching as well as learning. They will be people who recognize habits which they need to change, and habits that they need to work on. Finally, they will be people who make different choices regarding what they learn about and the environments in which they feel most comfortable learning.

In reflecting on this diagram, we need to remind ourselves that the purpose of education is not just about developing an understanding of situational themes, thinking routines, or even dispositions. It is about the formation of character. Educators, irrespective of their faith position, must begin their task by developing a clear picture of human potential. What is our image of the "complete" (adopting the Greek word *teleios*, which is best translated as "complete" rather than "perfect"[9]) person, and how do we provide students with opportunities to become complete human beings? To answer this question, we turn to the New Testament which sets out the character of God's people in the new creation. This distinctively Christian anthropology of human potentiality provides the endpoint which can shape a school's approach to the development of learning character. Whether students accept the Christian worldview as a framework within which to live their lives or not, Christian faith-based schools have an opportunity, through a focus on the development of learning character, to commend a distinctly Christian vision of humanity and humanity's potential.

One of the first things we notice in the New Testament, however, is that in this overlapping age before the establishment of God's kingdom

---

9. Wright, *Virtue Reborn*.

bringing heaven and earth together once and for all, the process of becoming a person of the kingdom never reaches a final endpoint or "telos."[10] In fact, within this age, our approach to education is not driven by the goal of reaching a particular "telos," but rather establishing our students on a lifelong trajectory of being who they are becoming[11]—whether this is as fully-fledged redeemed people of the new creation or as people who remain outside the kingdom of God with an appreciation of the Christian vision of redeemed humanity. And this lifelong journey does not begin at the point of graduating from educational institutions—it is evident in every lesson, establishing a pattern of building learning character that can shape a person's life as they seek to be/become a person of the new creation.

Prior to graduation, of course, those who locate themselves on this trajectory of being/becoming people of the new creation will approach their learning in very different ways to achieve very different ends. Good learners demonstrate graciousness towards one another—they care for those with whom they learn, and also recognize that if someone has a limited understanding of a concept or idea, this merely reflects their current state rather than their actual potential.

Good learners demonstrate compassion—they seek to serve other people and support the learning of those around them. It comes as no surprise that one of the most powerful ways to learn is to teach someone else. Compassionate learners recognize that they can contribute to the learning of others and their own learning by explaining their thinking and reasoning to other people. This idea that teaching and learning are intricately connected is evident in Russian where the one word *obuchenie* refers to teaching/learning without distinguishing between them.[12] Teaching as a strategy for learning reinforces the idea that we are made to be other-person centered rather than self-centered and that we flourish as learners when we seek first the learning of others.

Good learners display humility. In an article appearing in the *New York Times* in 2014, Laszlo Bock from Google identified humility as a necessary fundamental virtue if someone is to be a lifelong learner.[13] They need to know how to step forward in collaborative tasks and also how to step back and allow other people to present their ideas. Humility is a precursor to learning.[14] By recognizing our own limitations we look for ways to improve

10. Phil 1:6; 2 Cor 3:18. See also Lewis, *Till We Have Faces*.
11. MacIntyre, *After Virtue*.
12. Schmidt et al., "Obuchenie." See also Cole, "Perils of Translation," 291–95.
13. Friedman, "Job at Google."
14. Dickson, *Humilitas*, 113–32.

our understanding by listening to others, learning from experts, and seeking the wisdom of those who have gone before us.

And finally, good learners seek to know and understand the world around them so that they might be a voice for justice. Good learners want to be involved in restoring a broken world, a world that is fractured by injustice, oppression, hatred, and violence. They want to understand the world from a position of concern and love rather than a desire to control. They adopt an "epistemology of love,"[15] seeking the truth in such a way that both the knower and the known are dependent on one another. Love is the deepest mode of knowing, because it is love that, while completely engaging with reality other than itself, affirms and celebrates that other-than-self reality. This is the mode of knowing that is necessary if we are to live in the new public world, the world launched at Easter, the world in which Jesus is Lord and Caesar is not.

Our task as Christian educators, therefore, is to identify the habits associated with each learning disposition which, through being strengthened over time, can result in the formation of specific character traits associated with the restored creation. We recognize that the learning dispositions themselves can serve multiple masters and as educators we need to be constantly asking the question regarding character—what virtues and character traits are we building up through the competencies and habits of our classrooms? As we consider how best to reflect on our practice, we need to return time and again to this question of character formation. How might we be explicit about the character traits that we hope to promote amongst our students?

## Expansive Education

Building learning character as an approach to educating for the kingdom fits within the body of approaches to education described by Lucas, Claxton, and Spencer as "expansive education."[16] Drawing on Yrjö Engeström's notion of "learning by expanding,"[17] Lucas, Claxton, and Spencer identify many current approaches to education which seek to do four things. First, adopt goals that extend beyond conventional achievement on examinations; second, expand on our notions of intelligence and the kinds of dispositions that will enable young people to succeed at school and throughout their lives; third, see learning as something which takes place in many different

---

15. Wright, *Virtue Reborn*.
16. Lucas et al., *Expansive Education*.
17. Engeström, *Learning by Expanding*.

contexts as well as the classroom; and fourth, recognize that teachers also have the capacity to be ongoing, enthusiastic learners as well.

There are many expansive approaches currently being implemented across different countries using a range of conceptual frameworks within which to describe the process of learning and associated ideas about intelligence, mindsets, and culture. They include Project Zero run through Harvard University,[18] Art Costa's Habits of Mind framework,[19] and approaches focused on teaching philosophy to young children.[20]

The term "expansive education" refers to a unique aspect of educational activities when compared with other human activities. All human activities, according to Engeström (1987), involve the transforming of objects to achieve outcomes that meet human needs. Unlike other human activities where the object is typically some material good or service transformed to meet a human need, educational activities focused on learning (as distinct from educational activities focused on "schoolwork") have as their objects for transformation the members of this community of practice themselves. Drawing on Marx's interpretation of Hegel's dialectic, Engeström argues that human activities evolve over time in an attempt to resolve the fundamental production/consumption dialectic. But in expansive learning activities, the production/consumption dialectic resolves into a synthetic unity that drives the activity to a point of expansion or generation, producing new forms of human activity that have been made possible by the strengthening of learning capacity. Students at school grow and mature to be people who are able to participate in *other* forms of human activity that exist separate to the original learning activity.

The purpose of schooling, therefore, could be described as the process of identifying the human activities that our students will one day be engaged in, and determining what learning activities will generate the learning character required to participate in these human activities. This definition of purpose could be appropriated by all educators, Christian or otherwise. But what are the human activities in which our students will one day be engaged? We may answer this question with reference to our understanding of life in the twenty-first century and identify the ways in which our current practice needs to change away from transmission approaches to learning towards participatory approaches. Certainly, this is the intention of expansive approaches to education outlined earlier.

18. http://www.pz.harvard.edu/.
19. https://www.habitsofmindinstitute.org/about-us/.
20. Cam and Rinkel, *Thinking Stories*, 1.

For us, however, as people of the kingdom of God who look forward to the restoration of all things, there is a much larger picture of the types of human activities that students could be engaged in, associated with their participation in the new heavens and the new earth.[21] With this understanding of the future, we seek to develop students' learning character, teaching them the "language of heaven"[22] in anticipation of this eschaton evident throughout the Bible. While not all students will choose to be a part of this new creation, the speaking of this language by teachers, other students, and staff creates an opportunity within our schools for students from different faith backgrounds to gain an insight into God's plans and purposes for creation. The speaking of this language also challenges the dominant tongues of our age that speak of individuality, self-fulfillment, and greed. It has the potential to generate ways of thinking, acting, and doing that communicate something of God's character and the virtues that will characterize the coming kingdom of God.

## The Process of Developing Learning Character

Given that Christian education has as its focus the development of learning character, how might schools best achieve this goal? The initial answer to this question suggested by both educational theorists and theologians alike is "little by little." Claxton and colleagues regularly describe the classroom as a learning gym in which different "learning muscles" are exercised at different times:

> [*Building Learning Power*] . . . uses our knowledge of learning and the mind to create a coherent picture of the kinds of mental agility and emotional stamina the good learner has, and to make sure that schools give all these aspects the work-outs they need in order to develop.[23]

> We often use the analogy of a fitness coach in a gym. Such coaches are able to construct broad, balanced and effective exercise regimes that will help people get fitter, because they have a model of what the different ingredients are that go to make up "fitness." . . . They can get us to work on all those things, and gradually, in concert, they add up to improved fitness.[24]

---

21. Wright, *Surprised by Hope*.
22. Wright, *Virtue Reborn*.
23. Claxton, *Building Learning Power*, 14.
24. Claxton et al., *Learning Powered School*, 45.

This same fitness metaphor is adopted by Wright to describe the process of character formation through habits of practice:

> Working on one or two (muscles) isn't enough: there's no point having super-fit legs while the rest of the body is flabby, for example.... In the same way a complete and flourishing human being needs all the basic strengths of character.... The "virtues" are the different strengths of character which together contribute to someone becoming a fully flourishing human being.[25]

All students should have opportunities to build their learning character whether they (or we) identify these characteristics as strengths or weaknesses. While students might pursue their own individual interests within different areas of the curriculum and develop expertise specific to their interests (what might be described as finding their "element" by Sir Ken Robinson[26]), all students are encouraged to become more powerful learners and people committed to the project of restoring a broken world.

Peterson and Seligman[27] make a similar case for the necessary development of virtues. They identify six virtues which are related to twenty-four character traits—wisdom, courage, humanity, justice, temperance, and transcendence. "Good character" requires the development of each of the six virtues they identify, drawing on a range of cultural, spiritual, and ethical traditions (reflecting closely Aristotle's four cardinal virtues of prudence, temperance, justice, and courage). But Peterson and Seligman and their colleagues, in the development of their "signature strengths" approach, suggest that the existing character strengths of individuals provide the initial focus of teachers' attention as they attempt to strengthen students' character. The approach described here, as the development of learning character, challenges teachers to promote each of the different elements of learning character, building up the learning capacity of each student irrespective of their strengths and weaknesses.

## Pathways to Character Formation

Tom Wright identifies within the New Testament an ongoing discussion from a distinctively Christian perspective about the formation of character in his book, *Virtue Reborn*. The key to the development of virtues, according to Wright, is the transforming of the heart and mind. It is not by following rules

25. Wright, *Virtue Reborn*, chap. 2, §3, e-book.
26. Robinson and Aronica, *Element*.
27. Peterson and Seligman, *Character Strengths and Virtues*.

that we become truly human, nor is it by simply being true to our inner selves. The first way involves identifying rules for living within the biblical writings and then obeying such rules to the best of our ability. The second is to reject the notion of rule-following, instead living "authentically" by being true to our inner selves which have been transformed by the spirit of God.

Wright plots a third path which brings together these perspectives as he develops his Christian theory of virtue. Rules and guidelines help us to know what types of behaviors are more likely to build the character associated with the kingdom of God. And yet, the end result is not primarily obedience (although obedience is an outcome), but the transforming of our character such that our inner being is characterized by love, faith, hope, compassion, kindness, humility, and gentleness. However, this is our second nature rather than our first, and it only becomes second nature over a considerable period of time. Appealing to our inner selves as a guide for ethical decisions represents an unwarranted shortcut. Yes, the end result for those who await the coming new creation is a renewed heart and mind such that we reflect the character of God in this world. But the transforming of our hearts and minds does not happen overnight—indeed, it could take a lifetime.

## Developing the Virtuous Learning Character

How, then, can schools be places that promote the Christian virtues of love, kindness, patience, self-control, grace, compassion, humility, and seeking justice? Requiring adherence to a code of conduct is unlikely to change people's character.[28] Nor can we expect that students will simply know within themselves how to live in a manner that reflects the character of the kingdom of God. The third path suggested by Wright involves promoting behaviors (which would be described by Peterson and Seligman as *situational themes*) that become habit-forming, resulting in the transforming of character. In the context of schooling, therefore, character formation can occur through students (and teachers) engaging in carefully designed learning activities which, over time, result in the transformation of participants. As outlined by Paul in Colossians, we encourage students to "put on" the virtues of the new creation, to be a person of the new creation so that we might become this person in the future. By doing so, faith-based Christian schools can be conduits for the spirit of God—first, by transforming the lives of those

---

28. In fact, many approaches to character formation have been criticized for doing just this. "[Most] character education programs focus on rules per se (what to do and what not to do) and not on the students who are urged to follow these rules." See Peterson and Park, *Strengths of Character*, 25–33.

students who already acknowledge the lordship of Jesus in their lives, and second, by providing all students with an appreciation and insight into the character of the kingdom of heaven.

In *Virtue Reborn*, Wright identifies five related elements of Christian communities associated with virtue formation that he locates around a *circle of virtue*. Each element informs the next element around the circle such that it does not matter where someone starts in this circle of virtue—eventually, all five elements will come into play to provide a context within which the members of this community, be they Christian or not, are challenged and encouraged to become people of Christian virtue. These five elements are outlined below.

Figure 2

Wright outlines how these five elements operate and interact with each other in healthy Christian communities—typically in the form of church communities. However, these five elements are also evident in schools that see their role as sharing the vision of the "complete" humanity outlined in the New Testament. Schools whose purpose, character, and practices are shaped by the teachings of Jesus provide a context within which habit formation and subsequent character development are possible, incorporating the same five elements identified by Wright.

The first element identified by Wright (common to churches and schools) are their "texts" or "voices." Just as churches come together around the reading of Scripture, so schools have their own "texts" or "voices" (using the notion of voices from Bakhtin's theory of dialogical spaces[29]) that promote habits of mind in particular and ways of doing that are

29. Bakhtin, *Dialogic Imagination*.

foundational for the development of character. Many of these voices are heard through Scripture in Christian schools, through the teaching of the Bible, and conversations about the Christian worldview that emerge from the biblical story. Unlike most churches, however, schools are communities in which multiple voices contribute to the learning conversation. This conversation may include the voice of Scripture, alongside other voices drawn from scientific communities, historians, geographers, scholars in many different fields, as well as the voices of teachers and students. This conversation can be shaped, prompted, and directed towards the development of learning character.

The second element identified by Wright is the sharing of stories. Claxton describes the activity of teaching as an "epistemic apprenticeship."[30] Whether we do so intentionally or unintentionally, teachers communicate certain beliefs about learning. Is the practice of learning mathematics, for example, about avoiding making errors, or is it about taking risks and exploring where different ideas might lead? Teachers regularly tell stories that communicate beliefs about the capacity of students to improve their understanding—whether our learning capacities are relatively fixed, or whether it is always possible for us to develop as learners. Teachers also tell students stories about how learning occurs (intentionally and unintentionally). Does learning occur primarily through drill and practice, through the communication of ideas with others, or by asking the teacher what the correct answer is? Claxton argues that all teachers, whether they are conscious of it or not, are "epistemic coaches," training students to think about learning in a particular way. He suggests that teachers need to be conscious epistemic coaches, identifying those learning dispositions which they are trying to build up in students each lesson. He argues for a "split-screen" approach to each lesson where teachers are encouraged to consider how they might teach content and strengthen dispositions known to support learning.

Similarly, all teachers communicate something about *learning character*, intentionally or unintentionally. We do this through the stories we tell about the benefits of learning. Students may be encouraged, for example, to approach their learning as a pathway to personal empowerment, increasing their chances of happiness and prosperity later in life. Or they might view learning as a pathway to a life of service, whereby their skills, knowledge, and capacities can provide support and comfort to other people.

Learning might be viewed as an individual endeavor in which each individual is competing with those around them to gain the "rewards" of learning (which might be in the form of grades, acceptance into a university

---

30. Claxton, *School*.

course, or simply the praise of the classroom teacher). Or our individual learning could be seen as a process intimately linked with the learning of those around us and that we learn best when we learn from and teach each other. Finally, learning might be connected with our self-image and ego, or it might be an outworking of our intellectual humility. The stories that we tell about "learning power" as a means of self-advancement or as a means of serving others provide powerful insights into the values and virtues that are most valued within our school culture.

The third element is that students follow examples, most notably their teachers. We model how to interact with different conceptual ideas each lesson, but more importantly we model what learning looks like in our various disciplines. Our learning practice informs our students' practice. What do we do when we get stuck? How do we deal with the fact that our understanding of each subject area is also incomplete? We need to model the same learning character that we hope our students will one day exhibit, being intellectually humble, people who ask questions that extend our thinking, who collaborate with others displaying grace and compassion rather than arrogance and ego. We need to be people who listen to our students to hear their perspectives and value these perspectives as sources of new ways of understanding our subject area, approaching our learning as an opportunity to become a voice for justice in the world.

The fourth element in Wright's circle of virtue development is engagement in a community. As we reflect on our goal of building learning character, we seek to establish communities of practice within which students (and teachers) are able to transform themselves, growing in understanding and maturity. One of the features of Christian communities is that through their practice as people of the kingdom of God, they become a source of blessing to those communities around them. Schools are no different in this regard. School communities become places of blessing—blessing for students, but also blessing for the wider community. Sharing in the activities of a Christian school community that is intent on being a blessing to those around them communicates something to our students that is at the heart of what it means to be part of the kingdom of God.

The fifth element in Wright's circle of virtue is a common language to talk about learning character and establishing common practices in each class. This language associated with learning character should be evident across the school such that all members of the school community recognize that "learning" and "growing as people of character" are features of the school community, not just for students, but for all participants in this community of practice—as teachers, parents, and other staff working within the school are also encouraged to be people of grace, compassion, humility, and justice.

In summary, learning character is promoted in schools in many different ways. It is not by stating rules for the community to follow that hearts and minds are transformed, or by identifying the preexisting "goodness" of students' character. Instead, schools need to be places that support the development of habits, the shaping of character by shrugging off our first nature and putting on our second. Schools can do this in myriad ways by concentrating on developing character inside and outside the classroom. Teachers model learning character, encourage students to adopt different aspects of learning character, tell stories about what "good" learning involves, and promote the development of learning communities that are characterized by expansive learning activities which have as their outcome the development of learning character. Schools support the development of communities of practice through the way they structure learning activities, the language that is used to describe learning, and the way that all members of this community show an eagerness to learn and grow in maturity and understanding. Through the concerted effort of all members of the school community, Christian schools have the potential to encourage all students to put on the learning character that will enable them to participate in the coming kingdom of God.

# Bibliography

Aristotle. *The Nicomachean Ethics*. London: Penguin, 2004.
Bakhtin, M. M., and Michael Holquist. *The Dialogic Imagination: Four Essays*. Austin: University of Texas Press, 1981.
Cam, Philip, and Ken Rinkel. *Thinking Stories 1: Philosophical Inquiry for Children*. Sydney, NSW: Hale & Iremonger, 1993.
Claxton, Guy. *Building Learning Power. Helping Young People Become Better Learners*. Bristol: TLO Limited, 2002.
———. *School as an Epistemic Apprenticeship: The Case of Building Learning Power*. 32nd Vernon-Wall Lecture. Leicester: British Psychological Society, 2013.
———. *What's the Point of School: Rediscovering the Heart of Education*. Oxford: Oneworld, 2008.
Claxton, Guy, et al. *The Learning Powered School*. Bristol: TLO Limited, 2011.
Cole, Michael. "The Perils of Translation: A First Step in Reconsidering Vygotsky's Theory of Development in Relation to Formal Education." *Mind, Culture, and Activity* 16 (2009) 291–95.
Cooling, Trevor, et al. "What If Learning." http://whatiflearning.com.
Costa, Art L., and Bena Kallick, eds. *Habits of Mind across the Curriculum: Practical and Creative Strategies for Teachers*. Moorabbin, Victoria: Hawker Brownlow Education, 2009.

Dickson, John. *Humilitas: A Lost Key to Life, Love, and Leadership.* Grand Rapids: Zondervan, 2011.

Engeström, Yrjö. *Learning by Expanding: An Activity-Theoretical Approach to Developmental Research.* Helsinki: Orienta-Konsultit, 1987.

Friedman, Thomas. "How to Get a Job at Google." https://www.nytimes.com/2014/02/23/opinion/sunday/friedman-how-to-get-a-job-at-google.html.

Lewis, C. S. *Till We Have Faces: A Myth Retold.* New York: Harcourt, Brace, 1957.

Lucas, Bill, et al. *Expansive Education: Teaching Learners for the Real World.* Camberwell, Victoria: ACER, 2013.

MacIntyre, Alasdair. *After Virtue: A Study in Moral Theory.* 2nd ed. Notre Dame: University of Notre Dame Press, 1984.

Peterson, Christopher, and Nansook Park. "Classifying and Measuring Strengths of Character." In *Oxford Handbook of Positive Psychology*, 2nd ed., edited by Shane J. Lopez and Charles R. Snyder, 25–33. New York: Oxford University Press, 2009.

Peterson, Christopher, and Martin Seligman. *Character Strengths and Virtues: A Handbook and Classification.* Oxford: Oxford University Press, 2004.

Pietsch, James. *Character Reborn: A Philosophy of Christian Education.* Sydney: Acorn, 2018.

Ritchhart, Ron, et al. *Making Thinking Visible: How to Promote Engagement, Understanding, and Independence for All Learners.* Chichester: Jossey-Bass, 2011.

Robinson, Ken, and Lou Aronica. *The Element: How Finding Your Passion Changes Everything.* New York: Penguin Group USA, 2009.

Schmidt, J. A., et al. "*Obuchenie* in High-School Physics Classrooms: A Study of Students' *Perezhivanie* and Teacher Speech During Unfolding Activity." Paper presented at the annual meeting of AERA, Vancouver, 2012.

Smith, J. K. A. *Desiring the Kingdom: Worship, Worldview, and Cultural Formation.* Grand Rapids: Baker Academic, 2009.

Wright, N. T. *Surprised by Hope.* London: SPCK, 2011.

———. *Virtue Reborn.* London, SPCK, 2010.

# 4

# Exploring the Connections between Authentic Leadership and Evangelical Christian Leadership

*Framing Practice to Achieve Authenticity in Leadership*

Peter White

*Anglican EdComm—Anglican Diocese of Sydney*

## Abstract

THE AIM OF THIS chapter is to explore the construct of authentic leadership from an evangelical Christian perspective and illuminate the potential for an authentic leadership construct to inform faith-based educational leaders and teachers. This chapter critically reviews the literature on authentic leadership and determines the common components from each proponent. The chapter provides an overview of an evangelical Christian view of leadership and ethics to inform a view of authentic leadership. The aim is to progress a new framework for evangelical Christian leaders in faith-based educational leadership contexts where consideration needs to be given to: (1) personal identity and the transformational work of the Holy Spirit in leading us from the "old" and to a "new" identity in Christ; (2) belief as it impacts behavior, particularly in ethics and morality; (3) how personal identity and an ethical framework shape the leadership of others and the wider community to serve the common good under Christ.

## Introduction

Leadership is undergoing somewhat of a crisis in Australia. Recent sporting scandals have raised questions about on-field unethical practices.[1] Royal Commissions have uncovered institutional failures,[2] and political parties are undergoing endless leadership speculation and changes.[3] All of these have helped to reinforce misgivings in the Australian public towards anyone in positions of power and authority. Leaders who were once seen as stable forces in our community are now perceived as having limited moral standing, or a limited ability to provide the leadership that the Australian public desires. But this evaporation of trust in leadership is not just an Australian phenomenon.[4] It seems to be a trend worldwide, and, more startlingly, a scourge that has affected the perception of educational institutions and of those who work in and lead them.

It is unfortunate that educational institutions have not been immune from this rising suspicion and distrust of leaders.[5] It would seem the trend in wider society has crept through the gate of Christian institutions, be it real or imagined. What is true is that questions are emerging about the nature of service and whether a common good is being held in view by leaders. As one commentator remarked, the "rise of individualism erodes the idea of public good."[6] Leaders of institutions are now being questioned and having to defend their motives and intent, both within and from outside their organizations. The perception is that many leaders are self-seeking rather than acting as servants of their constituency. Research in educational institutions that has measured levels of trust, both institutional and relational, has shown a widening gap between the perceptions that leaders have of each other.[7] This will continue to impact churches and educational institutions until a new paradigm is forged that enables leaders to develop and establish themselves as trusted leaders, held in the highest esteem by their staff and the wider community.

1. The Ethics Centre, *Australian Cricket*.
2. Hayne, *Misconduct*; McClellan, *Institutional Responses*.
3. Gauja, "This Is Why."
4. Sullivan, "When Trust Evaporates"; Edelman, *2018 Edelman Trust Barometer*.
5. Fink and McCulla, "Final Thoughts"; Sullivan, "Governments and Leaders."
6. Sullivan, "Governments and Leaders."
7. Marks and McCulla, "Australia."

Investing time, energy, and effort in cultivating authentic leadership may be the antidote to this burgeoning malaise towards leaders, particularly those in churches and in educational institutions. More pointedly, for those leaders in faith-based educational institutions—including evangelical Christian churches, schools, and tertiary institutions—authentic leadership provides the means for leaders to express genuine and lived-out Christian faith, while expressing a sincere care of and rightful concern for those with varied backgrounds who are a part of the leader's community.

In the pursuit of becoming an effective leader, practitioners need to be wary of relying on off-the-shelf solutions for leadership development. Rather, effective leaders need to be self-aware, realizing that the art of leadership is a highly personal journey.[8] They need to be able to draw down on a whole suite of skills.[9] In this respect, authentic leadership offers a unique approach to leadership, one that is highly personalized and reliant on an individual's moral and value frame.[10]

## Background

The intent of this chapter is to explore the potential for authentic leadership among faith-based educational leaders. More specifically, my aim is to address the question: "What should characterize authentic leadership in practice for educational leaders in evangelical Christian educational contexts?" This chapter explores how evangelical Christian educational leaders can frame their practice to achieve authenticity in their leadership, along with understanding the measures of successfully applied authentic leadership.

In order to explore these questions, a critical review of the literature on authentic leadership is required, as is an exploration of the distinctive view of leadership in evangelical Christian institutions. In my opinion, an evangelical view of leadership and authentic leadership are not at odds with one another but operate to complement and strengthen each other. While *Authentic Leadership* is an emerging category of recognized leadership systems, what sets it apart is its focus on the interior life of the leader. Avolio et al. offer a tidy definition of the frame when they say, "we conceive of authentic leaders as persons who have achieved high levels of authenticity in that they know who they are, what they believe and value, and they act upon those values and beliefs while transparently interacting with others."[11]

---

8. Fuda, *Leadership Transformed*, xiv.
9. Fullan, *Change Leader*, xiv.
10. George, *Authentic Leadership*, 8–15.
11. Avolio et al., "Unlocking the Mask," 802.

While the framework offers no grounded or guiding center—the individual is left to self-determine what is right, ethical, and true—this enables evangelical Christian educational leaders a frame to grow and develop their leadership skills without fear of compromising their deeply held beliefs; in fact, it provides an opportunity to place Christ at the center. More than this, by approaching leadership from an authentic frame, leaders are able to consciously enact their faith to shape their practice as leaders. They will be empowered to encourage the same in others. This approach provides them with resources to lead faith-based educational institutions with integrity, being certain that the tenets and practices of their faith can sustain and grow their leadership capacity, no matter the context.

This study has emanated from my experience of and exposure to various church organizations and faith-based educational institutions. In these churches and institutions, many leaders and teachers express distrust for those around them. Some of the distrust is in the perceived effectiveness of a leader or the perceptions surrounding their intent. In many circumstances, faith-based teachers are uncertain how faith can be enabled in the practice of teaching and learning, let alone within leadership. In some cases, educators—particularly those involved in theological education—are concerned that many of the approaches to leadership in the "marketplace" encourage practices that do not accord with an evangelical Christian faith, and they are left wanting for direction on how faith and leadership practice can be homologous. An exploration of the literature around authentic leadership and a synthesis with an evangelical Christian theological understanding of faith and leadership will provide a means for faith-based leaders to understand the qualities of authentic leadership, frame their practice, and see potential for its success from a distinctly Christian point of view.

## Recurring Themes and Ideas

Academics consider authentic leadership as a recognized leadership category, albeit in its formative stages. The concept of "authenticity" has a long history within the academy.[12] However, it has struggled as a focus of study, in part, due to the lack of evidence-based measures to verify its validity,[13] and because of an overwhelming focus on the intra-personal understanding of the leader. Despite these weaknesses, there is a consensus emerging as to the core qualities and characteristics of authentic leaders

---

12. Gardner et al., "Authentic Leadership," 1120–45; Duignan, "Educational Leadership," 152–72; Northouse, *Leadership*.

13. Northouse, *Leadership*, 209–10.

and the actions that mark their behavior. Table 1 provides a summary of definitions of authentic leadership.

Table 1: Definitions of Authentic Leadership

| Source | Definition |
| --- | --- |
| Bhindi and Duignan[14] | [T]he authors argue for authentic leadership based on: *authenticity*, which entails the discovery of the authentic self through meaningful relationships within organizational structures and processes that support core, significant values; *intentionality*, which implies visionary leadership that takes its energy and direction from the good intentions of current organizational members who put their intellects, hearts and souls into shaping a vision for the future; a renewed commitment to *spirituality*, which calls for the rediscovery of the spirit within each person and celebration of the shared meaning with purpose of relationship; a *sensibility* to the feelings, aspirations and needs of the increasing globalizing trends in life and work. |
| Begley[15] | Authentic leadership may be thought of as a metaphor for professionally effective, ethically sound, and consciously reflective practices in educational administration. This is leadership that is knowledge based, values informed, and skilfully executed. |
| George[16] | Authentic leaders use their natural abilities, but they also recognize their shortcomings, and work hard to overcome them. They lead with purpose, meaning and values. They build enduring relationships with people. Others follow them because they know where they stand. They are consistent and self-disciplined. When their principles are tested, they refuse to compromise. Authentic leaders are dedicated to developing themselves because they know that becoming a leader takes a lifetime of personal growth. |

---

14. Bhindi and Duignan, "New Century," 119.
15. Begley, "In Pursuit," 353.
16. George, *Authentic Leadership*, 12.

| Source | Definition |
|---|---|
| Luthans and Avolio[17] | [W]e define authentic leadership in organizations as a process that draws from both positive psychological capacities and a highly developed organizational context, which results in both greater self-awareness and self-regulated positive behaviors on the part of leaders and associates, fostering positive self-development. The authentic leader is confident, hopeful, optimistic, resilient, transparent, moral/ethical, future-oriented, and gives priority to developing associates to be leaders. The authentic leader is true to him/herself and the exhibited behavior positively transforms or develops associates into leaders themselves. The authentic leader does not try to coerce or even rationally persuade associates, but rather the leader's authentic values, beliefs, and behaviors serve to model the development of associates. |
| Kernis and Goldman[18] | [W]e define authenticity as the unobstructed operation of one's true or core self in one's daily enterprise. Rather than viewing this as a single unitary process, however, we assert that authenticity can be broken down into four discriminable components. Specifically, we suggest that authenticity involves *awareness, unbiased processing, behavior,* and *relational orientation.* |
| Starratt[19] | First, authenticity is the vocation of every human being, the call to bring one's unique possibilities into realization. There is a fundamental moral imperative here. One either violates one's authenticity or chooses it. Second, authenticity is always relational, in dialogue with another, a cause, a career. Thus, while the manner of being authentic is self-referential, the content of authenticity is realized in relationships. One does not know who one is unless one can recognize oneself in the response of the other, and in that recognition choose to continue to be that kind of person. Third, one's freedom to choose and shape one's life is exercised in a society that guarantees, more or less, those freedoms for everyone. |

---

17. Luthans and Avolio, "Authentic Leadership Development," 243.
18. Kernis and Goldman, "Thought and Experience," 32.
19. Starratt, *Ethical Leadership*, 80.

| Source | Definition |
| --- | --- |
| Avolio and Gardner[20] | [A]uthentic leaders are anchored by their own deep sense of self; they know where they stand on important issues, values, and beliefs. With that base they stay their course and convey to others, often times through actions, not just words, what they represent in terms of principles, values, and ethics. |

The recurring themes and ideas that have emerged enable leaders to focus on the core components of authentic leadership. In drawing together the threads of each of the various definitions, it can said that the literature affirms authentic leadership as a journey that sets leaders on a path of discovering their true identity and a deep understanding of a sense of self that grounds a leader's thoughts and actions.[21] The literature gives focus to moral/ethical purpose as being the means of actualizing the leader's identity and giving purpose to their behavior and action.[22] These moral and ethical sensitivities are worked out in relationship. Many of the proponents expand on the notion of leader/follower relationships as a key component of authentic leadership. They see this as a means for leaders to seek the good of the community.[23] Finally, the literature points to a focus on leader behavior that facilitates the personal growth of the leader, the growth of others, and improved outcomes for the institution they lead.[24]

In addition to these categories, Bhindi and Duignan interestingly add spirituality as a key category in their frame. In presenting this as a part of their view of authentic leadership they explain that:

> [b]y spirituality a partisan religious view is not meant, but that individuals and groups should experience a sense of deep and enduring meaning and significance from an appreciation of

---

20. Avolio and Gardner, "Leadership Development," 329–30.

21. Bhindi and Duignan, "New Century"; Begley, "In Pursuit"; George, *Authentic Leadership*; Luthans and Avolio, "Authentic Leadership Development"; Kernis and Goldman, "Multicomponent Conceptualization"; Starratt, *Ethical Leadership*; Avolio and Gardner, "Leadership Development."

22. Kernis and Goldman, "Multicomponent Conceptualization."

23. Luthans and Avolio, "Authentic Leadership Development"; Kernis and Goldman, "Multicomponent Conceptualization"; Avolio and Gardner, "Leadership Development."

24. Bhindi and Duignan, "New Century"; George, *Authentic Leadership*; Luthans and Avolio, "Authentic Leadership Development."

their interconnectedness and interdependency, and from their feelings of being connected to something greater than self.[25]

This view certainly affirms the need for leaders and followers to be connected by relationships formed by a sense of common purpose. For the person striving to be an authentic leader, time spent casting vision beyond the here and now, creating agency, and developing moral purpose, amplifies a community's sense of being.[26]

Further to this, other proponents of authentic leadership, particularly those within education, affirm aspects of authentic leadership as being core purposes of the educational endeavor in general. Researchers such as Sergiovanni and Fullan speak of the importance of moral and ethical leadership as central components of educative leadership.[27] Positive psychologists and leadership academics would affirm the need for leaders to be attuned to their understanding of self and its effect on those around them.[28] This adds weight to the inclusion of these elements in any system or process of leadership development for educational leadership.

In an attempt to address concerns about the lack of empirical research to confirm the validity of the authentic leadership construct,[29] a number of researchers have sought to develop tools which assist leaders to begin the process of identifying authenticity as a leadership trait. Of note, there are currently two self-assessed inventory tests that have been developed within the literature on authentic leadership.[30] Both use a questionnaire and a self-assessment guide. Participants rank perceptions of self against a series of crafted questions that highlight a particular aspect of the proposer's frame for authentic leadership. Both questionnaires are validated, theory-based instruments, and provide a basis for future research in authentic leadership.

With these factors in mind, authentic leadership as a construct offers leaders an opportunity to focus on the self to refine and develop their skills, and to invest in the development of others around them. A strong moral and ethical focus serves to ground leaders more firmly in leading their organizations and people with firm, considered foundations at the

25. Bhindi and Duignan, "New Century," 126.

26. Starratt, *Cultivating an Ethical School*, 26–29; Starratt, *Ethical Leadership*, 67; Sergiovanni, *Moral Leadership*, 72–74; Fullan, *Moral Imperative*, 9.

27. Sergiovanni, *Moral Leadership*; Fullan, *Moral Imperative*.

28. Seligman, *Flourish*; Cameron, *Positive Leadership*; Kouzes and Posner, *Leadership Challenge*.

29. Northouse, *Leadership*.

30. Kernis and Goldman, "Multicomponent Conceptualization"; Avolio et al., *Authentic Leadership Questionnaire*.

core. An other-person focus serves to help leaders operate with the best intentions for their people, while a desire to thoughtfully develop the talents, skills, and abilities of people working in their organization provides an opportunity to build capacity for the future. While these elements may not be empirically validated,[31] they are certainly human qualities that are worth pursuing and provide evangelical Christian educational leaders with a positive framework in which to consider how they operate with a distinct moral frame in mind.

## Understanding an Evangelical Christian View of Leadership, Ethics, and Spirituality

Evangelical Christians operate with a particular epistemology. An evangelical Christian's view of the world is shaped by an understanding of the Bible and has led this branch of Christianity to frame leadership, morality, and ethics with certain tenets of faith in mind. Ledbetter et al. state that:

> Christians consider the Bible authoritative for life. The Bible affirms a God of history who revealed himself to humanity and established a foundation for being, purpose, morality, and community. So, we come to know by faith, by reason, and by experience—all guided by the biblical narrative. This foundation informs our efforts to understand leadership and acts as a filter for any research findings.[32]

Evangelical Christianity, then, accords a particular view of leadership. John Stott, a well-renowned and influential evangelical Christian scholar, who has had a profound effect on the evangelical Christian church and academy,[33] commented that: "Leadership is a word shared by Christians and non-Christians alike, but this does not mean that their concept of it is the same. On the contrary, Jesus introduced into the world a new style of servant-leadership."[34] In another volume, Stott states: "Leadership and lordship are two quite different concepts. The Christian leads by example, not force, and is to be a model who invites a following, not a boss who compels one."[35] Additionally, the former Archbishop of Sydney, the Right Rev. Dr. Peter Jensen, noted in a recent interview that "you can't separate the spiritual life of the

---

31. Northouse, *Leadership*, 210.
32. Ledbetter et al., *Reviewing Leadership*, 17–18.
33. Brooks, "Who is John Stott?"; The Telegraph, "The Rev. John Stott."
34. Stott, *Calling Christian Leaders*, 9.
35. Stott, *Challenges of Christian Leadership*, 90.

Christian leader from his leadership, because his leadership requires faith, expressed in prayer of course, but faith in the willingness to do things which otherwise you wouldn't do."[36] In context, Jensen is meaning that evangelical Christian leadership calls on its leaders to serve people in such a way that it requires them to encourage—but equally, to rebuke and exhort—people to a way of living that is consistent with the Bible.

Evangelical Christians are suspicious of leadership frameworks that call them to use power and assert authority over people outside of the biblical narrative. A Christian view of leadership is one that posits Jesus Christ at the center, as the person who commands all authority, and the one to whom all others need to reverence. Christians with authority to lead should be conscious that Jesus is Lord, and, in understanding this, strive to operate as his subject and servant. Ultimately, their authority comes from Jesus, and so there is an expectation that these leaders will live and lead like Jesus. Authenticity in this realm is to model life, thought, and action by the example of Jesus himself.

This raises some complications for evangelical Christians. Evangelical Christian leaders want to "do the right thing," to make decisions that are consistent and honoring to the Lord. The biblical narrative—the authoritative text—does not give an account of Jesus dealing with every conceivable issue that might be encountered, so evangelical Christians are required to understand the biblical text in such a way that they can build an ethical frame from which to operate. This requires evangelical Christian leaders to have a clear sense of self and direction as essential qualities for leadership. Herrington et al. put it this way:

> A leader who has the capacity to know and do the right thing understands himself or herself apart from others and so is able to achieve distance from a situation and observe what is really going on, without letting personal reactivity or anxiety get in the way.[37]

To this end, evangelical Christian leaders need to have a well-thought-out system of ethics and morality to help them understand how to apply the biblical narrative within their immediate personal context, institution, and wider community.

To aid in this endeavor, evangelical Christians have relied on an understanding of theology to develop their ethical frame. Evangelical Christian authors such as O'Donovan, Holmes, Hill, and Cameron have all created works

---

36. Interview with Archie Poulos.
37. Herrington et al., *Leader's Journey*, 18.

that frame an ethical model based on an evangelical Christian understanding of theology and the Bible.[38] O'Donovan summarizes this by saying:

> Purposeful action is determined by what is true about the world into which we act; this can be called the "realist" principle. That truth is constituted by what God has done for his world and for humankind in Jesus Christ; this is the "evangelical" principle. The act of God which liberates our action is focused on the resurrection of Jesus from the dead, which restored and fulfilled the intelligible order of creation; this we call the "Easter" principle.[39]

Further to this, Holmes states that "[o]ur highest end is to glorify God and enjoy him forever. Consequently, these principles of God's kingdom [love and justice] are the principles of a Christian ethic, to guide our judgements and our conduct."[40] Each of these Christian ethicists offer a vision of life for evangelical Christians that revolves around an ethic of love. That is, in response to God's love for his people, Christians are to love others as God has loved them. Additionally, they are to steward the world bearing the same concerns for and love of the world as God. This model shapes an evangelical Christian's view of themselves, of others, and the world, with Jesus Christ as the center of that understanding.

With regard to spirituality, Ledbetter et al.[41] claim that all religions espouse a view of spirituality and have deliberate spiritual practice. They argue that "Christian leaders have a unique opportunity to winsomely integrate the human spirit, fully engaged as part of their ventures."[42] This provides a way for the integration of faith with leadership theories, such as authentic leadership. Peter Scazzero asserts that "[w]ork for God that is not nourished by a deep interior life *with* God will eventually be contaminated by other things such as ego, power, needing approval of and from others, and buying into the wrong ideas of success and the mistaken belief that we can't fail."[43] If he is correct, then evangelical Christian leaders need to take seriously the potential for authentic leadership to not only deepen their understanding of self, their motivations, and behavior, but also to shape their practice of leadership.

---

38. O'Donovan, *Resurrection and Moral Order*; Holmes, *Ethics*; Hill, *How and Why*; Cameron, *Joined-up Life*.

39. O'Donovan, *Resurrection*, ix.

40. Holmes, *Ethics*, 55.

41. Ledbetter et al., *Reviewing Leadership*.

42. Ledbetter et al., *Reviewing Leadership*, 20.

43. Scazzero, *Emotionally Healthy Spirituality*, 32.

## What Should Characterize Authentic Leadership in Practice for Educational Leaders in Faith-Based Educational Contexts?

Bringing together the work of various researchers and academics in the realm of authentic leadership with a brief overview of evangelical Christian leadership, ethics, and spirituality, it can be argued that authentic leadership can be comfortably adopted by evangelical Christian leaders. Given the comments by Bhindi and Duignan that spirituality is not partisan,[44] it is conceivable that a community of like-minded people could be brought together as a community of faith. Authentic leadership lends itself to an overt evangelical Christian faith context. It will serve to strengthen the ability of its leaders to give "meaning and significance" to the communities of people they lead.[45]

With evangelical Christianity at the core, I contend that Christian leaders can rely on authentic leadership to frame and characterize their practice. Evangelical Christian leaders should already be committed to an understanding of self in light of their religious sensitivities. More specifically, authentic leadership provides these leaders with permission to pursue an evangelical Christian understanding of their identity and sense of self.[46] It gives evangelical Christian leaders permission to reflect on the development of the tenets and practice of their faith as a part of their leadership development. Further reflection on evangelical Christian theology will shape behavior and help these leaders to act with sensitivity towards their community. Naturally, this assists in developing moral and ethical awareness.

Given that an ethical frame is central to the faith, life, and work of evangelical Christians,[47] these leaders should focus on developing an understanding of their faith. It provides an epistemology from which evangelical Christian leaders can ground their morality and ethics. The practice of evangelical Christianity enables the leader to ground their actions and behavior in an understanding of their faith. Starratt affirms that becoming authentic is always done in relationship to others, including God.[48] Similarly, faith-based leaders can be confident that leading with an evangelical

---

44. Bhindi and Duignan, "New Century," 126.

45. Bhindi and Duignan, "New Century," 126.

46. Bhindi and Duignan, "New Century"; Begley, "In Pursuit"; George, *Authentic Leadership*; Luthans and Avolio, "Leadership Development"; Kernis and Goldman, "Multicomponent Conceptualization"; Starratt, *Ethical Leadership*; Avolio and Gardner, "Leadership Development."

47. Holmes, *Ethics*.

48. Starratt, *Ethical Leadership*, 70.

Christian faith at the center provides them with certainty of thought and action. This aids followers in understanding the standard and expectations for evangelical Christian leaders. This accords with Avolio et al., who state, "[w]e conceive of authentic leaders as persons who have achieved high levels of authenticity in that they know who they are, what they believe and value, and they act upon those values and beliefs while transparently interacting with others."[49] Evangelical Christian educational leaders who have a clearly articulated theological understanding that is communicated through relationship with the wider community will be empowered to lovingly serve their followers and develop future leaders.[50]

Evangelical Christian leaders should be characterized by a deep awareness of their faith as it shapes their understanding of leadership. It shapes their sense of identity, and their frame to live a moral and ethical life. It develops a deep concern for the welfare of those among whom they work by providing leadership, in their service and towards those in the wider community. These leaders should develop authenticity through a consistent approach that comes from a cogent faith. This is grounded and shaped, not arbitrarily, but in the person and work of Jesus Christ who acts as leader par excellence, and as the model for all human behavior and endeavor. In this respect, evangelical Christian educational leaders should not act as autonomous masters. Rather, they should see themselves as subject to a greater power and submit themselves to their Lord, Jesus Christ. Evangelical Christian educational leaders need to see that their journey in leadership is as much a work of knowing and understanding the mechanics of leading people, as it is a journey of spiritual formation.[51] Christian leaders can take confidence from this statement by Greenman who says:

> Spiritual formation is an ongoing process for Christians. It is not a program or project or course that is completed in a few weeks, but rather is a lifelong journey of transformation. . . . Faith in Jesus Christ sustains a lifelong pursuit of spiritual maturity or wholeness found in him. Despite the pressures of our activist, hurried culture, this process cannot be reduced to learning personal management techniques or how to "do things for the Lord" because it is primarily a matter of cultivating an intimate relationship with the triune God.[52]

49. Avolio et al., "Unlocking the Mask," 802.

50. Bhindi and Duignan, "New Century"; George, *Authentic Leadership*; Luthans and Avolio, "Authentic Leadership Development"; Kernis and Goldman, "Multicomponent Conceptualization"; Avolio and Gardner, "Leadership Development."

51. Ledbetter et al., *Reviewing Leadership*.

52. Greenman, "Spiritual Formation," 24.

## An Agenda for Future Research

Throughout this chapter, it has been apparent that while there is limited literature available on the specific topic of authentic leadership—and a subsequent limited availability of empirically validated measurement tools for authentic leadership—there is limited literature that examines authentic leadership from an evangelical Christian theological position. As a leadership construct, authentic leadership lends itself to a rich and enduring faith-based perspective. Further exploration of an evangelical Christian form of authentic leadership—with subsequent investigation into the effectiveness of this construct for evangelical Christian leaders, an understanding of the Christian "self" in light of authentic leadership, and leader/follower relationship benefits within authentic evangelical Christian leadership—are all potential areas of future research.

## Conclusion

The aim of this chapter was to explore the construct of authentic leadership from an evangelical Christian perspective, and to illuminate the potential for authentic leadership to inform faith-based educational leaders. To that end, I have sought to critically review the literature on authentic leadership, determine its major components, analyze an evangelical Christian view of leadership, and then determine if the ideologies were complementary. It is hoped that this is the beginning of a new framework for evangelical Christian leaders to further explore strategies in leadership development.

This chapter has highlighted a shortage of literature in the emerging field of authentic leadership study despite a multiplicity of definitions. However, there are consistent threads that can be synthesized to show that authentic leadership researchers are in agreement at many points. To this end, the literature establishes that authenticity in leaders is formed through the exploration and understanding of personal identity and a sense of self. Further to this, the literature identifies an ethical and moral frame as being critical to the pursuit of authentic leadership. This is seen as a deeply relational component in the practice of this form of leadership. The literature also shows the need for authentic leaders to be committed to ongoing personal growth, a commitment to the growth of others, and a desire to see improved outcomes for the communities/institutions that authentic leaders manage.

In reviewing an evangelical Christian view of leadership, it is apparent that there are synergies with the authentic leadership literature.

This opens the way for further research and investigation into building a faith-based frame for authentic leadership. This will provide evangelical Christian leaders with a construct to guide them in developing their skills as leaders, their leadership of others, and in the leadership of the communities that they serve.

## Bibliography

Avolio, Bruce J., and William L. Gardner. "Authentic Leadership Development: Getting to the Root of Positive Forms of Leadership." *The Leadership Quarterly* 16, no. 3 (2005) 315–38.

Avolio, Bruce J., et al. *Authentic Leadership Questionnaire*. Menlo Park: Mind Garden, 2007.

———. "Unlocking the Mask: A Look at the Process by which Authentic Leaders Impact Follower Attitudes and Behaviors." *The Leadership Quarterly* 15, no. 6 (2004) 801–23.

Begley, Paul T. "In Pursuit of Authentic School Leadership Practices." *International Journal of Leadership in Education* 4, no. 4 (2001) 353–65.

Bhindi, Narottam, and Patrick Duignan. "Leadership for a New Century: Authenticity, Intentionality, Spirituality and Sensibility." *Educational Management and Administration* 25, no. 2 (1997) 117–32.

Brooks, David. "Who is John Stott?" *The New York Times*, November 30, 2004. https://www.nytimes.com/2004/11/30/opinion/who-is-john-stott.html.

Cameron, Andrew J. B. *Joined-up Life: A Christian Account of How Ethics Works*. Nottingham: Inter-Varsity, 2011.

Cameron, Kim. *Positive Leadership: Strategies for Extraordinary Performance*. Oakland: Berrett-Koehler, 2012.

Duignan, Patrick. "Authenticity in Educational Leadership: History, Ideal, Reality." *Journal of Educational Administration* 52, no. 2 (2014) 152–72.

Edelman, Richard. *2018 Edelman Trust Barometer—Annual Global Study*. Chicago: Edelman, 2018.

The Ethics Centre. *Australian Cricket: A Matter of Balance*. A report commissioned by the Board of Cricket Australia. Sydney: The Ethics Centre, 2018.

Fink, Dean, and Norman McCulla. "Themes, Dreams and Final Thoughts." In *Trust and Verify: The Real Keys to School Improvement*, edited by Dean Fink, 205–34. London: University College London Institute of Education Press, 2016.

Fuda, Peter. *Leadership Transformed: How Ordinary Managers Become Extraordinary Leaders*. London: Profile, 2013.

Fullan, Michael. *Change Leader*. San Francisco: Jossey-Bass, 2011.

———. *The Moral Imperative Realized*. Thousand Oaks: Corwin, 2011.

———. *The Moral Imperative of School Leadership*. Thousand Oaks: Corwin, 2003.

Gardner, William L., et al. "Authentic Leadership: A Review of the Literature and Research Agenda." *The Leadership Quarterly* 22, no. 6 (2011) 1120–45.

Gauja, Anika. "This is Why Australia Churns Through Leaders So Quickly." *The Washington Post*, September 18, 2015. https://www.washingtonpost.com/news/

monkey-cage/wp/2015/09/18/this-is-why-australia-churns-through-leaders-so-quickly/.

George, Bill. *Authentic Leadership: Rediscovering the Secrets to Creating Lasting Value.* San Francisco: Jossey-Bass, 2003.

———. *Discover your True North: Becoming an Authentic Leader.* Hoboken: John Wiley & Sons, 2015.

Greenman, Jeffrey P. "Spiritual Formation in Theological Perspective." In *Life in the Spirit: Spiritual Formation in Theological Perspective*, edited by Jeffrey P. Greenman and George Kalantzis, 23–35. Downers Grove: InterVarsity, 2010.

Hayne, Kenneth M. *Royal Commission into Misconduct in the Banking, Superannuation and Financial Services Industry—Interim Report.* Canberra: Commonwealth of Australia, 2018. https://financialservices.royalcommission.gov.au/Pages/reports.aspx.

Herrington, Jim, et al. *The Leader's Journey: Accepting the Call to Personal and Congregational Transformation.* USA: CreateSpace, 2016.

Hill, Michael. *The How and Why of Love: An Introduction to Evangelical Ethics.* Sydney: Matthias Media, 2002.

Holmes, Arthur F. *Ethics: Approaching Moral Decisions.* 2nd ed. Downers Grove: InterVarsity, 2007.

Kernis, Michael H., and Brian M. Goldman. "From Thought and Experience to Behavior and Interpersonal Relationships: A Multicomponent Conceptualization of Authenticity." In *On Building, Defending and Regulating the Self: A Psychological Perspective*, edited by Abraham Tesser, Joanne V. Wood, and Diederik A. Stapel, 31–52. East Sussex: Psychology, 2005.

———. "A Multicomponent Conceptualization of Authenticity: Theory and Research." *Advances in Experimental Social Psychology* 38 (2006) 283–357.

Kouzes, James, and Barry Posner. *The Leadership Challenge: How to Make Extraordinary Things Happen in Organizations.* San Francisco: The Leadership Challenge, 2012.

Ledbetter, Bernice M., et al. *Reviewing Leadership: A Christian Evaluation of Current Approaches.* Grand Rapids: Baker Academic, 2016.

Luthans, Fred, and Bruce J. Avolio. "Authentic Leadership Development." In *Positive Organizational Scholarship: Foundations of a New Discipline*, edited by Kim S. Cameron, Jane E. Dutton, and Robert E. Quinn, 241–61. San Francisco: Barrett-Koehler, 2003.

Marks, Warren, and Norman McCulla. "Australia: Halfway to Anywhere?" In *Trust and Verify: The Real Keys to School Improvement*, edited by Dean Fink, 46–73. London: University College London Institute of Education Press, 2016.

McClellan, Peter. *Royal Commission into Institutional Responses to Child Abuse—Final Report.* Canberra: Commonwealth of Australia, 2017. https://www.childabuseroyalcommission.gov.au/final-report.

Northouse, Peter G. *Leadership: Theory and Practice.* 8th ed. Thousand Oaks: SAGE, 2019.

O'Donovan, Oliver. *Resurrection and Moral Order: An Outline for Evangelical Ethics.* 2nd ed. Leicester: Apollos, 1994.

Poulos, Archie. Interview by author, Sydney, August 14, 2018.

Scazzero, Peter. *Emotionally Healthy Spirituality: Unleash a Revolution in Your Life in Christ.* Nashville: Thomas Nelson, 2006.

Seligman, Martin E. P. *Flourish: A Visionary New Understanding of Happiness and Wellbeing*. New York: Free, 2011.
Sergiovanni, Thomas J. *Moral Leadership: Getting to the Heart of School Improvement*. San Francisco: Jossey-Bass, 1992.
Starratt, Robert J. *Cultivating an Ethical School*. New York: Routledge, 2012.
———. *Ethical Leadership*. San Francisco: Jossey-Bass, 2004.
Stott, John. *Calling Christian Leaders: Biblical Models of Church, Gospel and Ministry*. Leicester: Inter-Varsity, 2002.
———. *Challenges of Christian Leadership*. Nottingham: Inter-Varsity, 2014.
Sullivan, Helen. "What Can Governments and Leaders Do When Trust Evaporates?" *The Conversation*, February 9, 2015. https://theconversation.com/what-can-governments-and-leaders-do-when-trust-evaporates-37333.
The Telegraph. "The Rev John Stott." *The Telegraph*, July 28, 2011. https://www.telegraph.co.uk/news/obituaries/religion-obituaries/8668938/The-Rev-John-Stott.html.

# 5

# Christian Values and Economic Knowledge

*The Implications of Wolterstorff's Epistemology for a Christian Perspective on Economics*

PETER DOCHERTY[1]\*

*University of Technology Sydney*

## Abstract

THIS CHAPTER EXPLORES THE epistemological relationship between values and economic theory. It considers Nicholas Wolterstorff's critique of epistemological foundationalism and his argument that values of various kinds shape how theories are constructed and evaluated. It then unpacks some of the key values in mainstream economic theory as represented by Lionel Robbins's famous 1932 *Essay on the Nature of Economic Science* and compares these values with those derived from what Wolterstorff calls *authentic Christian commitment*. The chapter concludes that mainstream economics is problematic from a Christian perspective and that a reconsideration of economic phenomena is needed that employs alternative Christian values. These will include the values of *grace, justice,* and *righteousness,* as well as a recognition of God's abundant material provision.

---

1 \*Thanks to Andrew Sloane, Gordon Menzies, Paul Oslington, participants at the *Transforming Vocation Conference*, Morling College, July 3–4, 2019, and the late Douglas Vickers, for comments and suggestions.

## Introduction

Christians in the field of economics have been asking for some time what implications their faith might have for an understanding of how economic systems work. Answers to this question range from suggesting that biblical material, especially from the Old Testament, provide a blueprint for modern economic *practice*[2] to concluding that the Scriptures deal with matters other than economics, and that Christian economics is simply "good" economics.[3] A further possibility for the faith–economics nexus, however, arises from developments in Christian epistemology in the second half of the twentieth century. Nicholas Wolterstorff argued some time ago that *values* play a key role in theory construction whichever discipline is on view.[4] Since the Christian faith has a great deal to say about values, this suggests that economic analysis beginning from a Christian perspective may well generate different theoretical structures than one from some other ethical stance. This possibility has not received very much attention.[5]

This chapter, therefore, explores the potential for Wolterstorff's epistemology to provide an entry point for a Christian evaluation of economics. Next, it outlines Wolterstorff's epistemology, especially his critique of classical foundationalism, and what this critique implies for the role of values in theory construction. Following, it attempts to identify the key values that underpin modern mainstream economics. The chapter then provides a preliminary evaluation of mainstream economics from a Christian perspective by comparing these economic values with relevant Christian values derived from the Scriptures. Finally, it offers some conclusions and suggests directions for further consideration of these issues.

---

2. Such *theonomistic* approaches include, for example, North, *An Introduction to Christian Economics*.

3. See, for example, Hawtrey, "Evangelicals and Economics," 27–40; and Richardson, "Christian Economists," 251–71.

4. Wolterstorff, *Reason*.

5. There are a small number of exceptions. Hay, *Economics Today*, 91–124 draws on Holmes, *All Truth*, 60, who, in turn, cites Wolterstorff at a key point in his own analysis. Vickers, *Economics and Man*, 169–71; "Last of the Economists," 87–88; and Beed and Beed, "Christian Perspective," 101, all recognize the potential for values to influence facts. Wilber and Hoksbergen, "Ethical Values," 208–14 discuss values in economics but focus on the contribution of Thomas Kuhn rather than Nicholas Wolterstorff.

## Wolterstorff's Critique of Foundationalism

In *Reason within the Bounds of Religion*, Wolterstorff advances an argument for the rejection of classical epistemological *foundationalism* and the adoption of an alternative approach to theory construction and evaluation. According to foundationalism, a proposition is epistemically justified, and thus constitutes part of our knowledge, only when it is logically consistent with a chain of supporting propositions that ends with an empirical or introspective observation.[6] The statement "Inflation is caused by excessive increases in the money supply" will thus form part of our economic knowledge if excessive increases in the money supply are regularly observed to precede inflation in the real world. Or the statement "An increase in the price of a good, other things equal, will lead to a smaller amount being demanded by consumers" will form part of our economic knowledge if a logically consistent set of propositions implying this relation between price and quantity demand, can ultimately be linked to a statement about the economic objectives of a representative person, and I can corroborate this statement by looking within myself, and agreeing that this is how I would behave (i.e. by introspection). In general, propositions are regarded as constituting "knowledge" according to foundationalism, only if they correspond in a well-defined way to observed reality.

This approach to determining knowledge received strong support from the *logical positivist school* of the 1920s. This school drew a sharp dichotomy between what they called *analytical* statements, that depend for their truth simply on the rules of logic and language, and *synthetic* statements, that express propositions that may or may not be true but which can be evaluated by comparing them with experience.[7] In logical positivism, knowledge is comprised of only these two kinds of statement. Statements which fall into neither of these categories, do not count as knowledge.[8] Thus the statements "sunrises are beautiful" or "kindness is good" are neither true nor false. They may express *values* or *opinions*, but this is a completely separate category from the expression of truth or knowledge, because these statements cannot be assessed in a clear and definite way against reality. The well-known processes of induction and falsification,

---

6. These "foundational" propositions can alternatively be called "self-evident." A statement is *self-evident* if it can be known to be true *non-inferentially*, that is, by virtue of understanding the meaning of its words. Cf. Audi, *Epistemology*, 94–95.

7. See Blumberg and Feigl, "Logical Positivism," 282–83. The idea that synthetic statements could be compared to observed reality was called the *verification principle*. See Ayer, *Language, Truth and Logic*, 48.

8. Ayer, *Language, Truth and Logic*, 56, 152.

used extensively in science, are both examples of foundationalism.⁹ They generate specific propositions or theories which imply something about the world (synthetic statements), and these propositions or theories may be tested by observation. It is worth emphasizing that such approaches imply that knowledge is "value-free," as frequently asserted in economics.¹⁰ It is about what "is" not what "ought to be."

Wolterstorff observes, however, that there are serious problems with approaching knowledge this way. These problems largely flow from the famous Duhem-Quine critique of logical positivism, advanced in the 1950s, which identified a difficulty with the dichotomy between analytical and synthetic statements.¹¹ According to this critique, observational propositions are rarely framed as simple statements that may be compared directly with empirical data. Instead, they are made up of complex structures of statements, both analytical *and* synthetic, along with additional or auxiliary statements pertaining to things like appropriate experimental design and data collection processes. When observation predictions from such complex systems are falsified, i.e. when they are *not* consistent with observed reality, it is not necessarily possible to identify which point in the system is responsible for the lack of verification. Verifiability of particular statements is thus very difficult, and even distinguishing which statements are purely analytical and which are purely synthetic is often not possible. Wolterstorff expresses the implications of this critique as follows:

> [E]ven if there is a set of foundational propositions, no one has yet succeeded in stating what relation the theories that we are warranted in accepting or rejecting bear to the members of that set. Even if there is a set of foundational propositions, we are without a general logic of the sciences, and hence without a general rule for warranted theory acceptance or rejection.¹²

But he is very cautious in teasing out the implications of this conclusion. It implies, he argues, neither a denial of objective reality, nor a denial that true belief about such reality is attainable. It simply means that the foundationalist route to such knowledge is insecure and that the only alternative is the exploration of non-foundationalist approaches.¹³

---

9. Chalmers, *Science*, 41–73, 87–92; Pritchard, *Knowledge*, 101–28.

10. See, for example, Blaug, *Methodology of Economics*, 136.

11. Duhem, *Physical Theory*, and Quine, "Two Dogmas," 20–43; cf. Wolterstorff, *Reason*, 35–55.

12. Wolterstorff, *Reason*, 45.

13. Wolterstorff, *Reason*, 56–57.

Wolterstorff then offers a non-foundationalist alternative to knowledge construction and theory evaluation. At the heart of this alternative is a comparison of new propositions with the set of beliefs already held by the theorist. These existing beliefs fall into three categories: data beliefs; data-background beliefs; and control beliefs. *Data beliefs* are beliefs about the entities which fall within the scope of the theory.[14] These beliefs are likely to include those relating to certain characteristics of relevant entities and/or their behavior.[15] This first set of beliefs incorporates the empirical into Wolterstorff's process of theory evaluation. They give shape to how the scientist understands the world and it is against this understanding that the theory will be compared as part of its evaluation. *Data-background beliefs* are necessary in order to hold the data beliefs described above. These are beliefs about the processes by which data is collected and measured, and correspond to the auxiliary hypotheses identified in connection with the Duhem-Quine criticism considered above.[16] *Control beliefs* are those pertaining to "what constitutes an acceptable sort of theory."[17] They appear in Wolterstorff's thinking to be fairly wide ranging including what might be called *epistemic* beliefs, those pertaining to the characteristics a good theory ought to have, but they also include "beliefs about the entities to whose existence a theory may commit us, and the like."[18] It is at this point that moral and political values may enter the picture. We might decide, for example, that only explanations of social phenomena that are cast in terms of individuals are acceptable because we have a moral or political commitment to the social autonomy of the individual.

Control beliefs thus function in two ways. They can first lead us to reject theories either because those theories are not consistent with these beliefs, or because, even if they are technically consistent, they do not "comport well" with control beliefs.[19] Secondly, control beliefs also play a role in the *construction* of theories.[20] They lead us to put theories together in certain ways with particular emphases and relations among the various explanatory forces on view. And we cannot avoid the operation of these beliefs, which are likely to be informed by a range of epistemic, moral, and political values, because choices about the structure of theories, what

14. Wolterstorff, *Reason*, 63, 66.
15. Wolterstorff, *Reason*, 66.
16. Wolterstorff, *Reason*, 67.
17. Wolterstorff, *Reason*, 67.
18. Wolterstorff, *Reason*, 67–68.
19. Wolterstorff, *Reason*, 68.
20. Wolterstorff, *Reason*, 68.

to include, what to leave out, and what to focus upon, must be made, and there are no rules apart from the guidance offered by control beliefs that we can rely upon to make these choices. This point has also been made by Vivian Walsh and Hilary Putnam.[21]

For Wolterstorff, *control beliefs* are central for the possibility of a Christian approach to theory construction and evaluation:

> My contention in what follows is that the religious beliefs of the Christian scholar ought to function as *control* beliefs within his devising and weighing of theories. This is not the only way they ought to function. For example, they also ought to help shape his views on what it is important to have theories about. Nor does that exhaust their function. But their functioning as control beliefs is absolutely central to the work of the Christian scholar.[22]

The process by which this "functioning" operates revolves around the idea of *authentic Christian commitment* which Wolterstorff defines as:

> ... the complex of action and belief that [realization of being a Christ-follower] ought in fact to assume.[23]

It is made up of the body of ideas, propositions, principles, and values which emerge from belonging to a community that possesses a tradition, part of which is to regard its sacred writings as authoritative for thought and conduct. Those writings then inform and shape the content of authentic Christian commitment, and this, in turn, informs the Christian's control beliefs, and thus the approach he or she ought to take to theory construction and evaluation.[24] A particular Christian thinker may not, of course, actually theorize in this way, and may not explicitly draw upon authentic Christian commitment in the process of formulating and weighing theories in their discipline area. But this raises the question of what values they *are* using in this activity, whether implicitly or explicitly, since, as pointed out above, it is not possible to avoid bringing some values to bear on this process.

Wolterstorff's challenge for the Christian is firstly to develop a self-awareness of this process, and secondly to ask whether the appropriate values to be employed should not be explicitly Christian ones. We now turn

---

21. Walsh, "Philosophy and Economics," and Putnam, *Meaning* and *Fact-Value Dichotomy*.

22. Wolterstorff, *Reason*, 70.

23. Wolterstorff, *Reason*, 72.

24. Wolterstorff, *Reason*, 72–73 unpacks the broad features of the *details* of this content.

to ask what implications this perspective might have for a Christian view on economics, and the first step in this process is to ask what values might already be present in mainstream economics.

## Values in Mainstream Economics

Wolterstorff's assertion that all theoretical structures are likely to contain embedded values that inform control beliefs suggests that we should be able to identify key values within mainstream economics and then compare these to corresponding values arising from the Christian faith. We may then assess whether these economic values are acceptable from a Christian standpoint and consider what this implies for our understanding of modern economics.

A useful way to identify the values that might be present in mainstream economic knowledge might be to consider Lionel Robbins's celebrated *An Essay on the Nature and Significance of Economic Science* because it has been so influential in shaping the definition and structure of economics to the present day.[25] One of the striking features of the definition of economics advanced by Robbins in this essay[26] is that it defines economics not in terms of the issues with which economics deals or the general problems that it seeks to solve, but in terms of a *particular framing* of those problems. Thus economics is *not* about explaining the prices of goods and services, or the level and composition of economic activity, or the material welfare of the citizens of any particular country, but about how unlimited wants can be satisfied in the context of scarcity.[27] Such a framing immediately suggests the presence of values. We may see this by considering Robbins's justification for this framing, centered around the hypothetical case of a shipwreck survivor on a deserted island:

> Let us turn back to the simplest case in which we found this [alternative] definition [that according to which economics is about material welfare] inappropriate—the case of an isolated man dividing his time between the production of real income

---

25. Robbins, *Nature and Significance*.

26. This definition is: "Here, then, is the unity of subject of Economic Science, the forms assumed by human behavior in disposing of scarce means . . . . Economics is the science which studies human behavior as a relationship between ends and scarce means which have alternative uses." Robbins, *Essay*, 15, 16.

27. Robbins is explicit in the definitions he rejects. For example, "Whatever Economics is concerned with, it is *not* concerned with the causes of material welfare as such." Robbins, *Essay*, 9; original italics.

and the enjoyment of leisure. We have just seen that such a division may legitimately be said to have an economic aspect. Wherein does this aspect consist? The answer is to be found in the formulation of the exact conditions which make such division necessary. They are four. In the first place isolated man wants both leisure and income. Secondly, he has not enough of either fully to satisfy his want of each. Thirdly, he can spend his time augmenting his real income or he can spend it taking more leisure. Fourthly, it may be presumed that, save in the most exceptional cases, his want of the constituents of real income and leisure will be different. Therefore he has to choose. He has to economise.[28]

Since the isolated man must make choices about the allocation of his time between activities that serve his wants, Robbins regards the four parameters that constitute this formulation of the man's problem as fundamental to the nature of economics. These parameters may then be generalized to economic issues in a broader social context.[29]

A number of values may be identified within this argument. The first is a commitment to *individualism* which values explanations of social phenomena that are cast only in terms of the behavior of individuals. Social outcomes are thus *nothing more* than the sum of individual behaviors and *not* the outcome of forces that operate at any higher level of aggregation. That Robbins chooses to frame his analysis of fundamental economic forces in terms of an isolated person on a deserted island, and then generalizes the resulting characterization of those forces, explicitly reflects such a value. We shall categorize this as an *epistemic value*, i.e. a value about how we should theorize, although the possibility that it reflects an underlying ethico-political value according to which respect for individual freedom should be a fundamental feature of society cannot be ruled out.

The second value which Robbins's analysis evinces is some form of *utilitarianism*.[30] That *utilitarianism* is a key feature of the normative aspect

28. Robbins, *Essay*, 12.

29. Robbins is explicit about this transition: "This example is typical of the whole field of economics studies." Robbins, *Essay*, 12.

30. Slote, "Utilitarianism," 890 defines utilitarianism as "an approach to morality that treats pleasure or desire-satisfaction as the sole element in human good and that regards the morality of actions as entirely dependent on consequences or results for human (or sentient) well-being." Cf. Smart and Williams, *Utilitarianism*, 3–27. It should be noted that some theorists have attempted to modify utilitarianism as employed in economics to embody some form of *altruism*. See, for example, Becker, "Altruism," 817–26. This issue is worth more attention than can be given to it here, but these efforts tend to make altruism reducible to self-interest or to undermine the utilitarian nature

of mainstream economics is well known[31] but it is important to recognize that it also plays a role within what is regarded as its "*positive*" aspect.[32] Its influence is reflected in Robbins's statement that his "isolated man" does not have "enough of either [real income or leisure] fully to satisfy his want of each." In other words, "isolated man's" welfare is measured by the degree to which his unlimited wants are satisfied, and maximizing this welfare is the principle that governs his behavior. The "positive" nature of this explanation of human behavior might be defended on the grounds that such behavior is not being *affirmed* by this explanation, but simply *described* and analyzed. It thus reports and analyzes what *is* not what *ought to be*. But this is where methodological considerations become crucial. Robbins in particular cannot make this move because of his adherence to the so-called *Verstehen* doctrine.[33]

According to this doctrine, economics is an empirical science because its criterion for whether a proposition counts as economic knowledge depends on whether that proposition can be linked in a logically consistent way to introspective observations about human motivation. This use of the *Verstehen* doctrine is, however, *inherently* value dependent. For as the economist interrogates his or her own behavior and the objectives that underpin that behavior, he or she is effectively exploring his or her own *values* and how those values operate to shape their economic objectives and behavior. By deciding that *utility maximization* or the *satisfaction of preferences* is the fundamental objective that underpins all human economic action, Robbins is thus acknowledging that *he* values want satisfaction and that this drives *his* own behavior. He is identifying what he thinks is important enough to govern the decisions he makes in the economic sphere. In addition, by generalizing this value to all economic agents, Robbins is also deciding that *this* is the value upon which to focus and the one that should be used to characterize economic behavior generally rather than some other value or motivation, and this imputation carries with it a further dimension of ethical affirmation. This evaluative dimension is evident by the standard depiction in economic analysis of agents who pursue the form of self-interest identified by the *Verstehen* process as "rational."[34]

---

of the resulting construct.

31. Sen, *Ethics and Economics*, 30–31; and Hay, *Economics Today*, 125.

32. Those who have acknowledged such a role though not within the context of the Wolterstorff-Walsh-Putnam framework include: Hollis and Nell, *Rational Economic Man*, 48–50; Sen and Williams, "Introduction," 1–2; Wilber and Hoksbergen, "Ethical Values," 211; Hay, *Economics Today*, 104–5; and Birnie, "Utilitarian Economics," 12–14.

33. See Blaug, *Methodology*, 47–48.

34. See Sen, *Ethics and Economics*, 15–22; and Hausman and McPherson, "Taking

A third value embedded in Robbins's analysis is reflected in his use of the concept of *scarcity*. The "economic problem," that of how best to allocate resources, arises for Robbins because unlimited wants confront "limited" or "scarce" resources:

> The ends are various. The time and the means for achieving these ends are limited and capable of alternative application .... The external world does not offer full opportunities for their achievement. Life is short. Nature is niggardly.[35]

At one level, this observation is uncontestable. The world is finite, and this does appear to place limits on the satisfaction of unlimited wants. At another level, however, this observation too is value dependent. If my objective of satisfying as many of my material desires as possible is strong enough to be the determining force underpinning my behavior, as Robbins argues it is, this is likely to *shape* my orientation towards the world and the resources it contains. I am, therefore, likely to *see* the world in terms of scarcity rather than in some other way which I might do if my values and objectives were different. Robbins's "positive" description of resources then as "scarce" may not simply be a "fact" that interacts with the other "fact" of unlimited wants to produce the economic problem, but it may be a characterization that flows from the same value-disposition as the objective of unlimited wants. If this analysis is reasonable, characterizations of the world as "niggardly" and of resources as "scarce" employ what Hilary Putnam calls ethically "thick" concepts in the same way as does the characterization of economic agents as "rational."[36]

This brief analysis may not exhaust the value content of mainstream economic theory but it does demonstrate that the conception of economics in Robbins's influential 1932 *Essay* contains at least three value propositions in contradiction to the often repeated idea that economics is value-free. The next question is whether these values are consistent with what Wolterstorff calls authentic Christian commitment.

---

Ethics Seriously," 679–83.

35. Robbins, *Essay*, 12–13.

36. Putnam, *Collapse*, 34–35, describes "thick" ethical values as those which can be used simultaneously as *descriptive* and *evaluative*. Thick values have the potential to cause false impressions of objectivity. For example, some commonly used epistemic values champion the coherence, plausibility, reasonableness, simplicity, and "beauty" of a hypothesis. Putnam argues that the purpose of these values is "right description of the world" but he complains that because this is often associated with the idea of "objectivity" we have no way of knowing whether the epistemic values employed deliver "a right explanation of the world" independently of those same values.

## A Christian Assessment of Mainstream Economic Values

That values can be identified within the structure of mainstream economics is of the utmost significance for the development of a Christian perspective on the subject. Values are generally regarded as being contestable in a way that propositions perceived as being "factual" are not.[37] If economics and the conclusions it generates are value dependent, then one's acceptance of those conclusions depends crucially on how its embedded values are regarded. If one can offer plausible justification for holding *different* values, and those values are either inconsistent with mainstream economic analysis or require it to be significantly modified, mainstream economic conclusions may then justifiably be rejected. The values outlined in the previous section may, therefore, be compared with pertinent Christian values to ascertain whether or not mainstream economics is consistent with authentic Christian commitment.

A comprehensive survey of Christian values that might be pertinent to economic matters is also beyond the scope of the remaining space in this chapter. What we can do, however, is to reflect on a few central values that might be relevant. Even here we need to be selective, and we will take an *evangelical* perspective in identifying what values will be used.[38]

Our starting point is to consider the *utilitarian* value in economics of maximizing want satisfaction. This seems to directly contradict the central Christian principle of *grace*[39] which is used a number of times in the New Testament as a model for the Christian's own motivation and behavior.[40] With the associated concept of generosity and concern for others, it is central to Jesus's commendation in Matt 22: 40 which evokes the Old Testament law and its associated covenant principles of *justice* and *righteousness*.[41] The Old Testament prophets, of course, witnessed to precisely these principles in condemning

---

37. Blaug, *Methodology*, 132–33.

38. The word "evangelical" is used here in the broad sense outlined by Pierard, "Evangelicalism," 379–82.

39. See, for example, Rom 3:24; Gal 2:20–21; and Eph 1:7.

40. See, for example, 2 Cor 8:9; Phil 2:3–4. Hay, *Economics Today*, 123 shares this view of utilitarianism in mainstream economics, as does Birnie, "Utilitarian Economics," 18–19. Sen and Williams, "Introduction," 6, also share a negative view of utilitarianism but with a secular justification that may be argued to have some overlap with the Christian ethic outlined above.

41. The concepts of justice (*mispat*) and righteousness (*sedaqa*) are closely associated in Hebrew thought as the foundation for a social order that reflects the covenant with Yahweh. See Johnson, "Meet the Lion," 22–23; Birch, *Hosea, Joel and Amos*, 215–16; and Johnson, "*Mispat*," 92–93.

Israel's covenant breaches and by encouraging the Israelites to repentance and covenant faithfulness.[42] Wolterstorff summarizes the values associated with these passages in terms of the idea of *shalom*, a state of the world within which each person enjoys just and peaceable relationships with God himself, other members of society, and the natural world.[43]

The second economic principle of *individualism* may also be questioned from a Christian perspective. The Bible's conception of Israel as a society places considerable emphasis on the *communal* nature of that society and the character of Israel as a *whole*.[44] Thus, the values outlined in the Mosaic law were designed to shape and reflect that character. Christopher Wright thus argues that: [45]

> [Israel's] very existence and character as a society were to be a witness to God, a model or paradigm of his holiness expressed in the social life of a redeemed community.

Oliver O'Donovan similarly asserts that: [46]

> The various ideas associated with "individualism" in Western thought—the individual contracting into society from a state of nature, the primacy of the self-interested will etc.—are all quite inappropriate to Israel's self-understanding. In the Hebrew Scriptures the holy community is the prior and original fact; the individual member finds his or her significance within it.

---

42. Amos, for example, identifies the sins of Israel during the reign of Jeroboam II around the period 750–760 BC as "trampling" on the poor and taking "levies of grain" (Amos 5:11), and he announces impending judgment on Israel for these sins. See Dumbrell, *Faith of Israel*, 156. Hubbard, *Joel and Amos*, 181, argues that these sins included demanding too much rent from peasant sharecroppers, and Smith, "Amos 5:13," 168, asserts that such practices breached Levitical regulations that protected the poor. In contrast to these covenant breaches, Amos 5:24 calls upon Israel to "let *justice* roll down like waters and *righteousness* like an ever-flowing stream" (NRSV; italics added).

43. See Wolterstorff, *Justice and Peace*, 69–71; Sloane, *Home*, 28; and Stackhouse, *Humble Apologetics*, 73.

44. The catchphrase of the Sinai covenant and the new covenant promised by the prophets when Israel breached the Sinai and Davidic covenants was "I shall be your God and you shall be my people" (Exod 6:7; Lev 26:12; and Jer 31:33). Yahweh also refers to Israel as a "nation of priests" which signifies their corporate status in relationship to him (Exod 19:5; Ps 99:1–4). Finally, the purpose of the law was to enable Israel *as a nation* to reflect the character of God to the other nations of the world (Lev 20:26).

45. Wright, *People of God*, 43.

46. O'Donovan, *Desire of the Nations*, 73.

This communal dimension is also a feature of the New Testament's conception of the *church* as the spiritual descendant of Israel.[47] Paul's theology of the church, therefore, in such passages as 1 Corinthians 12:27, Ephesians 1:22–23, and Colossians 1:18 has at its center the idea of the *body of Christ*. It also entails the idea of the *unity* of this body (see, for example, 1 Corinthians 1:10–17 and Ephesians 4:4–6) and an emphasis on the church as a *community* of faith with different members having different gifts and functions that are given for the service of the whole body. Thus ideas of "communion" and "fellowship" are central to this doctrine (see Acts 4:32–37 and 1 Corinthians 12:26).

Within these conceptions, social outcomes may be understood as fashioned, at least partly, by the *parameters that govern the character of society*. That is, the Old Testament law and the principles that flow from the gospel are designed to *shape individual behaviour* so that it conforms to the social vision and in particular the character of God, reflecting that character to the world. This conception of society stands in contrast to the view that social outcomes should be understood as the summation of decisions made by individuals who possess their own, independent objectives. Note also the methodological implications of this perspective. One must be careful not to dismiss this perspective because of its apparent *ideal* nature, arguing that the secular world *does not* share the convictions of Old Testament Israel or the New Testament body of Christ and that individuals *do* have their own independent objectives that affect the nature of society. The *methodological* implications of the biblical view of Israel and the church *as communities* flow from its embedded ethical value that social parameters can and should shape behaviour and that we may *understand and interpret society in these terms*. The actual social parameters currently in operation in most modern societies may not be closely aligned with those of Old Testament Israel or the church and may even give explicit license to individuals to formulate their own, independent objectives. But the possibility of understanding society in terms of its social parameters is not denied by this state of affairs and this possibility stands in contrast to the individualism of mainstream economics.[48]

---

47. Compare 1 Peter 2:9 with Exodus 19:5 to see Peter's understanding of the church in this respect. See also Reymond, *Systematic Theology*, 825.

48. Stackhouse, *Need to Know*, 184–85 warns against sentimentalizing "community" to the point of suppressing individuality which he sees as an important Christian value. This perspective is consistent, however, with the above recognition of *methodologically* determinative forces at the community level since these forces may themselves (and do so in the case of biblical principles) protect and value individuals. Hence the injunction against murder in Exodus 20:13.

Third, we may question the mainstream economic value that perceives nature and material resources as scarce or niggardly. The Bible's characterization of the world's resources is quite the opposite. The Christian doctrine of *providence* stresses God's ongoing, sustaining commitment to the created order and part of this commitment is his provision for the needs of those he has created.[49] His provision for Israel in particular is described in terms that are better characterized by adjectives of superfluity such as "abundant" and "plentiful" rather than "scarce" or 'niggardly." Thus we see "the land flowing with milk and honey" promised in Exodus 3:8 and 33:3 and realized in the economic splendor of Solomon's reign (see 1 Kings 4:20–24), and God's provision for the Israelites in the wilderness where the needs of each person were *more than* met with ample supplies of bread and quail, and where "saving" was unnecessary since this provision was available every day (see Exodus 16:17–18).[50]

In the New Testament, Jesus also affirms God's material provision for the disciples, citing the abundance of nature and comparing it favorably with the splendor of Solomon's reign (Matt 6:28–33). In Paul's encouragement to the Corinthians in 2 Corinthians 8 and 9 to be generous, he assures them that "God is able to provide you with every blessing in *abundance*" (2 Corinthians 9:8). The word Paul uses here for "abundance" is *perisseun* which carries the connotation of being "more than enough" or "excess to need,"[51] precisely in the sense conveyed about God's provision in the Exodus 16 wilderness episode which Paul explicitly cites in support of his argument (see 2 Corinthians 8:15). The value which underpins perceiving the world's resources as scarce or niggardly stands, therefore, in distinct contrast to the perspective of Christian theology.

Each of the three value propositions identified above as constituting part of mainstream economic theory appear then to be in direct contradiction to central Christian values which can be understood as constituting Wolterstorff's idea of *authentic Christian commitment*. This suggests that serious questions must be asked about the legitimacy of mainstream theory as an acceptable Christian perspective on the science of economics, and that the consideration of alternative approaches which employ the values of grace, justice, and righteousness, and which see the world's resources in terms of God's abundant provision must form an important part of the

---

49. Ps 145:9, 13, 15–17; Neh 9:6; Acts 17:25; Col 1:17; Heb 1:3. See Erickson, *Christian Theology*, 414–16; and Reymond, *Systematic Theology*, 399–403.

50. Interestingly, the "manna" episode of Exodus 16 is cited by Robbins, *Essay*, 13, in his analysis of the "niggardliness" of nature, where it seems to be completely misunderstood: "The Manna which fell from heaven may have been scarce . . . ."

51. See Bauer et al., *Greek-English Lexicon*, 650.

research agenda for Christian scholars in this field. The precise structure that such alternatives might take is beyond the scope of this chapter but useful starting points for consideration might include Sen's "capabilities approach,"[52] Walsh's "second phase" revival of classical economics,[53] and Wolterstorff's later treatment of justice in terms of *rights*.[54]

## Conclusion

It is reasonable to conclude from the analysis presented in this chapter that, despite its assertion of being value-free, mainstream economics *does* contain embedded ethical as well as epistemological values. Those of note include *individualism, utilitarianism*, and the characterization of the world's natural resources as *scarce*. The first of these was interpreted as an *epistemological* value, while the second and third were shown to be *ethical* in nature. These values were then evaluated from a Christian perspective by comparing them with core Christian values derived from a consideration of relevant biblical and theological perspectives which can be understood as constituting Wolterstorff's idea of *authentic Christian commitment*. Included amongst these values were the notions of *grace, justice*, and *righteousness*, or what Wolterstorff collectively refers to as *shalom*, as well as a recognition of God's abundant provision in the doctrine of providence. These values appear to be inconsistent with those embedded within mainstream economic theory, suggesting that a Christian perspective on economics could profitably look to frameworks *other than* this approach for direction and guidance. A number of starting points for building such frameworks were suggested but their investigation must be left to further work.

## Bibliography

Audi, Robert. *Epistemology: A Contemporary Introduction to the Theory of Knowledge*. London: Routledge, 1998.
Ayer, A. J. *Language, Truth and Logic*. London: Pelican, 1971.
Bauer, Walter, et al. *A Greek-English Lexicon of the New Testament and Other Early Christian Literature*. 2nd ed. Chicago: University of Chicago Press, 1979.
Becker, Gary S. "Altruism, Egoism and Genetic Fitness: Economics and Sociobiology." *Journal of Economic Literature* 14, no. 3 (September 1976) 817–26.
Beed, Clive, and Cara Beed. "A Christian Perspective on Economics." *Journal of Economic Methodology* 3, no. 1 (1996) 91–112.

52. Sen, "Description as Choice", 432–49.
53. Walsh, "Freedom," 199–232.
54. See Wolterstorff, "Social Justice," 670–79; and Wolterstorff, *Rights and Wrongs*.

Birch, Bruce C. *Hosea, Joel and Amos.* Louisville, KN: John Knox, 1997.

Birnie, J. Esmond. "Utilitarian Economics: A Theory of Immoral Sentiments?" *Christian Scholar's Review* 29, no. 1 (Fall, 1999) 11–24.

Blaug, Mark. *The Methodology of Economics.* Cambridge: Cambridge University Press, 1980.

Blumberg, Albert E., and Herbert Feigl. "Logical Positivism." *Journal of Philosophy* 28, no. 11 (May 1931) 281–96.

Chalmers, Alan F. *What is This Thing Called Science?* 3rd ed. Maidenhead, UK: Open University Press, 1999.

Duhem, Pierre. *The Aim and Structure of Physical Theory.* Princeton: Princeton University Press, 1954.

Dumbrell, William J. *The Faith of Israel: Its Expression in the Books of the Old Testament.* Leicester, UK: Apollos, 1989.

Erickson, Millard J. *Christian Theology.* 2nd ed. Grand Rapids, MI: Baker Academic, 1998.

Hawtrey, Kim. "Evangelicals and Economics." *Interchange* 38, no. 2 (1986) 27–40.

Hay, Donald. *Economics Today: A Christian Critique.* Leicester, UK: Apollos, 1989.

Hausman, Daniel M., and Michael S. McPherson. "Taking Ethics Seriously: Economics and Contemporary Moral Philosophy." *Journal of Economic Literature* 31, no. 2 (June 1993) 671–731.

Hollis, Martin, and Edward J. Nell. *Rational Economic Man: A Philosophical Critique of Neo-classical Economics.* Cambridge: Cambridge University Press, 1975.

Holmes, Arthur F. *All Truth is God's Truth.* Grand Rapids, MI: William B. Eerdmans, 1977.

Hubbard, David A. *Joel and Amos: An Introduction and Commentary.* Downers Grove, IL: IVP Academic, 1989.

Johnson, B. "Mispat." In *Theological Dictionary of the Old Testament*, vol. 9, edited by G. Johannes Botterweck, Helmer Ringgren, and Heinz Joseph Fabry, 86–98. Grand Rapids, MI: William B. Eerdmans, 1998.

Johnson, Richard. "Prepare to Meet the Lion: The Message of Amos." *Southwestern Journal of Theology* 38, no. 1 (Fall, 1995) 20–28.

North, Gary. *An Introduction to Christian Economics.* Nutley, NJ: Craig, 1979.

O'Donovan, Oliver. *The Desire of the Nations: Rediscovering the Roots of Political Theology.* Cambridge: Cambridge University Press, 1996.

Pierard, Richard V. "Evangelicalism." In *Evangelical Dictionary of Theology*, edited by Walter A. Elwell, 379–82. Grand Rapids, MI: Baker, 1984.

Pritchard, Duncan. *What is This Thing Called Knowledge?* 3rd ed. London: Routledge, 2014.

Putnam, Hilary. *The Collapse of the Fact–Value Dichotomy and Other Essays.* Harvard: Harvard University Press, 2002.

———. *Meaning and the Moral Sciences.* London: Routledge & Kegan Paul, 1978.

Quine, W. V. "Two Dogmas of Empiricism." *Philosophical Review* 60, no. 1 (1951) 20–43.

Reymond, Robert L. *A New Systematic Theology of the Christian Faith.* Nashville, Tennessee: Thomas Nelson, 1998.

Richardson, David. "What Should (Christian) Economists Do? Economics." In *Economics and Religion, Volume II*, edited by Paul Oslington, 251–71. Cheltenham, UK: Edward Elgar, 2003.

Robbins, Lionel. *An Essay on the Nature and Significance of Economic Science*. 2nd ed. London: Macmillan, 1949.
Sen, Amartya. "Description as Choice." In *Choice, Welfare and Measurement*, edited by Amartya Sen, 432–49. Cambridge, Massachusetts: MIT Press, 1982.
———. *On Ethics and Economics*. Oxford: Basil Blackwell, 1987.
Sen, Amartya, and Bernard Williams. "Introduction: Utilitarianism and Beyond." In *Utilitarianism and Beyond*, edited by Amartya Sen and Bernard Williams, 1–22. Cambridge: Cambridge University Press, 1982.
Sloane, Andrew. *At Home in a Strange Land: Using the Old Testament in Christian Ethics*. Grand Rapids, MI: Baker Academic, 2014.
Slote, Michael. "Utilitarianism." In *The Oxford Companion to Philosophy*, edited by Ted Hoderich, 890–92. Oxford: Oxford University Press, 1995.
Smart, J. J. C., and Williams, Bernard. *Utilitarianism: For and Against*. Cambridge: Cambridge University Press, 1973.
Smith, Gary V. "Amos 5:13—The Deadly Silence of the Prosperous." *Journal of Biblical Literature* 107, no. 2 (June 1988) 289–94.
Stackhouse, John G. *Humble Apologetics: Defending the Faith Today*. Oxford: Oxford University Press, 2002.
———. *Need to Know: Vocation as the Heart of Christian Epistemology*. Oxford: Oxford University Press, 2014.
Vickers, Douglas. *Economics and Man: Prelude to a Christian Critique*. Nutley, NJ: Craig, 1976.
———. "Theology and the Last of the Economists." *Perspectives on Science and Christian Faith* 43, no. 1 (March 1991) 29–35.
Walsh, Vivian. "Freedom, Values and Sen: Towards a Morally Enriched Classical Economic Theory." *Review of Political Economy* 20, no. 2 (2008) 199–232.
———. "Philosophy and Economics." In *The New Palgrave: A Dictionary of Economics*, edited by John Eatwell, Murray Milgate, and Peter Newman, 861–69. London: Macmillan, 1987.
Wilber, Charles K. and Hoksbergen, Roland. "Ethical Values and Economic Theory: A Survey." *Religious Studies Review* 12, nos. 3–4 (July/October 1986) 208–14.
Wolterstorff, Nicholas. "How Social Justice Got to Me and Why It Never Left." *Journal of the American Academy of Religion* 76, no. 3 (2008) 664–79.
———. *Justice: Rights and Wrongs*. Princeton: Princeton University Press, 2008.
———. *Reason within the Bounds of Religion*. 2nd ed. Grand Rapids, MI: Eerdmans, 1984.
———. *Until Justice and Peace Embrace*. Grand Rapids, MI: William B. Eerdmans, 1982.
Wright, Christopher J. H. *Living as the People of God: The Relevance of Old Testament Ethics*. Leicester, UK: Inter-Varsity, 1983.

# 6

## Rehumanizing Precarious Work[1]

### Vocation in Location Versus a New Priesthood of Cosmopolitan Techno-Creatives

GORDON PREECE

*Director, Ethos: Evangelical Alliance Centre for Christianity and Society; Honorary Director, Religion and Social Policy Network, University of Divinity; Senior Policy Officer, Catholic Social Services Victoria*

### Abstract

THIS PAPER EXAMINES HOW increasing monopolization of Liquid Modernity's sense of vocation by celebrity techno-creatives (such as Amazon's Jeff Bezos), displaces, divides, dehumanizes, and destabilizes true vocation. Increasing numbers have little long-term sense of relational and creative role responsibility in real time and place—a vocation and location. This sense of dislocation, precarity, and vocational fragility, at work and home, challenges Luther's more medieval sixteenth-century notion of relatively universal and unchanging, located and integrated vocation. But Luther and the broader Reformed tradition may yet have more to say.

The rise of the creative class leads to its concentration in accompanying cities. Techno-creatives become a new vocational priesthood of cultural

---

1. This paper is completely revised and expanded from Preece, "Re-Humanising Work." Used with permission.

creatives. This esthetic elite sets the tone of cultural consumerism, as opposed to the surrounding precarious service class mired in material survival. But this produces its own urban and vocational crisis.

Much of the expectation of this rootless cosmopolitan technological and creative class is generated from our systems of international higher education. A sampling of Australian university advertising shows how this subverts what are seen as parochial and tradition-bound vocational and communal captivities to be fled rather than returned to and served. Many modern cosmopolitan techno-creatives are increasingly disconnected from particular places, family, and church loyalties.

The incessant mobility and top-down flexibility of this cosmopolitan techno-creative ideal in Liquid Modernity also raises the key question of whether "vocation" in such a system is psychologically and spiritually sustainable. It needs a relatively stable location or anchorage in households, communities, and churches—not just work in our turbulent times. The "heroic" techno-creative exemplars and institutional powers of "disruptive" technology need challenging and transforming so they can serve the social stability and economic equality of the most needy and precarious.

Liquid Modernity's work patterns produce an increasingly disruptive and inhumane technological pace of change which requires contemporary and classical theological resources for rehumanizing it. These include the priority of the general calling to and by Christ and his people over particular callings and individual choices of vocation, the priority of justification by faith—not justification by one's job—and the symbiotic relationship of vocation and location within a creation/new creation and Trinitarian framework.

## Vocation and Location: Sleepless, Workless, and Homeless in Seattle

In mid-2018 I spent some study leave in spectacular Seattle, focusing on faith and work in the archives of Seattle Pacific University. But the more I saw, read, and talked with locally engaged and creative-thinking Christians, the more anxious I felt about this fastest growing of major US cities. Seattle's growth is driven by a wave of high-tech companies such as Boeing and Microsoft, and fast-service companies like Starbucks. It is the face of the future, not just for the US, as research on other creative cities in New York and Miami confirmed,[2] but also for my city of Melbourne, Australia.

---

2. Gage, "Rising Sea Levels."

The fastest growing company of all, aptly named Amazon, is taking over Seattle's inner city, and exemplifying urbanist Richard Florida's three T formula for the economic development of creative cities—"talent, technology, and tolerance."[3] I will use *techno-creative* as shorthand for these three urbane characteristics which combine technological efficiency with creative talent for a cool esthetic. Under tolerance it includes liberal cultural values, being pro-gay marriage, as is the economically and sexually libertarian Amazon CEO Jeff Bezos, and what is called Silicon Valley Ethics—being more for homosexuals (or LGBTQI+) but less for the homeless.[4]

This climaxed in Amazon's shameless but successful overturning of Seattle City Council's high-wage tax on hundreds of corporates to provide for the homeless directly affected by increased rents due largely to the inner-city takeover by Amazon and others.[5] Furthermore, Amazon has since given a million dollars to ensure that city council was not elected.[6]

Amazon is not alone in the dehumanization and ethical inconsistency it often brings to its workplaces, neighborhoods, and wider society,[7] but its very size intensifies impact. Yes, it provided approximately 647,500 full- and part-time jobs worldwide in 2018.[8] But it also brings massive disruption, intractable traffic, and high homelessness levels to many people and places, including the locals I met at Seattle Union Gospel Mission.

3. Florida, *Creative Class*.

4. This comment is not about homosexuality or gay marriage in itself, but about hypocrisy. Silicon Valley Ethics is liberal culturally and sexually, given nearby San Francisco city and Berkeley and Stanford universities, but without liberalism's social justice element. Many Silicon Valley CEO's are libertarian, their favorite author being Russian émigré and egoist and individual freedom absolutist, Ayn Rand.

5. Beekman, "Amazon Backlash."

6. "The Church of Amazon."

7. Compare computer esthete Steve Jobs of Apple fame, and some infamy for abandoning his pregnant partner and icy indifference to mass rooftop suicides at Apple's Chinese supplier, FoxConn: https://www.business-humanrights.org/en/foxconn-suicides-2010. Note also the massive disparity in pay and conditions, and sexual harassment standards between "Do No Evil" Google core staff and its "expendable" contracted staff: https://www.theinquirer.net/inquirer/news/3076457/google-has-more-contractors-than-staff-and-theyre-p-ssed. More broadly, see Strom on Google, "Abstract and Control" and the Guardian on its 2019 US investigations of Silicon Valley: "This year, we exposed allegations of wage theft by [Google] one of the richest companies in the world, revealed how Amazon was working with police departments to create a vast surveillance system. We tracked extremism and hate from the dark corners of the web to the supposedly sanitized realm of Facebook, reported on the harsh reality of Uber drivers living in their cars as the founders made off with billions, and showed how the boom in 'kidfluencers' was enabling exploitation of child labor." See Wong, "Dark Side of Tech."

8. See https://www.statista.com/statistics/234488/number-of-amazon-employees/.

Amazon founder and CEO Bezos is the world's richest man, worth $167 billion. Amazon is the world's second largest company after Apple, worth a trillion US dollars. It has Amazonian ambitions to infinitely increase that wealth and to replace citizenship with consumer identity in an enveloping digital environment. Bezos praises customers for their "divine discontent," an aspect of our technological evolution.[9] This term hints at Amazon's idolatrous scale. American theologian William Cavanaugh exposes, on the one side, its obsessive, disenchanted, and rationalized efficiency sucking out workers' lives, and, on the other, breathing it back into its smile-branded products in a form of re-enchantment that demands total brand loyalty or vocation to the Church of Amazon.[10]

To expand on this first aspect, it is clear that the flip side of the growth of these techno-entrepreneurs and creatives is the inhumane pace demanded by Amazon's algorithms of their workers, often in extreme heat, without air-conditioning. It makes the obsessive-compulsive Frederick Taylor's mechanized stopwatch-measured methods look relaxed. Further, Amazon's ironically named *Fulfillment Center* workers and drivers have pee bottles so they don't delay deliveries by treks to the toilet and feel constrained not to drink water.[11]

Activists against such dehumanizing work, like unions, are anathema to Amazon. Communicating about them, "under her eye" that Shoshana Zuboff explores in *The Age of Surveillance Capitalism* (2019), can be a sackable offence if overheard, by human or Alexa's artificially intelligent, hearing.[12] Sadly, unions seem unable to connect with highly mobile and individualistic non-joiners from the hi-tech and gig economies, despite recent attempts to unionize, for instance, by striking Deliveroo workers.[13]

9. See Austin, "Constant Consumer."

10. See "Church of Amazon."

11. See Hatch, "Amazon's 'Hellscape,'" also https://www.businessinsider.com.au/the-disturbing-accounts-of-amazon-delivery-drivers-may-reveal-the-true-human-cost-of-free-shipping-2018-9?r=US&IR=T, both concerning the Dandenong Fulfillment Center in Melbourne. Also, from a UK perspective, see Bloodworth, "Amazon." Amazon distribution centers also have poor Operational Health and Safety (OH&S) standards that are routinely flouted. When workers are injured, they can find that insurers, influenced by Amazon, cut their cover, leaving them sometimes invalided and isolated. Again, Amazon is not the only exploiter, but it sets the standard with which others compete. Ken Loach's UK movie, "Sorry We Missed You," based on *in situ* reverse surveillance by workers, shows similar watering and toileting constraints in the life of a franchise owner-driver, lest they get penalized for lateness.

12. Zuboff, *Surveillance Capitalism*, 267–68, describes Amazon's ambitious and already partially implemented plans for voice-recognition surveillance at home and work via Alexa-like AI.

13. Note "Deliveroo, Geelong" and many places for strikes from 2016–2019 in

Deindustrialized and GFC (Global Financial Crisis) devastated areas outside Creative Cities are easy game for monopolizers like Amazon to demand big tax exemptions from desperate cities and wage and condition concessions from isolated, individual workers. Further, Amazon's barely minimum wages for extremely physical work (up to fifteen miles of fast walking per shift) exemplify the growing gap between the top one percent and the rest. Contrary to assumed economic law and employer/employee deals, productivity gains no longer translate into wage gains, neither for the last forty years in the US, nor ten years in Australia.

In Seattle, I was told of enlightened work practices at higher, creative, technological design levels of Amazon. And I heard of similar things from a gifted Christian Artificial Intelligence (AI) expert for Amazon, Tripp Parker,[14] at the October 2018 Chicago Faith and Work Summit. Even so, the system seems highly hierarchical in how it apportions more humanized or vocational work. Those with choices are "called" techno-creatives, like queen bees, and those without choices are the short-term and casual drones in the "Fulfillment" Centers.

I have highlighted Amazon as the epitome of inhumane high-tech entrepreneurialism because of its pronounced "priestly" divide between those with a visionary, entrepreneurial vocation—such as creatives and disruptive start-up founders—and those left floundering without continuity of *vocation* and *location*. The former view of vocation is focused on individual inclination or choice which makes vocation an upper-middle-class luxury.

## Creative Cities and Vocational Destruction and Monopolization

Amazon isn't the only company nor Seattle the only city with a dark side of techno-creative disruption. Atlantic journalist Matthew Stewart argues that the creative class of about "9.9% is the new American Aristocracy."[15] New York, San Francisco-Silicon Valley (of which Seattle is a northern extension), Boston, and other high-tech creative cities have followed similar patterns with good housing, education, and transport effectively concentrated in creative city centers and privatized in the Clinton Democrats' high-tech coastal and city-based model, largely followed by Obama. And Hilary Clinton's "basket of deplorables" outside those areas apprentice themselves to President Trump, impeachment or not.

---

Britain.

    14. Erisman and Parker, "Artificial Intelligence."

    15. Stewart, "9.9 Percent."

The above intersections of the economic, technological, and urban increasingly raise questions as to whether economist Joseph Schumpeter's depiction of capitalist "creative destruction," fueled by disruptively creative technologies and entrepreneurs, is increasingly destructive, including vocationally disruptive.[16] Destructive developments since Richard Florida's *The Rise of the Creative Class* (2002) have led to his *mea culpa*, *The New Urban Crisis* (2018). Florida admits that, while clustering of the "creative class"—professionals in the arts, media, and technology—has brought growth and innovation to cities, it also led to cascading crises with massively rising real estate costs, school fees, and a new creative class of hereditary wealth through monopolization of property and intellectual capital. "Well-being inequality" thus happens when creatives pay premium prices to live in neighborhoods with better food, education, entertainment, and jobs.[17] Lower-wage workers are relegated to lower-amenity neighborhoods farther out with less family time due to increased commuting and hence higher family breakdown rates due to less family time.[18] The ideological misuse of a secularized techno-creative esthetic indirectly undermines the calling of many to care adequately for their families.

Australian vocational, locational, and political dynamics are less extreme, but not so different—just a decade or so behind. We are largely an east-coast and city-clinging people in the world's most urbanized nation. Richard Florida's *The New Urban Crisis* has nothing indexed on Australia, however, the techno-creative dynamics of vocation and location are broadly Western. In Sydney and Melbourne our creative classes are close to the inner-city universities. And the call to "go West young man" is not an American call to unlimited fertile land and fruitful work but to desert heat and bushfires.

Here, too, while the "secession of the successful" is advancing, those left outside the creative cities are constantly "on call," increasingly at the whim of totalizing corporations whose workplace flexibility is only top-down. Their company's demands leave their "non-creatives" experiencing little continuity, sociability, humane concern, or predictability. These are traditional compensatory relational and vocational virtues, linked largely to stability of location, but they are becoming more scarce and harder to "choose."

16. Schumpeter, *Capitalism*, 139.
17. Solman, "Creative Class."
18. Egrahrari, "Long Commute."

## Precarious Work and the Precariat

Beyond Bezos's tech-creatives and Florida's creative cities, though related as part of the digital economy, is British academic and activist Guy Standing's concept of "The Precariat,"[19] the largely service workers outside the privileged techno-creative inner-circles of contemporary cities. Different to and yet building upon the old Marxist class division between capital endowed or propertied class and labor or the proletariat, the precariat is a new and pervasive global class, crossing old class boundaries even including "secure" academics, surviving from casual course to course, depending on enrollments.

Precarious work is part of "the honeymoon is over" stage of the gig-economy that was once seen with rose-colored glasses as an expression of the sharing economy of digitally enabled peers capitalizing their spare assets.[20] But Uber cabs and food, Deliveroo and so forth, operate often in defiance of the law and target taxis and restaurants with better wages and conditions. They offer their ultra-convenient services at the cost of a highly casualized, on-call, poorly paid, private risk-bearing, without paid leave or pensions, servant or precariat class.[21] Increasingly cities are trying to control or ban them, and their workers are protesting at wages that barely cover their vehicle or other costs. And Airbnb has been increasingly corporatized by real estate investors and criticized for exacerbating housing problems.[22] Strikes, some unionization, and a disappointing stock exchange float for Uber confirm that the gig honeymoon is over.

More centrally to my thesis, however, the increasing monopolization of a sense of vocational choice by celebrity tech-creatives in liquid or most-modernity (that is, the hyper-acceleration of late modern, technological capitalism) has led to many rapidly changing socially and ecologically

---

19. Standing, *Precariat*; *Precariat Charter*; further extended by his *Plunder of the Commons*.

20. See, for instance, Botsman and Rogers, *What's Mine is Yours*.

21. Garben, "Tackling Precarity" states: "To focus on online platforms in isolation would miss the point that they are part of a wider phenomenon of spreading and intensifying precarity at work. . . . Indeed, it appears that the online-platform economy is growing 'for the wrong reasons'—not to deliver new, innovative and better-quality services for the benefit of customers and with the side-effect of quality employment opportunities, but as 'unfair competition' undercutting existing industry operators. The profit is generated on the back of the individual worker's wellbeing and the welfare state's sustainability. If these 'externalities' were properly factored into the calculation of the economic effects of the online-platform economy, it is doubtful that it would generate a net benefit for most of the individuals working within it, or for society at large."

22. Dunlop, *Future is Workless*, 131–32.

unsustainable jobs for others. It becomes difficult to have a long-term sense of vocational, relational, and role responsibility in real time and place under this highly disruptive technological pressure. Nowadays, much working life is less a settled vocation *in* social and geographical location (1 Corinthians 7:17–24) than like a relatively short movie made "*on* location" before moving quickly onto the next creative, or merely survival project.

This sense of locational and vocational mobility, precarity, and fragility, at work and home, challenges Luther's more medieval sixteenth-century notion of relatively unchanging vocation. It also raises questions as to whether vocation in a liquid, constantly changing world, is psychologically and spiritually sustainable. The inhuman technological pace and lack of place is deeply opposed to the slow pace of grace,[23] and a sense of stable location, tailored to our finitude and frailty. We require such contemporary and classical theological resources for rehumanizing or transforming work. But we will explore these after we deal more deeply with factors causing dehumanization and distortion of vocation in an exclusive and divisive direction.

## Shifting from a Protestant Productive Ethic for All to Elitist Esthetic Vocation

We will now explore some key postmodern philosophical and sociological trends behind the shift to a more esthetic ethic of creative vocation. Zygmunt Bauman analyzes this as a shift from a "Solid Modernity" productive ethic anchored in almost monastically set times—such as the 9am–5pm workday, with set locations like factories and offices—to what his seminal book, *Liquid Modernity* (2000), sees as fast fluidity and flexibility across a series of capital, labor, information, relational, migration/refugee, and other "flows" while connected 24/7.[24]

The Reformation-originated modern work ethic sought to equally humanize and sacralize all lawful work—pleasurable or unpleasurable—as "vocation" before God. By contrast, the Romantic era and postmodern consumerist work esthetic[25] stresses differences in felt degrees of internal

---

23. See https://www.livegodspeed.org/, and book by Canlis, *Theology of the Ordinary*, and article, "School of the Parish." Canlis speaks of "slowing down to the pace at which people are known (and God incarnate walked)." See also the website and tagline http://donteatthefruit.com/: "Technology is Fast, But Redemption is Slow." Thanks to Dave Benson for the references. I will only add Koyama, *Three Mile*.

24. This framework is summarized and developed further in my chapter, Preece, "Post-Vocational World," 192–215.

25. See Campbell, *Romantic Ethic*.

choice and hence authenticity. Some "elevated" professions are works of art or poetic. Other more prosaic work is relatively worthless.

The liquid-modern revised Romantic consumer esthetic is stratifying. It is as if we are constantly auditioning or, in reality, digitally objectifying and expressively authenticating ourselves,[26] by comparison online in Instagram, or reality TV, whether romantically or creatively, via music, mating, or cooking shows. Perceptive psychologists see this as a substantial factor in the epidemic of anxiety and lack of resilience among young people today. It also makes it difficult to develop a clear sense of vocation when you are facing constant self-reflection online about your own esthetic acceptability and creativity. From another angle, this is an economically rational response to disruptive neoliberalism and an overload of choice.

Contrary to many exclusivist postmodern and contemporary Christian esthetic perspectives dividing a creative priesthood and uncreative plebs, musician and Fuller Seminary Professor Andrew Peterson draws on the biblical principle of the priesthood of all believers that:

> All of God's creatures are creative in some way. To use J. R. R. Tolkien's word, we're all *subcreators* made in the image of a Creator. That's why I object when people refer to themselves as "creatives," not only because it sets up a sort of "creative class" (which strikes me as presumptuous) but also because it implies that non-artists aren't called to create.[27]

Instead of the relatively equalizing and stabilizing—albeit secularized—Protestant work or production ethic or vocational view, Bauman claims that Liquid Modernity requires most people to take a liquid view of vocation: "in the present-day flexible labour market, embracing one's work as a vocation carries enormous risks and is a recipe for psychological and emotional disaster." An "until further notice" sign is permanently hung over the postmodern work esthetic.[28]

This is particularly dangerous if our identity is inseparable from our vocation and its educational formation, especially through the US's rite of passage into autonomous adulthood through leaving home for college. We

---

26. See Charles Taylor's "Age of Authenticity," in his *Secular Age*, chap. 13.

27. Peterson: "Creativity," citing Jonathan Rogers: "that the arts make up a smaller slice of the creative pie than, say, friendship or a family dinner. . . ." Note also Holt, "Men in the Kitchen," for a similar egalitarian and affirming approach to ordinary, domestic, and feeding work, largely by unknown females, unlike male celebrity creative chefs in top restaurants or on television.

28. Bauman, *Work*, 31–34.

will now explore via Australian university advertising how this still happens here, where less local university students leave home to study.

## Higher Education Expectations for Cosmopolitan Techno-Creatives Low on Vocation in Location

To understand the relative pervasiveness of the effects of the liquid modern esthetic or consumer ethic, and its dislocating and divisive vocational effects through an exclusive techno-creative priesthood, we will examine a small Australian sample of recent university advertising to see how it shapes younger generations. Both universities and their big corporate technology employer partners to whom they supply graduates,[29] commonly adopt a pretense—particularly to university students—of offering a creative, humanizing vocational pathway, while in reality selling them short, due to the mass production process of corporatized education. Even so, with Bauman we need to ask: can and should vocation stay afloat in a corporate university-fostered, destabilizing liquid modernity?

The advertisements I will consider are from Melbourne universities, which unsurprisingly demonstrate shifts largely in the liquid modern direction. Deakin University featured a Deakin "Worldly" ad in 2012 with that catchword intended to represent a positive liquid or postmodern "look at all sides" approach to complex questions. Judging by the many "world as your oyster" images, however, it offers provincial students the opportunity to become progressive cosmopolitan consumers, traveling the world, but with little loyalty to place, and making choices based on whatever techno-creative projects they want to pursue.[30]

Deakin's "Worldly" ad is particularly like what British Canon Giles Fraser identifies, with help from conservative political philosopher

---

29. Cooper et al., "Scholars and Entrepreneurs," provide a broad base for my approach to the university-technological (and military) industrial complex updated since by many articles on US, UK and Australian universities, especially by Simon Cooper at *Arena*: https://arena.org.au/?s=%22Simon+Cooper%22.

30. https://www.deakin.edu.au/about-deakin/media-releases/articles/2012/deakin-wraps-train-to-spread-worldly-message-to-regional-victoria. For one negative reaction, see https://forums.whirlpool.net.au/archive/1952188. Later campaigns such as Deakin's 2016 campaign "Think Young" (https://campaignbrief.com/deakin-university-challenges-t/) reflect the young, vibrant, and cutting edge, ambitious image it seeks to project as a top 2 percent world ranked university. Its 2018 "Be Ready" campaign stresses Deakin's practical, pragmatic, skill-based technological approach to future challenges. In some ways, both are similar though more positive than Monash University's anti-tradition campaigns below. See https://unherd.com/thepost/labours-problems-start-at-university/.

Michael Oakeshott, as the delocalizing role cosmopolitan-oriented universities play for working-class students:

> Oakeshott describes . . . an educational system in which the local . . . is the enemy from which one has to be "emancipated." Being educated is all about turning one's back on the local, so that its "din" is no more than a "distant rumble."
>
> This, according to liberal apologists like Kwame Anthony Appiah, is precisely what a university exists to achieve: to cancel out the view from somewhere and replace it with the view from everywhere which is, of course, also the view from nowhere. And if this is what it does, then there is always going to be a tension between the university educated and the working class—or, to put it philosophically, a tension between the universal and the particular.[31]

My point in borrowing from Oakeshott and Fraser is not primarily political—though it is a kind of colonizing of the mind—but rather to note a parallel with what also happens for many young Christians at university. They are separated, physically or culturally, from their parents' allegedly parochial (whether rural or suburban), non-progressive faith and view of humble vocational and community service, which is not necessarily techno-creative class.

What Deakin's advertising agency calls the "hero"-ing of various graduates in their advertising, creates aspirations for certain techno-creative cosmopolitan vocations or character types. In Australia's thirty-second ranked "innovative business," they use technological and entrepreneurial means to disrupt parochial bonds, although on a smaller scale than in the US college and techno-creative system. Even so, it is still problematic for a Christ-centered view of vocation and character, as we will see.

Australia's largest university, Monash University,[32] also utilized an ultramodern technological theme in its 2016 advertisement themed "challenge the status quo." It appealed to the critical, creatively destructive entrepreneurial, and technologically innovative instincts of its ideal students. Technological creatives were clearly to see stability and tradition as things to be smashed in a reversal of the alleged nineteenth-century Luddites smashing of job-threatening machines and in an incarnation of Facebook founder Mark Zuckerberg's famed motto of "move fast and

---

31. Fraser, "Labour's Problems."

32. https://www.monash.edu/news/articles/our-new-ad-campaign-challenges-the-status-quo. See also https://campaignbrief.com/monash-university-rallies-peop/.

smash things."[33] Similarly, while a 2018 Monash ad stresses global impact in its quest for high fee-paying international students across many campuses, it is still negative or at best indifferent towards the past and students' particularity. The global future swallow locality and history, the very stuff of vocation in finite time and space.

The technologically utopian optimism of some university ads is the visible tip of the iceberg of an innovative techno-informational complex, fueled by entrepreneurial idealism. It has scaled-down echoes of Amazon and Silicon Valley morality, sometimes neglecting local needs as international students and techno-creatives take over inner cities close to universities causing housing hardship and homelessness, and pushing others further out from the techno-creative hub, which I witnessed as Director of Urban Seed homeless ministry in Melbourne.

This distancing from vocational dreams is further added to by the time it takes—on average four years—to enter the field for which one trained. This easily leads to a sense of vocational crisis, cynicism, or betrayal, which my own son felt, by big promises that vocationally oriented university courses often make of jobs upon graduation. With little general education these courses can then feel like a waste of time.

The massive inflation of educational expectations for creative, hi-tech work are concerning. They are driven in Australia—and likely elsewhere—by chronic government underfunding of higher education, and its necessity for increased international student numbers plus false promises from corporate partners of jobs and good money upon conclusion.[34]

The great reformed polymath and technology critic, Jacques Ellul, was ahead of his time when he recognized the obligatory and utilitarian necessity of much of his paid university work in a degree factory. He sought out air pockets of freedom within this sinking ship at his voluntary summer university or "Prevention Club" for teenage dropouts and misfits. It was still work, yet in a relatively free relationship to young people of a different and closer kind to his core Christian vocation to the outsiders than to his professional obligation to his university students.

---

33. An internal motto used by Facebook until 2014, and also the title of Jonathan Taplin's book, *Move Fast and Break Things*. See also Taneja's review, "Era."

34. This consumerizing of education is an international problem, most extreme in the US as highlighted in Tom Nichols' 2017 book, *Death of Expertise*, with its aptly entitled chap. 3, "Higher Education: The Customer is Always Right." Compare India where Prime Minister Modi's hopes of a hi-tech India are producing many engineering and especially computer trained graduates, but some of whom end up in the service-class driving taxis or working for Uber in Australia.

What would Ellul make of the all-enveloping corporate technological universities of today with their restrictions on academic freedom of opinion and public engagement? He would probably not seek escape but work to flesh out his sense of vocation in tension with the constraining university system. His, and our, Christian freedom is worked out by grace but under necessity, within a job's limitations.[35] This is not confining vocation as techno-creatives tend to today, to areas of completely uncoerced, authentic choice. Ellul's countercultural perspective is important for both academics and students thinking vocationally.

## Re-meaning Vocation against Techno-Creative Elitism

Having strongly critiqued the de-meaning and dislocating of a liquid modern consumerist esthetic view of vocation for cosmopolitan techno-creatives, we come now to the previously promised re-meaning and resourcing of a renewed Christian view of vocation.

The classical Reformed view of vocation is perhaps best summarized by the Puritan William Perkins, in *A Treatise of the Vocations* (1603),[36] which I have summarized in the diagram below. First, it clearly prioritizes the Christian's general calling to Christ and his people over our particular callings. Second, this provides the dynamism and critical christological leverage to challenge potential distortions and dehumanization of particular callings in the household economy, church, or politics/citizenship.

General Calling:

to conversion and conduct as God's people

("to walk worthy of your calling" Ephesians 4:1)

Particular Callings:

(Ephesians 5:21—6:9; Romans 13)

Household Economy    Church    Citizenship

A third critical theological tool against the elitist techno-creative monopolization of vocation, where often only creatives are considered "called,"

---

35. Ellul, *In Season*, chap. 11, "Toward a Forum-Style University." Note also his *Ethics of Freedom* and my positive analysis of it in my *Changing Work Values*, 183–85.

36. In Perkins, *Work of William Perkins*, 441–76.

is provided by Lutheran public theologian Robert Benne. He helpfully retrieves Luther's signature doctrine of justification by faith as a way of freeing us from justification by a job, both before God and others.[37] I would add that if, in Luther's terms, our "alien dignity" is in Christ, we do not have to primarily earn dignity or status through our work(s).

Also, though I am wary of possible ideological distortion by the powerful, we can still therefore exercise patience and hope in the midst of alienated labor. And yet, we do this while simultaneously seeking a modest share for ourselves and others, now, of the firstfruits of the full harvest of unalienated labor in "the new heavens and new earth" (Isaiah 65:17–25). We are both "waiting for and hastening the coming of the day of God" (2 Peter 3:12). This is our better balanced, less cynical, and more eschatological equivalent of Bauman's "until further notice" shingle hung over any earthly job.

Fourth, for Benne,

> [f]reedom from placing work in an idolatrous position means freedom for work as a penultimate good.[38] For those whose work is on the absorbing and demanding side of the ledger, the promises of the gospel allow proper distance. For those whose work is on the routine and pedestrian side, the gospel frees people from [the anxiety of] needing significant work as a way of earning their self-esteem before God.[39]

Christians thus, fifthly, simply serve neighbors in a matter-of fact way, incognito, doing so by God's common grace "which the Creator showers on the whole creation" as much as those in "important," or—we might add—techno-creative work.[40]

Justification by grace through faith, not work(s), is a helpful antidote to the increasing precarity of work and the inversely related proud propaganda of work as "co-creation"[41] beloved by Christian techno-creatives and scientists today. It also reminds us of the precarious nature of work in

---

37. Benne, *Ordinary Saints*, 169.
38. Drawing on Bonhoeffer, *Ethics*, 98–127.
39. Benne, *Ordinary Saints*, 169.
40. Benne, *Ordinary Saints*, 170. See also Matt 25:31–46.
41. See, also, Preece, *Changing Work Values*, 223, quoting Barth, *Church Dogmatics*, III/4, 110, 474, 482: "God's work in creation is incomparable and unique. Humanity does not participate in it. God finished his work of creation on the seventh day, and the work of redemption by the cross is finished also. [Karl] Barth rightly insists that by themselves, 'Christians are not collaborators, co-creators, co-saviors, or co-anything.' And yet paradoxically in Christ, human action can 'co-respond' to and co-operate with God's prior initiative."

Scripture (especially the Lord's Prayer's "give us this day our daily bread"), church history, and the majority world today.[42]

Sixth, our worth is in Christ's finished work on the cross, not our work. Out of our worth in Christ and worthwhile work under the risen Son, our work—however precarious—is not in vain (1 Corinthians 15:58; Romans 8:20), under the sun of death and the transient vanity of Ecclesiastes. Here, work flows into our daily sacrificial offering of our bodies and renewal of our minds, our rational or *logikos* worship (Romans 12:1, 2), worth-ship, or "Workship."[43]

Seventh, another Lutheran, Uwe Siemon-Netto, sees rediscovery of vocation as "the most effective antidote" to the "narcissism" of today's Western worldview, "because it directs the individual to the "You," the other person, and therefore away from the "Me"[44] and its anxious obsession with my creativity. Siemon-Netto blames Max Weber's anxiety-ridden, secularized, and utilitarian Protestant work ethic, which sees earthly success as proof of predestination, as an example of this "me-centeredness." Many self-conscious tech-creatives could be characterized this way, but there is nothing particularly Christian or Protestant about their anxiety.

By contrast, Luther's richer view of vocation sees it as rather a means for those already justified by faith, not justified by a job, to worship God and freely love and serve God's images/icons in necessities, not just if they are inclined or choose to be creative. He sees callings as "masks" or relational roles, enrolling humble actors in the everyday cosmic drama of salvation and God's constant preservation and re-creation of the world against evil powers, through various vocations of loving service.[45] Such earthy, other-centered vocations forestall a focus on the individual self's fragile identity, creativity, and frenetic pursuit of freedom at others' expense.[46]

---

42. See Sloane, "Biblical Reflections," 9–10.
43. See Martin, *Workship* and *Workship*, 2.
44. Siemon-Netto, "Vocation Versus Narcissus," 149.
45. See Preece, *Vocation Tradition*, 66, n. 20 on masks, and 67.
46. Siemon-Netto, "Vocation Versus Narcissus," 150. Luther's earthy illustrations of vocation include apparently uncreative work of a father washing diapers as justified or sanctified "in faith": "God, with all his angels and creatures, is smiling—not because that father is washing diapers, but because he is doing so in Christian faith." See also "Washing Diapers."

## Conclusion and Hopeful Alternatives

In this paper I have used Amazon as a typical example of an elitist, techno-creative notion of vocation as an upper-middle-class luxury, dehumanizing drone-like workers in their robotic Fulfillment Centers, in a mockery of biblical flourishing. The homeless evictees of Amazon's effective takeover of downtown Seattle and the effects, intended or not, by analogous creative class compatriots in Miami, New York, and Melbourne, are joined by the peripheral precariat and service class seeking to stay connected to these new creative city centers. This "secession of the successful" to live and work in concentrated areas of creativity leaves the allegedly "vocation-less" poor floating like flotsam and jetsam, the first victims of social and ecological instability—in a kind of literal liquid modernity.

My critique of cosmopolitan techno-creatives or creative class members for creating a new kind of monopolizing vocational priesthood, above the precariat outside the sacred core of creative cities, demands an articulation of a positive alternative. In the concluding chapter of my book *The Viability of the Vocation Tradition* (1998), I contrasted creation as the area of location or necessity (prioritized by Luther and later the modern secularized or Deistic Protestant work ethic), with that of the Spirit-transformed new creation focused on inclination or spiritual gifting stressed by my doctoral mentor Miroslav Volf's seminal *Work in the Spirit* (1991). I argued for holding these two dimensions together within a Trinitarian creedal framework with Christ as the pivotal Alpha and Omega, beginning and end, calling us vocationally to *stay* in our creational location, and yet also calling us *away* towards the new creation.

The key texts for this vocational tension are firstly in Luke 8:26–39 and parallels where Jesus calls the healed Gerasene demoniac to follow him, not on the road, as the demoniac wanted, but back home where his community could see the miraculous difference Christ made in his life. Later in 1 Corinthians 7:29–31—which Luther's creation-focused view neglected, compared with his majoring on "staying" in your calling in verses 17, 20, and 24—we are called to live our Christian calling within the conditions of marriage and work or commerce in the world's passing "present form" however "as if not" totally bound to them.

Volf in some ways similarly connects vocation to location in his and Matthew Croasmun's new book, *For the Life of the World* (2019). This allows for "cultural differences and individual uniqueness." It lays the foundation for a truly creative, "improvised," "individual life" within the two poles of Christ and vocation-location. Christ's life is the "genre-defining performance" carrying "normative weight," mimicked, but with meaningful particularity and creativity in time and place, in the "individual performances of ordinary Christians" on our finite stage for serving God, people, and creation.[47]

We need no heroic stories of techno-creatives or a creative class when we operate between the story of Christ and our locational vocations. What we do require is a much more focused and radical reenacting and practicing of this process in communities of faith and with cobelligerents. Such communities are both islands of stability in this creation but also of transition and mobility toward the shores of the new creation of fruitful, rehumanized work.[48]

## Bibliography

Austin, Drew. "The Constant Consumer." *Real Life*, September 10, 2018. https://reallifemag.com/the-constant-consumer/.
Bauman, Zygmunt. *Liquid Modernity*. Oxford: Polity, 2000.
———. *Work, Consumerism and the New Poor*. Maidenhead: Open University, 1998.
Beekman, Daniel. "Amazon Backlash Spurs Seattle City Council to Repeal 'Head Tax.'" *Governing*, June 13, 2018. https://www.governing.com/topics/finance/tns-seattle-head-tax-repeal.html.
Benne, Robert. *Ordinary Saints: An Introduction to the Christian Life*. 2nd ed. Philadelphia: Fortress, 2003.
Bloodworth, James. "Amazon: The New Victorian Workhouse." UnHerd, May 4, 2018. https://unherd.com/2018/05/amazon-new-victorian-workhouse/.
Bonhoeffer, Dietrich. *Ethics*. London: SCM, 1953.
Botsman, Rachel, and Roo Rogers. *What's Mine is Yours*. New York: Harper Collins, 2010.
Bottomley, John. "Theological Research Work in a World of Precarious Work." *Zadok Perspectives* 140 (Spring 2018) 18–22.
Campbell, Colin. *The Romantic Ethic and the Spirit of Modern Consumerism*. Oxford: Basil Blackwell, 1987.
Canlis, Julie. "The School of the Parish: Learning to Live a Theology of the Ordinary." *The Regent World* 29, no. 2 (Fall 2017). https://world.regent-college.edu/profile/the-school-of-the-parish.
———. *A Theology of the Ordinary*. Wenatchee: Godspeed, 2017.

---

47. Preece, *Vocation Tradition*, 310–11, and Volf and Croasmun, *Life of the World*, 108, 110–11.

48. See Preece, "New Churches?" for examples from two Anglican parishes I have led for six and eleven years respectively at Malabar in Sydney and Yarraville-Spotswood in Melbourne. Both are in partly working-class areas where considerable transformation in work and unemployment through the job creation and business incubator WorkVentures (Malabar) and community life (Spotswood) has been achieved. See *Changing Work Values*, chap. 3, 113–69 on the former.

"The Church of Amazon." Andrew West Interviewing William Cavanaugh. *Religion and Ethics Report, ABC*, November 6, 2019. https://www.abc.net.au/radionational/programs/religionandethicsreport/being-consumed/11676630.

Cooper, Simon, et al., eds. "Scholars and Entrepreneurs: The Universities in Crisis." *Arena Journal*, special ed., nos. 17/18 (2002).

Dawson, Claire Harvey. "The Changing World of Work: Crisis and Opportunity." *Zadok Perspectives* 140 (Spring 2018) 25–27.

"Deliveroo, Geelong: Pay Rates Won't Increase for Riders." *Geelong Advertiser*, September 4, 2019. https://www.geelongadvertiser.com.au/news/union-says-conditions-for-geelongdeliverooriderstoworsen/newsstory/a6229a51806ba02dc6308137615e45f7.

Dunlop, Ian. *Why the Future is Workless*. Sydney: NewSouth, 2016.

Egrahrari, Mark. "A Long Commute Could Be the Last Thing Your Marriage Needs." *Forbes*, January 21, 2016. https://www.forbes.com/sites/markeghrari/2016/01/21/a-long-commute-could-be-the-last-thing-your-marriage-needs/#6d44368e4245.

Ellul, Jacques. *The Ethics of Freedom*. Grand Rapids: Eerdmans, 1976.

———. *In Season and Out of Season*. San Francisco: Harper & Row, 1982.

Erisman, Albert, and Tripp Parker. "Artificial Intelligence: A Theological Perspective." *Perspectives on Science and Christian Faith* 71, no. 2 (June 2019) 95–106.

Florida, Richard L. *The New Urban Crisis: Gentrification, Housing Bubbles, Growing Inequality, and What We Can Do About It*. London: One World, 2017.

———. *The Rise of the Creative Class: And How It's Transforming Work, Leisure, Community and Everyday Life*. New York: Basic, 2002.

Fraser, Giles. "Labour's Problems All Start at University." *The Post, by UnHerd*, December 16, 2019. https://unherd.com/thepost/labours-problems-start-at-university/.

Gage, Julienne. "How Rising Sea Levels Are Gentrifying Miami." *Sojourners*, August 2018. https://sojo.net/magazine/august-2018/how-rising-sea-levels-are-gentrifying-miami.

Garben, Sacha. "Tackling Precarity in the Platform Economy—and Beyond." *Social Europe*, July 31, 2019. https://www.socialeurope.eu/tackling-precarity-in-the-platform-economy-and-beyond.

Hatch, Patrick. "In Amazon's 'Hellscape,' Workers Face Insecurity and Crushing Targets." *The Sydney Morning Herald*, September 7, 2018. https://www.smh.com.au/business/workplace/in-amazon-s-hellscape-workers-face-insecurity-and-crushing-targets-20180907-p502ao.html.

Holt, Simon Carey. "Men in the Kitchen: Food, Gender, Church and Culture." *Simply Simon*, July 29, 2019. https://simoncareyholt.wordpress.com/2019/07/29/men-in-the-kitchen-food-gender-church-culture/.

Koyama, Kosuke. *Three Mile an Hour God: Biblical Reflections*. Maryknoll: Orbis, 1980.

Loach, Ken, dir. *Sorry We Missed You*. Screenplay by Paul Laverty. UK: Sixteen Films, 2019.

Martin, Kara. *Workship: How to Use Your Work to Worship God*. Singapore: Graceworks, 2017.

———. *Workship 2: How to Flourish at Work*. Singapore: Graceworks, 2018.

Montgomery, John W., and Gene E. Veith, eds. *Where Christ is Present: A Theology for All Seasons on the 500th Anniversary of the Reformation*. Irvine: NRP, 2015.

Nichols, Tom. *The Death of Expertise: The Campaign Against Established Knowledge and Why it Matters*. New York: Oxford University Press, 2017.

Perkins, William. *The Work of William Perkins*. Edited by Ian Breward. Appleford: Courtenay, 1970.

Peterson, Andrew. "Creativity Isn't Just for 'Creatives.'" Interview by David O. Taylor. *Christianity Today*, October 21, 2019. https://www.christianitytoday.com/ct/2019/november/andrew-peterson-adorning-dark-creativity-art.html.

Preece, Gordon. *Changing Work Values: A Christian Response*. East Brunswick: Acorn, 1995.

———. "Churches, Unions and the Ensuring Integrity Bill." *Ethos*, October 29, 2019. http://www.ethos.org.au/online-resources/Engage-Mail/churches-unions-and-the-ensuring-integrity-bill.

———. "New Churches for Anglicans and Baptists? Missional Transitions in an Age of Chronic Economic and Ecological Crises." In *Cultural Diversity, Worship, and Australian Baptist Church Life*, New Wineskins vol. 2, edited by Darrell Jackson and Darren Cronshaw, 101–19. Macquarie Park: Morling, 2016.

———. "Rampant Lawlessness in the Workplace." *Vision Christian Radio*, March 22, 2017. https://vision.org.au/radio/2017/03/22/rampant-lawlessness-in-the-workplace/.

———. "Re-Humanising Work: From Vocation to Precarious and Robotised Work." *Zadok Perspectives* 140 (Spring 2018) 1–6.

———. *The Viability of the Vocation Tradition in Trinitarian, Credal and Reformed Perspective*. Lewiston: Edwin Mellin, 1998.

———. "Vocation in a Post-Vocational World: Meaning, De-Meaning and Re-Meaning of Work." In *The Bible and the Business of Life: Essays in Honor of Robert J. Banks' 65th Birthday*, edited by Simon Carey Holt and Gordon R. Preece, 192–215. Hindmarsh: ATF, 2004.

Schumpeter, Joseph A. *Capitalism, Socialism and Democracy*. London: Routledge, 1994.

Siemon-Netto, Uwe. "Vocation Versus Narcissus." In *Where Christ is Present: A Theology for All Seasons on the 500th Anniversary of the Reformation*, edited by John W. Montgomery and Gene E. Veith, 149–64. Irvine: NRP, 2015.

Sloane, Andrew. "Biblical Reflections on the Precariat." *Zadok Perspectives* 140 (Spring 2018) 9–10.

Solman. Paul. "Is the 'Creative Class' Saving Our Cities, or Making Them Impossible to Live In?" Interview of Richard Florida. *PBS News Hour*, June 1, 2017. https://www.pbs.org/newshour/economy/creative-class-saving-cities-making-impossible-live.

Standing, Guy. *Plunder of the Commons*. Milton Keynes: Pelican, 2019.

———. *The Precariat: The New Dangerous Class*. London: Bloomsbury, 2011.

———. *The Precariat Charter: From Denizens to Citizens*. London: Bloomsbury, 2014.

Stewart, Matthew. "The 9.9 Percent Is the New American Aristocracy." *The Atlantic*, June 2018. https://www.theatlantic.com/magazine/archive/2018/06/the-birth-of-a-new-american-aristocracy/559130/.

Strom, Timothy Erik. "Abstract and Control: Twenty Years of Google." *Arena Magazine* 156 (October/November 2018) 35–39.

Taneja, Hemant. "The Era of 'Move Fast and Break Things' Is Over." *Harvard Business Review*, January 22, 2019. https://hbr.org/2019/01/the-era-of-move-fast-and-break-things-is-over.

Taplin, Jonathan. *Move Fast and Break Things: How Facebook, Google and Amazon Have Cornered Culture and Undermined Democracy*. New York: Little, Brown, 2017.

Taylor, Charles. *A Secular Age*. Cambridge, MA: Belknap, 2007.

Volf, Miroslav. *Work in the Spirit: Toward a Theology of Work*. New York: Oxford University Press, 1991.

Volf, Miroslav, and Mathew Croasmun. *For the Life of the World: Theology That Makes a Difference*. Grand Rapids: Brazos, 2019.

"Washing Diapers for God's Glory: How Martin Luther Transformed Work." *Intersect*, October 31, 2017. http://intersectproject.org/faith-and-work/washing-diapers-gods-glory-martin-luther-transformed-work/.

Wong, Julia Carrie. "The Dark Side of Tech: Why the Guardian Asks Tough Questions about Silicon Valley." *The Guardian*, December 20, 2019. https://www.theguardian.com/us-news/2019/dec/19/dark-side-of-tech-silicon-valley-guardian.

Zuboff, Shoshana. *The Age of Surveillance Capitalism: The Fight for a Human Future at the New Frontier of Power*. London: Profile, 2019.

PART 2

Church and Pastoral Ministry

# 7

# Sustainability and Preventing Dropout in the Human Services Industry

*A Study of Pastors in the Australian Context*

KEITH MITCHELL

*Morling Theological College, an affiliated institution of
the Australian College of Theology*

## Abstract

THE SUSTAINABILITY AND PREVENTION of dropout in workers serving in the human services industry is a challenge, particularly for pastors. This study presents research utilizing interpretative phenomenological analysis (IPA) to unearth themes of sustainability and the prevention of dropout regarding pastors serving in church-based ministry within Australia. The results of this research show convergence and divergence in various features surrounding social support, emotionality, conflict, spiritual expression, and spousal relationships. After analysis of these themes, this study proposes that the key to sustainability and preventing dropout in pastors is the development of emotional intelligence (EI). The study concludes that people assisting pastors in this vocational area be attentive to developing EI.

## Introduction

Imagine a society without individuals to serve the vulnerable in our communities, or a communal village where those who need support had minimal human contact. Conceptualize a place where there were lessened numbers of people to care, encourage, and celebrate with others in communal settings such as churches. If such a reality evolved then this would mean the demise and deconstruction of the human services industry, as we know it today. This scenario if left unchecked would put society on a trajectory towards greater dehumanization.

Our civilization relies on the human services industry to deliver levels of support, care, and direction to people in our country; but it is anecdotally evidenced and generally accepted that these vocational areas incur high dropout rates. Workers in the human services industry—such as counsellors, psychotherapists, social workers, teachers, medical professionals, police officers, emergency service workers, and religious practitioners—face stressors different to other vocations because of the relational factors with which they contend. The level of relational pressure from direct human contact is accentuated for the human services industry, which means that unique causes of dropout exist.[1]

## *Australian-Based Pastors*

Amongst the human service industry are Australian pastors, who face distinctive stressors comparative to other human service workers. This profession, as with other human service workers, faces the incurrence of dropout. Although overall numbers of pastors who have dropped out is mostly unsubstantiated, there are stories and some denominationally based statistics that indicate dropout is an issue in the profession. For instance, amongst the Baptist Association of pastors in New South Wales and the Australian Capital Territory, substantiated figures revealed that between 1994 and 2013, 42 percent of pastors had dropped out from church-based ministry. Of this 42 percent who had dropped out:

- 20 percent of Baptist pastors had moved to a non-church-based approved Baptist ministry and so were no longer pastoring
- 3 percent had moved to another denomination
- 5 percent had retired

---

1. Dollard et al., "Unique Aspects of Stress," 84–91.

- 14 percent were no longer serving in any Christian ministry.[2]

This shows a 39 percent dropout from the face of church-based ministry over a nineteen-year period.

The loss of religious ministers in church-based ministry would have a profound effect on our society at both communal and government levels. Over the centuries, pastors have been at the forefront of societal transformation and government changes regarding aspects such as the support of the unborn by ensuring abortion laws remain; the medically frail through development of palliative care; the emotionally disturbed by ensuring dignity in their care; the disenfranchised such as asylum seekers; the enslaved and the release of sex slaves; and so on. The incurrence of dropout not only means a diminished influence of biblical ethics being initiated in our society but also means the incurrence of personal, familial, and financial cost to:

- pastors
- their families
- the communities in which they have served
- Australian taxpayers who encounter higher social support costs.

In response to these significant societal impacts, my primary research question is this: what aspects in clergy experiences have been assisting clergy in their sustainability in church-based ministry, and what facets of pastoral experiences are causing dropout from church-based ministry?

Besides the main question, are sub-questions surrounding:

- training and formation of people for pastoral ministry and its efficacy
- the ongoing development processes of those in pastoral ministry
- ongoing developmental procedures that denominations have engaged.

Essentially, what would the person who has remained in longer-term ministry and those who have dropped out of church-based ministry want to say to: the newcomer into pastoral ministry; educators of pastors in training; and denominational leaders who liaise with and have oversight of church-based congregations?

---

2. Clendinning, "BUNSW Ordinations."

## Pastoral Context

Most pastors generally face different stressors and experiences than other human service professions. Some of these more unique aspects surround areas such as finances, time allocation, personal identity and image, expectations, role conflict and ambiguity, life boundaries, the first few years of ministry, social support, relocation, church tensions, secularization, unique church structures, and religious upbringing.[3] A pastor, for instance, can feel that they are "on call" twenty-four hours a day, seven days a week, having conflicts with multiple people at the same time, and facing a crisis in their own personal lives whilst feeling incredibly isolated.

## Previous Studies on Pastoral Sustainability

Previous studies conducted in the area of preventing dropout of pastors have tended to enfold an amalgamation of specific factors such as:

- a particular country and its culture
- a specific or unspecified gender of clergy
- certain or combined denominations
- the utilization of a stipulated methodology, often quantitative
- extra-ecclesial research perspectives conducted by those—usually psychologists—who have not worked in the field of pastoral ministry
- a focus on burnout issues rather than explanations for dropout
- examination of a cohort of people still in ministry rather than those who have dropped out.

A review of these studies affirms that there are gaps in the research that allows the involvement of more specific cohorts of participants involving such factors as the country, denominational distinctiveness, gender, and culture of pastors. These studies also reveal gaps in literature that utilize other methodologies such as phenomenology, allowing for further research to be conducted by people more attuned to the field of research rather than non-pastors; in turn, researchers may look at broader issues in pastors' experiences rather than predefined assumptions of what has been causing dropout, such as burnout.

---

3. Cotton et al., "Clergy in Crisis," 311–57.

## Reason for Conducting an Interpretative Phenomenological Analysis (IPA) Study

In response to the research questions, current literature, and pastoral context, this chapter discusses a qualitative study utilizing an interpretative phenomenological analysis (IPA) methodology amongst Baptist pastors in Australia. Epistemologically connected to the phenomenological stream in research,[4] IPA differs from descriptive or pure phenomenology by claiming that:

> every experience entails immediately and necessarily the position of both a subjective and an objective pole and phenomenology aims to study not the psychological rules of the relation between a specific consciousness and its particular objects, but instead the general and universal laws of this correlation, its different structures and its different properties.[5]

Phenomenology emanates from the Greek word *phainomenon* and is understood as something visible or that which arises in contrast to reality.[6] By examining a person's experience, phenomenologists aim to describe the *lebenswalt* (the lived experience of a person) acting on the assumption that there "exists an essential perceived reality with common features."[7] Discoveries found through phenomenology can often then be utilized in further research through other means such as other qualitative or quantitative studies.

Pure or descriptive phenomenology has its critics because of its philosophical inception and appearance of bias and subjectivity. However, IPA is a methodology that aims to counteract subjective biases that can exist in pure or descriptive phenomenological research. It instead provides a response that gives a focus upon the researcher themselves in forming meaning from the phenomena expressed.[8] As a result, data—when analyzed—provides attention to more than just a person's narrative. In essence, IPA has attempted to *operationalize* phenomenology, and enable its engagement in a wide range of research areas, especially in psychology where quantitative studies tend to proliferate.[9]

---

4. Smith et al., *Interpretative Phenomenological Analysis*.
5. Aurora, "Realism and Idealism," 253.
6. Rockmore, "Hegel and Husserl," 67–84.
7. Starks and Trinidad, "Choose Your Method," 1373.
8. VanScoy and Evenstad, "Interpretative Phenomenological Analysis," 338–57.
9. Pringle et al., "Interpretative Phenomenological Analysis," 20–24.

An interpretative lens is utilized in IPA when working with participant stories and their lived experience.[10] This process allows researchers to be more investigative and inquisitive than in pure or descriptive phenomenology. This process of interview technique enables findings and analysis to be richer.[11] As Pringle and others highlight, "IPA stresses the interpretative and hermeneutic elements, seeking to capture examples of convergence and divergence, rather than focusing solely on commonalities."[12]

IPA achieves the interpretative process in its unique method amongst phenomenology. In comparison to pure or descriptive phenomenology, its method differs in that it utilizes a threefold process surrounding biases, to ensure an appropriate interpretative lens is enabled.[13] IPA studies tend to be smaller in sample, and in its threefold process engage in phenomenology, a double hermeneutic, and idiography (study of the specific). Hermeneutics is a familiar term in Christian-based studies as this is the exposition of text in its context.[14] In phenomenological studies, a person's story is exegeted through the contextual and cultural aspects of the person's *lebenswalt*. This process is known as "*lecture de texte*, or textual exegesis."[15] The employment of a double hermeneutic, however, is the exposition of both text and the researcher who is actually interpreting the text. It is these features which makes IPA unique amongst the world of phenomenology and, thus, makes it more palatable to someone who might specify themselves as a "critical realist."[16] Critical realism is posited between realism and relativism ontologically and epistemologically.[17]

Besides being inductive, IPA looks for patterns procured through themes unearthed from a person's *lebenswalt*. Analysis of these themes aims to deconstruct and evaluate current theory whilst creating new understandings where necessary. It works from source data, moving from the particulars into conceptual and theoretical frameworks.[18]

---

10. Lyons, *Analysing Qualitative Data*.
11. Pringle et al., "Interpretative Phenomenological Analysis."
12. Pringle et al., "Interpretative Phenomenological Analysis," 22.
13. Eatough and Smith, "Interpretative Phenomenological Analysis"; Shinebourne, "Theoretical Underpinnings," 16–31.
14. Smith and Eatough, *Interpretative Phenomenological Analysis*.
15. Davidson, "Introduction," 1.
16. Jeong and Othman, "Interpretative Phenomenological Analysis."
17. Coyle, "Qualitative Psychological Research."
18. Coyle, "Qualitative Psychological Research."

## Method of this IPA Study

In the IPA study in this chapter, I have considered two cohorts of Baptist pastors in Australia who were gathered and interviewed in a semi-structured approach, whilst maintaining anonymity and confidentiality. Recorded interviews were transcribed verbatim and analyzed, whilst themes that arose were examined for convergences and divergences between the two cohorts. The first cohort of Baptist pastors comprised three pastors still serving in church-based ministry and who had served over ten years since being ordained, known as PIMs (Pastors in Ministry). The second cohort of three participants were people who had previously served in Baptist settings but had dropped out of church-based ministry prior to serving ten years after ordination, known as OPMs (Out of Pastoral Ministry). Considering ease of procurement, accessibility, and homogeneity of the sample, all participants were middle-aged male pastors or ex-pastors, who had studied at the same theological college, were married, and had served in Baptist churches in New South Wales, Australia. They differed in the number of children that they had, ministry roles they served in, level of theological qualification attained, and church settings encountered.

## *Results of this Study*

The main themes gathered through participant interviews are presented in the following categories:

- similar church-based experiences and pastoral training, excepting that OPMs had exposure to church planting contexts, whereby PIMs did not. All candidates initially experienced urban-based contexts prior to other settings like inner city, or semi-rural

- analogous positive expression around leadership experiences and the identification of the challenges of pastoral leadership. All participants expressed that their pastoral experience was both good, and challenging or bad

- the incurrence of conflict in ministry, with OPMs also raising issues of unresolved conflict in both their marital relationships and church contexts. All participants raised that conflict existed at various times. However, PIMs mentioned that they tended to face conflict even if they did not like it. OPMs tended towards avoiding conflict, and/or blaming others

- the importance of the call of God, yet with variance amongst participants in both cohorts whether this was a predominant feature for them. This theme did not arise as a common aspect for all participants and was mentioned by both cohorts.
- the place of self-care, including spiritual expression. Inconsistencies were identified between the two cohorts in the manner that self-care strategies were employed. PIMs were inclined to being more intentional in self-care than OPMs
- social supports of various kinds for both cohorts but recognizing the differences in manner of employment of these sources between OPMs and PIMs. There was variance as to the amount of internal and external support amongst all participants, but it was the engagement of emotionality with support services that stood out for PIMs compared to OPMs
- denominational support identified inversely between the two cohorts. PIMs saw denominational support positively and realistically, whereas OPMs tended to see support as insufficient and expected more
- family and spousal support being dissimilar between cohorts. PIMs spoke favorably of spousal support compared to OPMs who discussed challenges with their spouse. In fact, all OPMs had either divorced or separated since dropping out of ministry, and mentioned animosity and relational strains throughout their years as a pastor.

## Main Findings and Discussion from this Research

Through analysis of the results the main finding in this IPA study was the impact that Emotional Intelligence (EI) played upon participants. EI is a recent theory in research instigated by Daniel Goleman[19] and essentially examines one's ability to discern events in life from an emotional perspective. Studies engaging with EI have expanded since Goleman's first work and have created conjecture over how EI can be measured.[20] It was Steven Stein who said that essentially all definitions and understandings basically claim that EI is:

1. the ability to identify emotional information in oneself and in others

---

19. Goleman, *Emotional Intelligence*.
20. Jordan et al., "Application of Emotional Intelligence," 171–90.

2. the ability to manage emotional information in oneself and in others
3. the ability to focus emotional energy on required behaviors to get things done.[21]

The results from this study establish that the employment of EI in pastoral leadership was a predominant aspect of sustainability in pastors and preventing dropout. This was identified through a variety of factors. First, PIMs had near double the variety of emotional language expressed in the interviews as they discussed their experiences compared to the OPMs. These words were both positively and negatively charged, and varied in balance between each OPM and PIM. The cohort of OPMs recorded a variety of forty emotional words compared to PIMs, with an average of fifty-seven. One OPM had been in high levels of therapy since dropping out of ministry, and so this may have caused a higher average for OPMs since his engagement in therapy, as therapies tend toward the processing of emotional well-being.

Second, PIMs seemed to be more aware and able to identify emotional dynamics that were occurring and were able to process emotion. They were cognizant of the deprecating effect of ministry events upon them compared to OPMs. For instance, all PIMs stated that they had been made aware of near burnout at some point in their ministry and were able to employ remedial actions to counteract burnout occurring. OPMs did not recognize near burnout and eventually dropped out from a range of unresolved ministry issues that they had incurred.

Third, there was a greater ability by PIMs to recognize that there was a limitation on what the theological college, their spouse, friends, colleagues, and denominational sources could supply as support during ministry challenges. This brought a sense of realism to their experiences. For instance, one PIM stated that theological college training had done all it could to assist them in pastoral ministry. They recognized that college training could not prepare them for everything in church ministry. This PIM also stated that denominational leaders were there to help if needed. In contrast, the OPMs tended to blame the college, the denomination, the church, and even one's spouse for what they incurred in their experiences. One OPM referenced the denominational leaders as not doing enough to assist them, and criticized the college for not preparing them for ministry like church planting. It must be noted though that after college, this OPM was serving in a traditional church setting and that their church planting experience came a few years later.

21. Stein, *EQ Leader*, 38.

Fourth, OPMs did not seem to be able to remain in challenged and emotive circumstances over as long a time span compared to PIMs. PIMs learnt to be more accepting of the challenges that they faced and saw these exposures as the reality of pastoral ministry. In fact, when it was time to change church contexts from a senior role, PIMs were happy to move back to an associate role instead of remaining in a senior role. OPMs instead moved to a church plant where pressures were accentuated.

Fifth, PIMs demonstrated intentionality in self-preservation by taking time out and/or changing their church context when required. They tended to have employed external support that was able to assist them to process emotional aspects. OPMs, instead, seemed to remain in the same state of emotionality until they dropped out. They did not have an intentional plan to engage in emotional processing with external sources. Some OPMs may have engaged in prayer counselling but this did not involve emotional processing.

Some North American-based studies[22] had expressed that EI had been a contributor to sustainability or preventing dropout, compared to Australian-based research where EI has not been mentioned. National Church Life Survey Research,[23] and Maureen Miner and others[24] indicated that the occurrence of low exhaustion and high job satisfaction were key to sustainability of clergy. This study supports these findings by claiming that the key to low exhaustion and increasing job satisfaction is by means of the development of a pastor's EI. Research amongst other professions, by the likes of Ortin and Camgoz,[25] and Jordan and others,[26] support these results as well. These other studies argue that EI is conducive to lower stress and higher job satisfaction. In essence, lower stress could be conflated with lower emotional exhaustion.

However, despite the importance that EI is in pastors to avoid leaving pastoral ministry, other aspects around sustainability and preventing dropout arose. These other factors seem to have affected the pastor's development of their EI. Four pertinent factors were unearthed.

---

22. Burns et al., *Resilient Ministry*.
23. NCLS Research, "Ministry Satisfaction."
24. Miner, "Ministry Orientation," 167–88.
25. Orta and Camgoz, "Exploring Emotional Intelligence," 346–63.
26. Jordan et al., *Application of Emotional Intelligence*, 171–90.

## Approach to Conflict

Amongst all OPMs it was identified that there tended to be a conflict avoidant style instigated in their ministry compared to PIMs. Despite the PIMs not necessarily enjoying conflict, they recognized that conflict was inevitable and were prepared to engage for the sake of leadership. Their emotional resolve seemed more developed than the OPMs.

## Type of Social Support Engaged

PIMs tended to engage with support people—such as denominational leaders, counsellors, and mentors—who were more highly skilled and attuned emotionally compared to OPMs. OPMs may have had support people, but these people were not identifiable as highly skilled in emotional processing. In fact, denominational support people were often rejected by OPMs who, in turn, formulated a more hostile relationship towards them. Having internal church support was helpful, but not always a reality for all participants at all times. Overall, it seemed that it was the type of social support which was important in sustainability for PIMs.

## Place of Spousal Support

All OPMs were either divorced or in high-level marriage therapy since they dropped out of ministry. There was a level of blaming and unresolved marital issues that were voiced from OPMs regarding their spouse or previous spouse, compared to PIMs. PIMs spoke favorably of their spouse and indicated a positive level of support in their ministry. It could be conceived that the level of EI ability within OPMs translated itself similarly in relationship to their spouses, but this is conjecture at this stage, warranting further research.

## Manner in Which Spiritual Practices Were Employed

All participants spoke of some level of spiritual practice and a sense of call. However, the manner in which PIMs described these practices, and their sense of call, tended to be more emotively connected to God than the OPMs. This is an indicator that the manner in which pastors employ spiritual practices could benefit sustainability. In a sense, it indicates that emotional attachment to God was an important aspect in this regard. Attachment is a theory which postulates that healthily expressed emotionality with another person is developed through secure connection and bonding.[27]

## Conclusion

This study has promulgated that sustainability for pastors serving in the human service industry revolves around developing their own emotional intelligence and implementing appropriate social and familial support. It postulated that the manner in which pastors deal with conflict and instigate spiritual practices should aim to improve emotional intelligence by processing emotional aspects and focusing on emotional attachment to God. Consequently, in the procurement of pastors into pastoral ministry, in forming pastors in theological training, and in the provision of ongoing developmental aspects, attentiveness to emotional intelligence needs to predominate for the sake of sustainability and preventing dropout.

### *Recommendations*

As a result of the findings this study presents an assortment of recommendations related to a range of people involved with pastors. First, for supervisors and counsellors, it recognizes the importance of developing emotive words and handling conflict in order to develop a greater level of EI in clergy. Therapists, therefore, need to provide attention to a pastor's ability to differentiate themselves from their ministry context.

For theological educators, this study proposes that for pastors there needs to be education and training that ensures EI development is included in pastoral formation. These formation processes need to engage in self-awareness, personal insight, and differentiating self in relational and ministry situations especially regarding conflict.

Finally, for denominational leaders, this study urges attention is given to EI in the procurement and ongoing development of pastors. These efforts need to check ongoing EI and awareness within applicants for accreditation, and—prior to ordaining—communicate the essential nature of appropriate professional support and supervision, encourage and provide programs to develop spousal relationships, and provide updated conflict development services.

---

27. Pines, "Adult Attachment Styles."

## Further Research

Due to IPA's idiographic nature, the findings in this research are restricted in its extrapolation. This means that there is scope for further studies to include consideration of factors concerning ministry context, culture, gender, denomination, country, age, and theological education. This study engaged cohorts of serving pastors up to the ten-year mark, and so a variation on years of service may also be another consideration in sample selection in future IPA studies.

The results from this study identified possible correlation between spousal relationships and relational dynamics in ministry situations, thus further explorations in this area of individuals serving as pastors is also highly recommended.

## Bibliography

Aurora, Simone. "Between Realism and Idealism: Transcendental Experience in Truth in Husserl's Phenomenology." In *Truth and Experience: Between Phenomenology and Hermeneutics*, edited by Dorthe Jørgensen, Gaetano Chiurazzi, and Søren Tinning, 243–60. Newcastle-upon-Tyne, UK: Cambridge Scholars, 2015.

Burns, Bob et al. *Resilient Ministry: What Pastors Told Us About Surviving and Thriving*. Downers Grove: IVP, 2013.

Clendinning, Kenneth. "BUNSW Ordinations/Accreditation 1994–2013." Personal communication, 2014.

Cotton, Sarah J. et al. "Clergy in Crisis." In *Occupational Stress in the Service Professions*, edited by Maureen Dollard, Helen R. Winefield, and Anthony H. Winefield, 311–57. London: Taylor & Francis, 2003.

Coyle, Adrian. "Introduction to Qualitative Psychological Research." In *Analysing Qualitative Data in Psychology*, 2nd ed., edited by Evanthia Lyons and Adrian Coyle, 9–30. Los Angeles: SAGE, 2016.

Davidson, Scott. "Introduction: Translation as a Model of Interdisciplinarity." In *Ricoeur Across the Disciplines*, edited by Scott Davidson, 1–11. New York: Continuum, 2010.

Dollard, Maureen, et al. "Unique Aspects of Stress in Human Service Work." *Australian Psychologist* 38 (2003) 84–91.

Eatough, Virginia, and Jonathan A. Smith. "Interpretative Phenomenological Analysis." In *Analysing Qualitative Data in Psychology*, 2nd ed., edited by Evanthia Lyons and Adrian Coyle, 193–211. Los Angeles: SAGE, 2016.

Goleman, Daniel. *Emotional Intelligence*. New York: Bantam, 1995.

Jeong, Hyeseung, and Juliana Othman. "Using Interpretative Phenomenological Analysis from a Realist Perspective." *The Qualitative Report* 21, no. 3 (March 19, 2016) 558–70.

Jordan, Peter J. et al. "The Application of Emotional Intelligence in Industrial and Organizational Psychology." In *Assessing Emotional Intelligence: Theory, Research, and Applications*, edited by James D. A. Parker, 171–90. Boston: Springer, 2009.

Lyons, Evanthia, and Adrian Coyle, eds. *Analysing Qualitative Data in Psychology*. Los Angeles: SAGE, 2007.

Miner, Maureen H. et al. "Ministry Orientation and Ministry Outcomes: Evaluation of a New Multidimensional Model of Clergy Burnout and Job Satisfaction." *Journal of Occupational and Organizational Psychology* 83 (2010) 167–88.

NCLS Research. "Ministry Satisfaction and Emotional Exhaustion." NCLS, n.d. http://www.ncls.org.au/default.aspx?sitemapid=6973.

Newton, Cameron et al. "Emotional Intelligence as a Buffer of Occupational Stress." *Personnel Review* 45 (2016) 1010–28.

Orta, Irem Metin, and Selin Metin Camgoz. "Exploring Emotional Intelligence at Work: A Review of Current Evidence." In *Handbook of Research on Organizational Culture and Diversity in the Modern Workforce*, edited by Bryan Christiansen and Harish C. Chandan, 346–63. Hershey: IGI Global, 2017.

Pines, Ayala Malach. "Adult Attachment Styles and Their Relationship to Burnout: A Preliminary, Cross-Cultural Investigation." *Work and Stress* 18 (2004) 66–80.

Pringle, Jan et al. "Interpretative Phenomenological Analysis: A Discussion and Critique." *Nurse Researcher* 18 (2011) 20–24.

Rockmore, Tom. "Hegel and Husserl: Two Phenomenological Reactions to Kant." *Hegel Bulletin* 38 (2017) 67–84.

Shinebourne, Pnina. "The Theoretical Underpinnings of Interpretative Phenomenological Analysis (IPA)." *Existential Analysis: Journal of the Society for Existential Analysis* 22 (2011) 16–31.

Smith, Jonathan A., and Virginia Eatough, eds. *Interpretative Phenomenological Analysis: Theory, Method and Research*. Los Angeles: SAGE, 2009.

Starks, Helene, and Susan Brown Trinidad. "Choose Your Method: A Comparison of Phenomenology, Discourse Analysis, and Grounded Theory." *Qualitative Health Research* 17 (2007) 1372–80.

Stein, Steven. *The EQ Leader: Instilling Passion, Creating Shared Goals, and Building Meaningful Organizations through Emotional Intelligence*. Hoboken: John Wiley & Sons, 2017.

VanScoy, Amy, and Solveig Beyza Evenstad. "Interpretative Phenomenological Analysis for LIS Research." *Journal of Documentation* 71 (2015) 338–57.

# 8

## Church as Formative Ecology

*The Youth Work Vocation in Secular Settings*

DAVID FAGG

*Deakin University*

### Abstract

CHURCH COMMUNITIES PLAY A significant role in shaping the youth work vocation. The presence of affirming and respected adults, combined with opportunities for responsibility and service, often results in a strong sense of call to serve young people. However, many talented and passionate youth workers become dissatisfied with church-based youth ministry, and leave to engage in secular youth work contexts, resulting in a diaspora of Christian youth workers. To understand this process, we ask, "How does the ecology of the church shape the vocation of these youth workers?"

This chapter draws on extensive interviews with youth workers to answer this question. It finds that: (1) the vocation of Christian youth workers is formed through the participatory community of the church; (2) discontent with the "safe" nature of church-based youth ministry is the dominant reason for the departure of Christian youth workers; and (3) there is a problematic divide between Christians in secular youth work, and leaders in church-based youth ministry. In response, the church needs to better recognize its formative role in the youth work vocation, and youth ministry leaders need to engage in dialogue with Christian youth workers.

## Introduction

Youth work in Australia is "secular," separate from "youth ministry," and not reliant on any religious worldview for its operation. It is thoroughly rationalized and regulated through government funding and guidelines. Yet, this secularized and rationalized sector still desires its workers to be "called" to the work. One cohort that possesses a strong sense of calling is Christians who work in secular youth work settings. This chapter asks: (1) In what ways does the Christian community form the vocation of Christians in secular youth work?; and (2) What are the consequences of such formation for their youth work vocation?

To answer these questions, this chapter draws on wider doctoral research in which fifty Australian youth workers (past and present) were interviewed to explore their sense of calling and practice of their faith in secular youth work settings. It finds that churches act as ecologies in which the youth work vocation is formed through participatory community, experiences of discontent, and diasporic connection.

To frame these empirical findings, the chapter commences with a review of the rationalization of Australian youth work, against which the persistent desire for vocationally oriented youth workers makes sense, and advocates that the youth work vocation be understood as a "virtue ethic" which necessitates an understanding of the community (the church) in which such an ethic is shaped.

## Definitions

### *Youth Work*

In this chapter, "youth work" takes the meaning commonly assigned to it in the Australian youth work sector:

> Youth work is a practice that places young people and their interests first. Youth work is a relational practice, where the youth worker operates alongside the young person in their context. Youth work is an empowering practice that advocates for and

facilitates a young person's independence, participation in society, connectedness and realisation of their rights.[1]

The Australian youth work sector tends to distinguish between *youth work* (as defined above) and *youth ministry*, which consists of work with young people that is authorized or implemented by churches and other religious organizations.[2] Though I am not overly satisfied with this distinction, for the sake of clarity I will use it in this chapter, recognizing that much "youth ministry" is also called "youth work" in Australia, the United Kingdom, and Aotearoa/New Zealand. Thus, in what follows, the term "youth workers" refers to personnel in the secular workforce, and "youth ministry leaders" refers to personnel who work in church-based youth ministry.

*Secular*

Defining "secular" has recently consumed much intellectual energy as theologians, philosophers, and sociologists have attempted to understand the post-Christian reality of most Western societies.[3] For this chapter, I use "secular" to denote:

> Youth work settings where active religious belief, commitments, action, and institutions are treated as irrelevant to the youth work task.

Attentive readers may ask where this leaves organizations such as Anglicare or UnitingCare, who have links to "parent" Christian denominations. After all, organizations of this type employ the bulk of youth workers in Australia. I treat these as secular organizations (excepting those linked to the Catholic Church), as in my judgment they are essentially autonomous from the religious authority that denominations attempt to exert.[4]

---

1. Australian Youth Work Coalition, "AYAC Definition," para. 17.
2. Sercombe, *Youth Work Ethics*, 37.
3. Smith, *How (Not) to Be Secular*; Taylor, *Secular Age*.
4. Chaves, "Denominations"; Chaves, "Secularization."

## Literature Review

### The Youth Work Vocation and Its Enemies

Max Weber set the tone for sociological understandings of "vocation" when he described it as an "irrational" element that nonetheless aids (in part) the rationality of modern capitalism:

> [T]he entire notion of a "calling" must appear fully irrational from the vantage point of the person's pure self-interest in happiness. Yet the dedication to work in the manner of a "calling" has in the past constituted one of the characteristic components of our capitalist economic culture. It remains so even today.[5]

Later sociological investigations of vocation are primarily found in studies of occupations or "professional identity," an important field of research which examines how individuals become committed to the norms, boundaries, and practices of modern professions. In these studies, a "sense of call" or "vocation" is subsumed within the umbrella of the concept of a "profession," and seen as one possible motivation for the professional.[6] Alternatively, some researchers see "calling" as the inner aspect of an outer, more occupational or professional "vocation."[7]

In theological treatments of vocation, however, "calling" is clearly distinguished from an occupation. For example, Gordon T. Smith uses a helpful three-part model of calling, starting with (1) a "general call" to follow Jesus, moving to (2) a life's mission that is specific to each person ("vocation"), and ending with (3) the call to perform immediate tasks or duties.[8] The call that we are concerned with here is that of "vocation," but we see it in the larger picture of the call to follow Jesus. The "youth work vocation" is distinct from, but can be partially fulfilled in, the youth work profession. Thus, the youth work vocation is an ongoing experience of purpose in an individual's life, stemming from the ultimate call to follow Jesus. What is this purpose? To work for and with young people, for their development and benefit.

However, the whole question of vocation is a source of anxiety in the youth work sector, and its literature. This makes sense when placed against

---

5. Weber, *Protestant Ethic*, 88. By "rationality," Weber does not simply mean a stance of the mind that values reason, but the way modern societies prioritize reason as an organizing principle over, for example, tradition.

6. Vasudevan, "Occupational Culture."

7. Erickson and Price, "Vocation and Professional Identity."

8. Smith, *Courage and Calling*.

the background of the increasing rationalization of the youth work sector. Youth work's history is rooted in the chaotic philanthropic and missionary impulses of the youth work pioneers of the nineteenth century, and shaped by the social upheavals of the late 1950s to 1970s. However, Australian youth work has gradually conformed to increasing government regulation, leading to what we have today—an efficiency-focused, outcomes-driven approach to youth work, which is a far cry from youth work's relational heart.[9] The rationalization of the youth work sector can be broken down into three components: marketization, secularization, and professionalization.

Trudi Cooper describes the marketization of the youth work sector clearly:

> Large charitable organizations compete with each other and with commercial organizations, to provide outsourced government services: more cheaply; under tighter government control, exercised through specification of "performance measures"; and, under threat that, if they did not perform, the contract would be given to another provider.[10]

The influence of the market paradigm on youth work funding and practice is fiercely criticized within the youth work sector, resisted wherever possible, and has played a central role in two further processes: secularization and professionalization.[11]

The market paradigm, while not the prime driver of secularization, contributes to the hollowing out of religious organizations in which youth work takes place. When government funding calls for a narrow set of expertise and knowledge, then an organization's religious character becomes less significant, and priorities are gradually changed to meet the needs of the market.[12] Hence, welfare agencies linked to denominations (e.g., Salvation Army, Anglicare, Wesley Mission, and so on) often undergo a process of "internal secularization," whereby religious influence is gradually removed from an organization's practice and ethos:

> The basic idea is that when agency structures representing substantial denominational resources are run by executives who are increasingly autonomous from a denomination's religious authority structure, such a development is likely to result in

9. Martin, *Invisible Table*; Rodd and Stewart, "Glue."
10. Cooper, "Institutional Context," 118.
11. Bessant, "Free Market Economics"; De St Croix, "Marketisation."
12. Gallet, "Christian Mission."

organizational changes that are appropriately understood as internal secularization.[13]

Of course, there are youth workers with a faith or "spirituality" in the sector, as well as organizations with an explicitly faith-based vision, and much work that happens in the sector could be interpreted as "Christ-like." However, "secularization" here means that these things are not seen as determinative of the character of the youth work sector; rather, they are incidental.

Professionalization has been hotly debated in the youth work sector at least since the early 1970s with the publication of seminal works by Elery Hamilton-Smith and Donna Brownell.[14] However, its advocates have decisively won the argument, even if the institutional arrangements for professionalization have not been firmly established, and the reasons for the transition have varied.[15] Nonetheless, the market paradigm accelerated professionalization in two main ways. First, youth work organizations must employ trained personnel who can achieve the outcomes required by governments. Second, the focus on competitive tendering for funding, and a move to skills-based training, has prompted youth workers to advocate professionalization as a bulwark against these foes.[16]

Given the twin moves of modern youth work to a secular framework with a professionalized workforce, and the advent of competitive tendering with a market paradigm, many commentators feel that "calling-based" or "organic" youth work is on its last legs. Does a "youth work vocation" make any sense in a sector that has secularized and professionalized? Do new entrants to the profession possess a powerful sense that they are "called" to do this work? Tony Jeffs, a long-time youth work academic, articulates the anxiety:

> The notion that becoming a social worker, teacher, community or youth worker axiomatically entails financial sacrifice, a selfless willingness to serve others, a lifetime commitment to demanding values and possess a high measure of education and "intellect" is no longer taken as a given.[17]

---

13. Chaves, "Denominations," 165.

14. Hamilton-Smith and Brownell, *Youth Workers*; Hamilton-Smith and Brownell, "Dilemmas."

15. For a sense of the literature, see Bessant, "Youth Work"; Goodwin, "Youth Worker Perception"; Maunders, "Professional Lions"; Sercombe, "Youth Work"; Youth Affairs Council of Victoria, "That Old Chestnut!"

16. Corney et al., "Youth Workers."

17. Jeffs, "Too Few, Too Many," para. 8.

This anxiety is also present in the Australian youth work sector. I interviewed Peter Wearne, a veteran youth worker with YSAS (Youth Substance Abuse Service) for the historical part of my doctoral research. Though a key worker in the establishment of "Theos,"[18] Peter is no longer a Christian, but he still sees a central role for the vocational ethic that youth workers of faith hold:

> *Interviewer*: To what extent do you think that faith has a legitimate role to play in youth work or not?
> 
> *Peter*: I think it has a legitimate role. . . . I think it's about values and attitudes and behavior . . . And what I was saying to [a coworker] . . . "the problem with the sector now, there's no vocation anymore." And I think what faith gives you is a purpose outside yourself and a framework and a paradigm outside yourself.

## *The Persistent Call to Youth Work*

How can we explain the persistent use and desire for "calling" language in the youth work sector and literature? I suggest three main sources.

First, the roots of youth work are overwhelmingly Christian. Early youth work (though not named as such at the time) was perceived as a divine calling, with Christian terminology, belief, and understanding widespread.[19] This work was often despised, and unsupported by the governments of the day, leading these early youth workers to see themselves as missionaries in their own land.[20]

Second, Australian governments began to take an interest in the field during and after World War II. "Fitness Councils" were set up, reports were written on youth work, and the need emerged for a trained workforce to meet the educational and social needs of young people.[21] This coincided with the late 1950s to 1970s, a time of great social ferment. The youth workers of that time were creating a craft that no one could really name. It encompassed camping, new forms of Christian outreach and community, political action, street youth work, and drop-in centers. This entailed being on the margins, being poorly paid, and thus imbued a sense of newness and adventure that combined to fuel a righteous passion.

---

18. Parachurch agency Scripture Union Victoria established "Theos" in the 1960s to 1970s. At the time it was a highly experimental form of youth outreach program.

19. Clyne, "Genealogy."

20. Smith, "Thomas John Barnardo."

21. Irving et al., *Youth in Australia*.

Third, the idea of youth work as a calling is strengthened by the view that the youth worker is the primary resource in the youth work relationship. Teachers focus on their discipline, and social workers depend on statute. But though youth work sometimes uses these things, youth work insists that the character of the youth worker is paramount.[22] This is because youth work is focused on an organic encounter between youth workers and young people. A personal relationship develops; young people feel safe and trusted to express their real desires for life, and youth workers assist young people to achieve these desires.[23] If youth work depends on the youth worker's character, then more than knowledge and skill is needed. Vocation is needed—an inner conviction that the youth worker's purpose is being expressed through this practice of relational youth work.

## *Vocation, Virtue, and the Church as "Formative Ecology"*

Given the anxiety about the decreasing role of vocation in youth work, the fact that the majority of youth workers in this study affirm a strong calling to youth work is significant. Therefore, it is important to understand how this calling is formed. As well as hearing from youth workers themselves, I posit that this question of formation is helpfully framed if we understand the youth work vocation as a type of "virtue ethic." Virtue ethics draws on philosophers like Aristotle and later interlocutors such as Alasdair MacIntyre. It asks, "What is human flourishing?" and thus, "What virtues must we cultivate, such that this vision of human flourishing can be lived out?" It recognizes that visions of human flourishing are rooted in communities or traditions that accumulate wisdom for what virtue looks like, and what a person needs to do to become virtuous.

Many youth work academics advocate virtue ethics as a more promising meta-frame for youth work practice than deontic or utilitarian ethics. These writers recognize that these latter ethical pathways are inadequate to the practical task of youth work—they cannot cope with the complexity of the youth work task, and they do not help to cultivate ethical character in the youth worker. In contrast, virtue ethics recognizes *phronēsis* (practical wisdom) as a fruitful way for youth workers to navigate the ethics of youth work relationships.[24]

---

22. Smith and Smith, *Art of Helping*.

23. Jeffs and Smith, "Valuing Youth Work."

24. For example, see Bessant, "Aristotle Meets Youth Work"; Hart, "Reality of Relationships"; Sercombe, *Youth Work Ethics*.

However, an aspect of virtue ethics that youth work academics usually neglect is the role of "community" in the formation of a virtuous disposition. Practitioners of an ethic cannot rely on a cognitive assimilation of its spirit and practices, but need to be formed in a community of practice that fosters the ethic over time, in a similar manner to an apprenticeship.[25] I call such a community an "ecology"—not to submit vocational formation to a thoroughgoing analysis via ecosystems theory, but simply to draw attention to the interdependent nature of the elements that constitute this process of formation.[26]

For youth work academics, this ecology is the professional community of youth workers. But Christians entering the profession have been formed in a prior ecology of practice—the Christian community. This is not to say that the church is the only ecology that forms the youth worker. Obviously, there are personal experiences, family systems, and other influences that spark a sense of life direction. Nonetheless, my research strongly suggests that the church community is the location within which Christians begin to seriously explore youth work as a vocation. Thus, we return to our research questions: "How does the church form the vocation of Christians in secular youth work?" and "What shape does this formation give to the youth work vocation of Christians in secular youth work?"

## Method

This chapter forms part of a larger doctoral project that I am undertaking at Deakin University. The project is a study of Christians who are youth workers in secular organizations—current youth workers in schools, welfare agencies, local councils, and so on (n=29), and secondary school chaplains (n=11). I also interviewed retired youth workers from the 1960s to 1970s for historical perspective; some of these are Christians, and others are not (n=11). Through semi-structured interviews and a focus group, I examine the ways in which Christians in secular youth work integrate their faith with their youth work, in particular: (1) the story of their faith, and of their entry into youth work; (2) their perceptions of their workplaces and colleagues in relation to their faith; and (3) the ways they express their faith in their work with young people.

---

25. Hauerwas, *Community of Character*; MacIntyre, *After Virtue*; Van Hooft, *Understanding Virtue Ethics*.

26. Bronfenbrenner, *Human Development*; Siporin, "Ecological Systems Theory."

## Findings

For the purposes of this chapter, I have limited my attention to the role that the church community plays in shaping vocation, rather than detailing the personal and theological views of youth workers. Suffice it to say, a vocational ethic is ubiquitous amongst the youth workers I interviewed, notwithstanding varying levels of articulacy about the connections between a sense of call on one hand, and practical youth work on the other. This research finds that the church ecology forms the vocation of Christian youth workers through three interdependent elements: *participatory community*, experiences of *discontent*, and *diasporic connection*. In the exploration of these three elements, we will hear from youth workers about their experience, and provide a brief comment on the ways these elements shape the youth work vocation of Christians in secular settings.

### *Participatory Community*

First, this research finds that church ecologies form the vocation of youth workers through *participatory community*. This element consists of three interdependent dimensions: (1) supportive mentors/advocates; (2) exercising practical responsibility in youth ministry; and (3) the conjunction of those dimensions with a renewal of, or entry into, Christian faith. Most of the interviewees (n=30) had experience of being a leader in a congregational youth ministry, with several having previously occupied paid "youth pastor" roles. Of the remainder (n=10), several had volunteered in other Christian ministry (e.g., Scripture Union, Fusion, camping). They viewed these experiences as formative of their vocation, even before they had an articulated sense of calling.

Phil is a manager of a youth agency in Western Australia, and his story is typical:

> I think I was asked to volunteer at a camp, and I found that I actually got along really well with the youth. And it got me thinking I guess about whether or not that might be something worth pursuing. So, I guess I just tested the waters, just volunteering and helping out where I could and found that I did enjoy it and young people seemed to be able to relate to me. I was able to develop rapport fairly easily, and it sort of went from there.

Many youth workers had their formative experiences of youth ministry in conjunction with a renewal of their faith, or their conversion into it:

> Yeah, growing up as a kid I grew up in [north-east Melbourne] and got into a bit of trouble as a young bloke and ended up having a bunch of youth workers get alongside me and support me. They were actually from a Christian organization called [Agency 1] at the time. They kind of supported me and got alongside me and really encouraged me and eventually after I tried my hand at a few different things they were looking for someone to help out with their Friday night youth groups and as a twenty-odd-year old I threw my hat in the ring and helped them with their Friday night youth group for about a year. (Cameron, mental health youth worker)

These experiences of mentoring, responsibility, and renewal/conversion were very affirming for the interviewees, and often the spark for taking the next step in their vocation, such as further study or through deeper investment in youth activities, both within and outside the church. This was the case for Rob; being mentored and encouraged in youth ministry led to parachurch ministry, study, and then his current position as a school wellbeing co-ordinator:

> I think, I think really just that relationship I had with my minister back home in [regional Victoria]. Yeah, I mean, I think I see, seeing him as my mentor and you know, sort of, you know him sort of encouraging and pushing me into you know having a go with that stuff early on was really key. You know, sort of basically fighting for me to give me that chance within the church.

In addition, youth workers would identify inspiring experiences of the church reaching out to young people beyond its boundaries:

> Probably going back to when I was a teenager, I was involved in—it was kind of like a girl's group originally—and then it kind of formed into a youth church that was really led by us. So, it had a youth band and we would have a go at preaching and go away on youth conferences and I think I really enjoyed that atmosphere of anyone being welcome. Because I probably found growing up that churches and church youth groups to be really cliquey and really not inviting and welcoming. (Joletta, youth worker)

Participatory community instilled interviewees with a conviction that youth development and participation is central to youth work, along with a focus on nurturing relationships and community, rather than programs or narrowly defined service provision. There is a deeply spiritual approach to practice, resulting from experiences of religious renewal and/or conversion.

## *Discontent*

Despite the affirmation of participatory community, most Christians in secular youth work experienced a deep sense of dissatisfaction with church-based youth ministry. This leads to our second finding: that the church forms the youth work vocation through *discontent*. Youth workers often spoke of the imperative to reach out to young people who were suffering or in some other need, they used the language of Christianity to explain this task, and critiqued the church for not living up to this mission. Frequently, discontent stems from hurtful experiences of disillusionment and disappointment. These youth workers often entered church youth ministry believing that the church could serve the most broken and difficult young people, but now seriously doubt its capacity to do so. For those with youth ministry experience, this discontent is the driving motivation for their departure to the secular youth work sector, rather than professional advancement or simple opportunity.

For example, Heather describes non-Christian young people coming to her church's youth ministry, but being marginalized in favor of existing members:

> Well, I just thought that a lot of the kids that were coming to church needed a lot of extra help and there wasn't the help in the church to help them and there were a lot of non-Christians where I thought we need to be helping people, they need to know Jesus . . . they're homeless or they've got really crappy life backgrounds and we should be helping them a lot more and I just felt like the church was focused on the Christians that were coming to church and sitting in the pews and just helping them every week. (Heather, case manager)

There was a strong desire to work with broken, poor, unchurched young people, and the youth workers found that they could not do this within the church context:

> I really felt like God was calling me to work with the most vulnerable kids. And those kids weren't in the church, so I felt like I was often with very middle-class, young people, with relatively, yeah relatively stable lives as opposed to the kids that I work with now, kind of engaged in a different, you know, child protection, juvenile justice, et cetera. So yeah, that was a very distinct decision. (Ange, manager of a youth work team)

Cameron describes pursuing a career as a youth pastor, but was advised that his calling to young people would likely not be served in such a role:

> I think the nail in the coffin so to speak was I had a meeting with [a denominational youth director] and we were chatting away and kind of talking through the steps of potentially moving into a youth pastor role and the like, and over a number of weeks we chatted. The final conversation we had was him saying, "Cameron, I see you have a real heart to release the last and the lost, you've got a real social justice bent, that would be wasted in the church. Most of our churches just want someone who will run their Friday night youth group and keep their kids out of trouble," he said.

In addition, this discontent was sometimes broader than the youth ministry practice of the church; it extended to the general direction their church was taking:

> I know what the realization moment was . . . . I had a group of our young leaders, and we were doing a six-week mission experience in the Philippines, so we were living in a little brick hut with mud floors . . . then receiving an email from our church council that our church had decided to spend $30,000 on nicer chairs for our church, and it was, for me, that was the moment where I realized how far my heart was from some of the things that our church was heading towards. (Ryan, local government youth worker)

The experience of discontent shapes the youth work vocation such that Christians in secular settings usually hold a critical stance towards church-based youth ministry, including a lack of confidence that "their" young people could find a home in the church. There is a corresponding deepening of commitment to the ethics, ethos, and aims of the youth work sector, and solidified commitment to young people at the margins.

## *Diasporic Connection*

This ongoing sense of discontent leads to our third finding: that the church forms the youth work vocation by fostering a *diasporic connection* with Christians in secular youth work. Because of the departure of youth workers from ministry within church congregations, there is now a diaspora of Christian youth workers in the church. I call them a "diaspora" not because they are not attending church. Indeed, the majority are regular attendees, and many find church a very positive experience. However, in relation to their vocation and work, they are generally disconnected from the church's ministry to young people. What is the nature of this diasporic connection?

First, the youth workers consistently affirmed that their work was not supported or understood by church members or leadership. Michael, a residential care worker in Victoria, says:

> Yeah, I think it's been particularly a journey for my church obviously . . . because when people hear the word "youth work" in church circles, they immediately think "ministry," so to gradually get the message over—"this is what I do, this is what it entails and what it doesn't entail" . . . . I mean to this day there are people that wouldn't have a clue. And I've been telling them for years. They wouldn't understand it.

Fiona, a high school chaplain in the west of Melbourne, testifies to an isolating lack of interest in her work after she invited her church congregation to a support evening:

> So I don't know where [people in the church] sit, because it's not on their radar, because there was no youth ministry . . . . So, it wasn't important to them. And then when I then got involved and became a chaplain, I guess, the same idea . . . . I did invite a lot of people to a, like a night, info night, storytelling night, and there was hardly any, I guess people from the church who came.

Youth workers found this lack of interest and support an isolating experience, and many chose simply not to discuss their work, while at the same time hoping that they might receive support.

Second, though they are trained and competent practitioners, their expertise is not sought out or heeded. For example, Cameron relates attempting to contribute to his church's youth ministry thinking:

> We've got a youth think tank [at church] that gets together once a quarter and chat about what's happened in the youth group . . . . [W]hen I interject any youth work thinking into that space I get blank stares like I'm an alien or something. An example of that is early last year I was talking about Roger Hart's "Ladder of Participation"[27] and that if we really wanted to see our youth group flourish . . . we needed to engage them to start having some participatory say in the work that they were doing, and

---

27. The "Ladder of Participation" is a well-known framework for youth participation. See Hart, *Children's Participation*.

the youth leader at the time said, "That's a fantastic model but it won't work." And I'm like, "I see it work every day. I can show you one hundred examples of where this works."

Despite this, there was a high degree of positivity from the youth workers for increased communication with youth ministry leaders. Helen, who was a paid youth pastor and now works in local government, speaks to the need for youth ministry leaders to become equipped with skills and knowledge from the secular youth work sector:

> I would highly welcome conversation with people who are working in ministry . . . . I think they could definitely work together better. I think they could glean from each other . . . . I would highly recommend people working in Christian ministries to get further education . . . . I would encourage people in leadership to encourage their twelve-year-old or seventeen-year-old or eighteen-year-old leaders that are leading young people to equip them with more skills that may be seen as secular skills, but some of these skills are transferable. I think people aren't speaking into some of these needs in the Christian circles and the Christian ministries.

At some risk of speculation, I would suggest that the lack of uptake of youth work expertise in churches is due to a misguided perception that youth ministry is "more Christian" than youth work in the secular sector. Certainly, that is the perception of the youth workers in my study. Though they generally reject this characterization, they claim that it is a widespread view in their churches:

> I think they would presume [youth ministry] is more Christian. Because again, it's very overt. You know, you're worshipping with kids, you're teaching kids about the Bible et cetera. Whereas I guess I'm coming at it from the point of view of, "does what I do reflect Jesus?" And so I think, if I was to answer that in both contexts, I would have said "yes," in both contexts, it just looks different. (Ange, manager of youth work team)

Diasporic connection leads to alienation from church-based youth ministry, and "vocational isolation"—a sense that their work is not understood and valued by their Christian community.

Through participatory community, discontent, and diasporic connection, the Christian community shapes the youth work vocation. First, Christian community is a "blessing" to the youth work vocation. It inculcates (1) a conviction that youth work is deeply Christian and equips Christians to practice (2) a relational approach to youth work which prioritizes marginalized young people, and their development. This is a strong witness against the depersonalizing nature of rationalized youth work. Second, Christian community is a curse on the youth work vocation. It tends to create (3) division between youth workers and youth ministry leaders, and (4) fails to adequately support the vocation or work of youth workers. Third, and neutrally, Christian community fosters (5) a commitment to the youth work sector, and (6) a critical stance towards youth ministry practice.

## Discussion

I have chosen three areas for a brief discussion, which focus on the areas of concern for the church that arise out of this research. This is not to claim that my research is all bad news for the church; the summary of findings shows the opposite. Nor is it to claim that all youth ministries are afflicted by the difficulties I discuss below. There is much room for hope because, despite the disillusionment of many youth workers with youth ministry, they are definitely not cynical about it.

### Youth Workers Need the Church to Value and Honor Their Work

Youth workers struggle to see how their work is valued or understood by the church and conclude that it is not. Though they are motivated by the desire to see the kingdom of God come into the lives of the young people they serve, they feel that they are not seen as partners in this work by their churches.

Without the church and its leadership reaching out to youth workers, and honoring the work they do, the church risks further alienation of youth workers. However, if they do include youth workers as coworkers, not only will the church gain ambassadors in the workplace, but the church will also gain a cohort of professionals who can contribute to the church's youth ministry.

### Youth Ministry is Losing Out

Given the division between youth workers and youth ministry leaders, and the alienation youth workers feel from church-based youth ministry, youth ministry is losing out in several ways. First, youth workers could be contributing to the skills and knowledge of youth ministry leaders in many areas: relationship building and boundaries; mental health of young people; safe ministry; and enabling young people to participate more fully in youth ministry. Second, youth ministry could be instigating creative mission ventures, through combining youth ministry aims with youth work frameworks and practices. Many parachurch organizations are doing exactly this, and there is scope for church-based youth ministry to do the same. Third, youth ministry is losing skilled and passionate people to the secular workforce. This is not necessarily a negative, as it places capable workers alongside young people who need their assistance. But the church would benefit from the presence of skilled personnel who are devoted to long-term ministry with young people. Fourth, youth workers bring a critical stance to youth ministry which could hone youth ministry practice through constructive input.

### *The Tension Between Participatory Community and "Safe" Youth Ministry*

The church needs to resolve this tension. When functioning well, church communities are participatory—they mentor and support young leaders, and give them powerful experiences of responsibility, thus equipping them for effective service in secular organizations. However, this research raises a question. Is this supportive and empowering community so "safe" that youth leaders with a heart for marginalized young people must leave to serve them?

### *How Could the Church Respond?*

There are several ways that churches could respond to this research, in areas that concern the practice of youth ministry at a congregational level, the place of youth workers within the church community, and theological education. First, codify the powerful processes of participatory community so that all young people are given the opportunity to exercise responsibility. Second, encourage youth ministry activities beyond the church. If youth ministry leaders want to experiment with activities in the community, support these and talk about them as "core" youth ministry. Third, create settings for connection between youth ministry leaders and youth workers, such as inviting youth workers to youth ministry retreats and meetings, encouraging constructive criticism from youth workers on youth ministry initiatives, and engaging youth workers to deliver training for youth leaders. Fourth, if youth leaders (or others) choose to enter secular youth work, commission them to do so, and support them. This communicates that youth work is a legitimate form of ministry to young people. Fifth, theological colleges must broaden their remit to include training for the practice of youth work in secular settings, as well as for church-based youth ministry. This could include engaging youth workers as lecturers and creating a major in youth work studies to equip those who wish to work in secular settings. This is happening to some extent with units on school chaplaincy, but it needs to be extended and deepened.

## Conclusion

Vocation is central to the motivation of Christians in secular youth work, and significant given the over-rationalization of youth work in Australia. This chapter has explored the crucial role of the church ecology in forming this vocation, in ways that are both a blessing and a curse. The dynamics of participatory community, discontent, and diasporic connection combine to inculcate a sense of calling that is deep and abiding, but also alienates Christians in secular youth work from their coworkers in youth ministry. There is much room for connections between youth workers and youth ministry leaders, in ways that will benefit youth workers and hone youth ministry practice.

In addition, this research touches on several other themes which could be fruitfully examined. Not all churches are the same; hence, what are the characteristics of church ecologies which form the youth work vocation most positively? If we cast our gaze to youth workers with no faith or other faiths, is a "vocational ethic" similarly present, and under what conditions has it developed? To what extent does a motivation of "calling" provide a bulwark against the rationalization of the sector, or (following Weber) does a vocational ethic simply enable it? Finally, how could the youth work sector incorporate lessons from the Christian community into its training and supervision processes? The model of the church works in terms of mentoring and practical responsibility, but can it be codified for broader application while retaining its relationality?

## Bibliography

Australian Youth Work Coalition. "The National Definition of Youth Work in Australia." https://ayac.org.au/uploads/131219%20Youth%20Work%20Definition%20FINAL.pdf.

Bessant, Judith. "Aristotle Meets Youth Work: A Case for Virtue Ethics." *Journal of Youth Studies* 12, no. 4 (2009) 423–38.

———. "Free Market Economics and New Directions for Youth Workers." *Youth Studies Australia* 16, no. 2 (1997) 34–40.

———. "Youth Work: The Loch Ness Monster and Professionalism." *Youth Studies Australia* 23, no. 4 (2004) 26–33.

Bronfenbrenner, Urie. *The Ecology of Human Development: Experiments by Nature and Design*. Cambridge: Harvard University Press, 1996.

Chaves, Mark. "Denominations as Dual Structures: An Organizational Analysis." *Sociology of Religion* 54, no. 2 (1993) 147–69.

———. "Secularization as Declining Religious Authority." *Social Forces* 72, no. 3 (1994) 749–74.

Clyne, Allan R. "A Genealogy of Youth Work's Languages: Founders." *Concept* 7, no. 3 (Winter 2016). http://concept.lib.ed.ac.uk/article/view/2453.

Cooper, Trudi. "Institutional Context and Youth Work Professionalization in Post-Welfare Societies." *Child and Youth Services* 34 (2013) 112–24.

Corney, Timothy, et al. "Why Youth Workers Need to Collectively Organise." *Youth Studies Australia* 28, no. 3 (2009) 41–46.

De St. Croix, Tania. "The Marketisation of Youth Work." In *Grassroots Youth Work: Policy, Passion and Resistance in Practice*, 21–54. Bristol: Policy, 2016.

Erickson, Mark, and Jem Price. "Vocation and Professional Identity: Social Workers at Home and Abroad." In *Professional Identity and Social Work*, edited by Stephen A. Webb, 79–93. New York: Routledge, 2017.

Gallet, Wilma. "Christian Mission or an Unholy Alliance? The Changing Role of Church-Related Organisations in Welfare-to-Work Service Delivery." PhD diss., University of Melbourne, 2016.

Goodwin, Veronica. "Youth Worker Perception of the Term 'Professional': A Victorian Study." *Australian Educational Researcher* 18, no. 2 (1991) 43–63.

Hamilton-Smith, Elery, and Donna Brownell. "Dilemmas of an Infant Profession." *The Australian and New Zealand Journal of Sociology* 9, no. 3 (1973) 54–58.

———. *Youth Workers and Their Education*. Melbourne: Youth Workers Association of Victoria, 1973.

Hart, Peter. "The Reality of Relationships with Young People in Caring Professions: A Qualitative Approach to Professional Boundaries Rooted in Virtue Ethics." *Children and Youth Services Review* 83 (2017) 248–54.

Hart, Roger. *Children's Participation: The Theory and Practice of Involving Young Citizens in Community Development and Environmental Care*. New York: UNICEF, 1997.

Hauerwas, Stanley. *A Community of Character: Toward a Constructive Christian Social Ethic*. Notre Dame: University of Notre Dame Press, 1981.

Irving, Terry, et al. *Youth in Australia: Policy, Administration, and Politics: A History Since World War II*. South Melbourne: MacMillan Education Australia, 1995.

Jeffs, Tony. "Too Few, Too Many: The Retreat from Vocation and Calling." http://www.infed.org/talkingpoint/retreat_from_calling_and_vocation.htm.

Jeffs, Tony, and Mark K. Smith. "Valuing Youth Work." *Youth and Policy* 100 (2008) 277–302.

MacIntyre, Alasdair. *After Virtue: A Study in Moral Theory*. 2nd. ed. Indiana: University of Notre Dame Press, 1984.

Martin, Lloyd. *The Invisible Table: Perspectives on Youth and Youthwork in New Zealand.* South Melbourne: Thomson/Dunmore, 2003.

Maunders, David. "Professional Lions and Multi-Skilled Kangaroos: Youth Work Professionalism in South Africa and Australia." *Youth Studies Australia* 18, no. 1 (1999) 37–42.

Richards, Samantha J. "An Exploration of the Notion of 'Sense of Vocation' among Christian Youthworkers." EdD diss., King's College, 2005.

Rodd, Helen, and Heather Stewart. "The Glue that Holds Our Work Together: The Role and Nature of Relationships in Youth Work." *Youth Studies Australia* 28, no. 4 (2009) 4–10.

Sercombe, Howard. "The Watchmaker's Chainsaw: Why New Public Management is the Wrong Tool for Youth Work (and Most of the Professions). *Journal of Applied Youth Studies* 1, no. 1 (2015) 97–121.

———. "Youth Work: The Professionalisation Dilemma." *Youth Studies Australia* 23, no. 4 (2004) 20–25.

———. *Youth Work Ethics.* Los Angeles; London: SAGE, 2010.

Siporin, Max. "Ecological Systems Theory in Social Work." *Journal of Sociology and Social Welfare* 7, no. 4 (1980) 507–32.

Smith, Gordon T. *Courage and Calling: Embracing Your God-given Potential.* Rev. and expanded ed. Downers Grove: Intervarsity, 2011.

Smith, Heather, and Mark K. Smith. *The Art of Helping Others: Being Around, Being There, Being Wise.* London: Jessica Kingsley, 2008.

Smith, James K. A. *How (Not) to Be Secular: Reading Charles Taylor.* Grand Rapids: Eerdmans, 2014.

Smith, Mark K. "Thomas John Barnardo ('The Doctor')." http://infed.org/mobi/thomas-john-barnardo-the-doctor/.

Taylor, Charles. *A Secular Age.* Cambridge: Belknap Press of Harvard University Press, 2007.

Van Hooft, Stanley. *Understanding Virtue Ethics.* Hoboken: Taylor and Francis, 2014.

Vasudevan, Deepa Sriya. "The Occupational Culture and Identity of Youth Workers: A Review of the Literature." PhD diss., Harvard Graduate School of Education, 2017.

Weber, Max. *The Protestant Ethic and the Spirit of Capitalism with Other Writings on the Rise of the West.* Rev. ed. New York: Oxford University Press, 2011.

Youth Affairs Council of Victoria. *That Old Chestnut! The Professionalisation of Youth Work in Victoria.* Melbourne: Youth Affairs Council of Victoria Inc., 2014.

# 9

## The Attitude of Queensland Baptist Pastors to the "Whole-Life Discipleship" and "Faith and Work Integration" Movements

*Where Are We and What Do We Need to Do?*

IAN HUSSEY AND DAVID BENSON

*Malyon Theological College, an affiliated institution
of the Australian College of Theology*

## Abstract

KANSAS PASTOR TOM NELSON made a famous pastoral "apology" to his church for failing to train and equip them in whole-life discipleship to live their faith through their frontlines. He confessed, instead, to seeing congregants as serving his agenda as a pastor. Nelson's apology was documented in a 2014 *Christianity Today* article which CT rated as one of their top forty articles from the thirty-six-year history of *Leadership* journal.

This paper positions his apology within a larger movement, and reports on research into the current attitudes of Queensland Baptist (QB) pastors to the propositions inherent in Nelson's apology and article (see appendix 1). Various statements capturing the heart of the "Whole-Life Discipleship" (WLD) and "Faith and Work Integration" (FWI) movements were used to elicit responses from QB pastors, regarding the theological views, attitudes, and strategies of pastors with respect to these propositions. Analysis was conducted with a view to implications for training at Malyon Theological College and equipping the emerging generation of pastors in QB.

A series of recommendations are made, including stronger institutional alignment with WLD language and frameworks, alongside intentional partnerships with leading parachurch networks; adoption of a more holistic anthropology for formation and theological reflection; and clarity when defining terms and communicating this vision, avoiding overstatement that tends to come with a narrower FWI frame, instead centering on *shalom* as the heart of God's mission to bless the world.

## Introduction

Kansas Pastor Tom Nelson (founder of the Made to Flourish Network and part of the Oikonomia Network[1]) made a famous pastoral "apology" to his church for failing to train and equip them in whole-life discipleship to live their faith through their frontlines. He confessed, instead, to seeing congregants as serving his agenda as a pastor. Nelson's apology was documented in a 2014 *Christianity Today* article which CT rated as one of their top forty articles from the thirty-six-year history of *Leadership* Journal.[2]

This paper reports on research into the current attitudes of Queensland Baptist (QB) pastors to the propositions inherent in Nelson's apology and article (see appendix 1). Various statements capturing the heart of the "Whole-Life Discipleship" and "Faith and Work Integration" movements were used to elicit responses from QB pastors, regarding the theological views, attitudes, and strategies of pastors with respect to these propositions. Analysis was conducted with a view to implications for training at Malyon Theological College, equipping the emerging generation of pastors in QB.

## The "Whole-Life Discipleship" (WLD) and "Faith and Work Integration" (FWI) Movements

Nelson's confession of "pastoral malpractice" in his Kansas City Evangelical Free Church was not composed in a vacuum. Through his theological education in a "fine evangelical seminary," he spoke of a growing realization that from creation to consummation, the biblical concern for "salvation" was located in a larger story of God's creational design serving human flourishing

---

1. See https://www.madetoflourish.org/.
2. Nelson, "Who's Serving Whom?," 68–71.

and "ontological wholeness." This theme was particularly strong for his Reformation forebears who "connected Sunday to Monday with a rich theology of vocation." For instance, in challenging the presupposition that only church-based workers had a calling—that is, "the Catholic Distortion" of vocation, according to Os Guinness[3]—Martin Luther protested,

> I advise no one to enter any religious order or the priesthood—no, I dissuade everyone—unless he be forearmed with this knowledge and understand that the works of monks and priests, however holy and arduous they may be, do not differ one whit in the sight of God from the works of the rustic laborer in the field or the woman going about her household tasks. . . . all works are measured before God by faith alone.[4]

Nelson was not alone in his realization. In due time he would be instrumental in the Oikonomia Network, bringing theological educators and pastors together for "faith–work integration."[5] And this network, in turn, was directly influenced by a wider "Faith at Work" movement since 1985,[6] spearheaded by the John Stott founded London Institute for Contemporary Christianity (LICC).[7] Through flagship programs like "Fruitfulness on the Frontline," they deconstructed the "sacred–secular, Sunday–Monday gap," instead offering new language and vision for coherent Christian discipleship.[8] As LICC Director, Mark Greene, challenged evangelical Christian leaders globally at the 2010 Cape Town Third Lausanne Congress on World Evangelization,

> Here in the UK, the church's primary mission strategy has been: *To recruit the people of God to use some of their leisure time to join the missionary initiatives of church-paid workers.* It's a strategy that has yielded much fruit . . . . Still, this is mission that most Christians can only participate in during their leisure time. What about the rest of their time? The reality is that 98 percent of Christians—i.e., those not in paid church work—are not properly envisioned or equipped for their mission in the 95 percent of their waking time that they aren't involved in church activities, wherever that might be—workplace, schoolplace,

---

3. Guinness, *The Call*, 31–35.
4. Luther, *Babylonian Captivity*, §3.42.
5. See https://oikonomianetwork.org/.
6. Miller, *God at Work*, 63–78.
7. See https://www.licc.org.uk/about/#history.
8. See https://www.licc.org.uk/ourresources/fruitfulness/#resources; Greene, *Fruitfulness*.

clubplace. And that is a tragic waste of the church's missional potential. Too few Christians have eyes to see what God might be doing in the places they already naturally spend their time, and where they already have relationships with those who don't know Jesus.[9]

The FWI movement, initially focused on bridging the Sunday to Monday gap has recognized a deeper *discipleship* issue. What pastors in particular need to offer Sunday Christians in the church pews is not a new program or better pastoral care contract, but rather a larger vision of forming "whole-life missionary disciples" which becomes the church's "core vocation."[10] *Church*, then, "is not something we do; it's who we are"—whether gathered on Sunday for training and equipping, or scattered throughout the week to our various "frontlines" as "place[s] where we realize God's calling to engage with non-Christians in mission."[11] *Whole-life disciples* are simply "people who are learning the way of Jesus in their context at this moment. . . . This call . . . is not some elitist form of Christianity. It's just taking seriously the call to follow Jesus in the everyday lives we are already living."[12]

But one of the key questions facing the movements is, "How far have these ideas penetrated into the day-to-day life of churches and their congregations?" Many important insights and correctives to church life have emerged from scholars and theological educators alike, but often this just accentuates the sometimes-present gap between the academy and the praxis of church life.

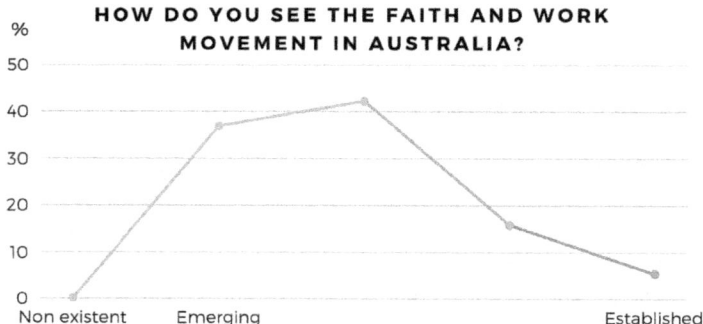

Figure 3: Faith and Work in Australia Survey Results (Reprinted with permission)

9. Greene, "One More Wall."
10. See Hudson, *Imagine Church*, 13, 22, 38.
11. Hudson, *Imagine Church*, 44, 54–65.
12. Hudson, *Imagine Church*, 63.

An online survey conducted by Reventure (n=19), for instance, found that among its dedicated partners in theological education and the marketplace—despite nearly a decade of collective strategic action and promotion from the parachurch—only 6 percent saw the faith and work movement in Australia as "established"; the majority saw the movement as "emerging" with culture change still needed for normalization.[13] Our rhetoric is not yet matched by action. Churches may be somewhat impervious to the efforts of the parachurch to change their culture. This is, however, the perception by external observers with a reforming mindset, often frustrated with what they believe to be a lack of change within pastoral leadership and congregational life.

This research, then, seeks to measure how far the ideas of the "Whole-Life Discipleship" and "Faith and Work Integration" movements have penetrated and shaped church life amongst Queensland Baptists in 2019, as subjectively weighed by QB pastors. In turn, we will consider implications for theological education through Malyon Theological College, that this cause may be further advanced.

## Methodology

The research instrument was a survey offered to QB pastors both at the annual Queensland Baptist Convention and online during April and May 2019 (see appendix 1). The survey involved presenting the pastors with a range of statements emerging from the WLD and FWI movements and asking them to indicate their agreement or disagreement with them on a five-point Likert scale. Definitions of the various terms used in the survey were provided in order to bring consistency to the responses. The survey also invited the participants to explain their response to each statement. At the end of the survey there was also the opportunity for pastors to indicate in what ways (if any) their church fostered the ideals of "Whole-Life Discipleship" and "Faith and Work Integration."

Of the four hundred Queensland Baptist pastors, fifty-seven completed the survey using pen and paper and twenty-three responded online. The margin of error of a survey reflects how much you can expect your survey results to reflect the views from the overall population. The margin of error (with a confidence level of 95 percent) for this survey, based on a sample of eighty from a population of four hundred pastors, was 10 percent. This means that, for example, if 60 percent of the sample agreed with the statement, you could be 95 percent confident that between 50 percent and 70 percent of the

13. McMillan and Koh, *Faith + Work*.

general population would also agree with the statement. For the purposes of this research, this margin of error was considered tolerable.

## Findings

The age distribution of the respondents is represented in this graph:

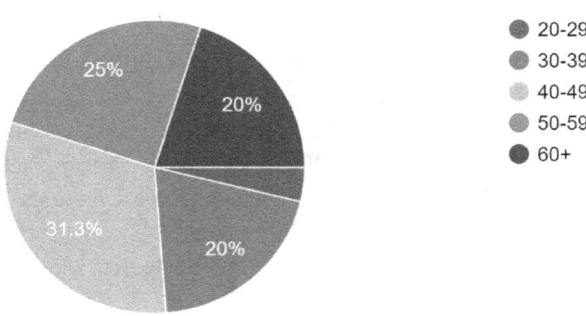

Figure 4: Age Distribution of Participants

The similar proportion of the various age groups in the sample added confidence to its representation of the view of the whole population of Queensland Baptist pastors. The survey also asked the participants to indicate how long since they had completed their primary theological education. The results are presented in figure 5:

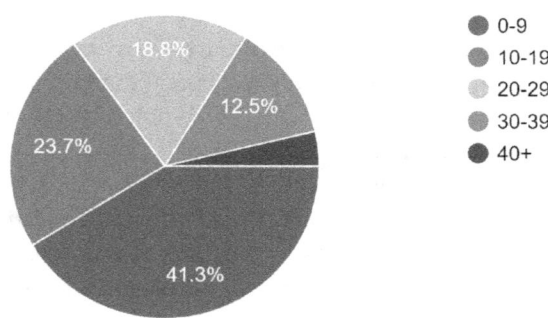

Figure 5: Years Since Completion of Theological Education

Over 40 percent of the participants have completed their theological training in the previous nine years. Only three of the participants completed their training more than forty years ago.

## Age and Support for Statements

A Spearman's Rho calculation was performed to check for a correlation between age and average agreement with the statements in the survey. It was found that $r_s$ = 0.05082, $p$ (2-tailed) = 0.65649. By normal standards, the association between the two variables would not be considered statistically significant. Hence it can be concluded that support for the ideas of the "Whole-Life Discipleship" and "Faith and Work Integration" movements is not age dependent. Pastors both young and old support or reject the ideas. Similarly, there was no correlation between length of time since completing primary theological study and average agreement with the statements ($r_s$ = -0.01786, $p$ [2-tailed] = 0.87586).

## Strongly Affirmed Statements

There were a number of statements in the survey which the majority of pastors strongly affirmed. The statement "I see, from Genesis to Revelation, the high importance of work and the vital connections between faith, work, and economics" was agreed with or strongly agreed with by 92.5 percent of the participants. As one participant said, "God put a stick in Adam's hand and told him to tend the garden pre-fall."

Similarly, 98.8 percent of participants agreed with the statement "The gospel speaks into every nook and cranny of life, connecting Sunday worship with Monday work in a seamless fabric of Holy Spirit empowered faithfulness." "Gospel living is not compartmentalized," said one of the participants. "That is what lordship is about," and "It is not all about Sunday," were other insightful comments.

The statement "As image bearers of God we are designed to image a working God" was also warmly affirmed (88.7 percent agreed or strongly agreed). Similarly, 95.0 percent agreed or strongly agreed that "Work is a gift from God, but we are also gifted by God for our work." However, one pastor inserted the caveat, "It can be, but in most of the world people don't experience blessing in their work." Further, 77.5 percent of pastors agreed or strongly agreed that cultivating an integral theology of vocation was at the heart of the church's gospel mission.

Finally, 75.0 percent of pastors agreed or strongly agreed with the statement that much of our accounting before God will be answering for the stewardship of the work we have been called to do.

### *Aspirational Statements*

Alongside the statements which pastors were able to strongly affirm were a number where participants affirmed the statements but recognized a dissonance with practice. For example, the participants wrestled with the statement "I restrict the language of 'full-time ministry' to describe pastoral or missionary work." While 53.8 percent of participants disagreed with the statement, 38.8 percent indicated that they *did* restrict the term "full-time ministry" to describe pastors and missionaries. This doesn't mean they were comfortable doing so, though. One said, "I probably do, but I know that it is wrong." Another said, "I try not to!" but "It is a useful label until someone comes up with a better one."

Similarly, the issue of visiting members of the congregations in their workplaces was a source of dissonance for some pastors. Although 33.8 percent said they regularly visit, 40.8 percent did not. A relatively high 25 percent were neutral about the statement. Several expressed regret: "Not as regularly as I would like" and "Definitely should do more of this." A number indicated that it was not because they did not want to visit, but that it was not appropriate because of busyness or the workplace context. "Most people I know wouldn't welcome that—nor would their employers." "Often this is not possible from their workplace perspective."

Although 72.5 percent of pastors agreed or strongly agreed that "Our Sunday worship services seek not only to connect Sunday to Monday, but to bring Monday into Sunday," one commented "We should, but we don't," and another "But it should." Similarly, the statement "Our church regularly celebrates the diversity of locations," was affirmed by 61.3 percent of the pastors although 23.8 percent were neutral. This is probably because some pastors aspired to this ideal but it did not happen, as reflected by comments like "We try to," and "No, but we should."

Further, 67.5 percent of participants agreed or strongly agreed that they "almost always" make applications to the workplace in their preaching, although a number indicated that it strongly depended upon the passage they were preaching on. As one said, "I apply where I think it applies. Sometimes it is in the workplace, sometimes not." Another said, "If it is clearly in the text, not contrived or forced."

## Controversial Statements

As expected, a number of statements in the survey were either disagreed with or questioned. There was only one statement where more pastors disagreed or strongly disagreed (36.3 percent) than agreed or strongly agreed (28.8 percent): "Our congregant's vocation is the primary work of the church." The participants indicated that although vocation was important, it was not the primary work of the church. As one respondent said: "No. Our primary work is to glorify Christ in whatever sphere of life we live. This includes our paid work, but most people are also fathers, mothers and spouses or children . . . ." Another said, "Mission is the purpose of the church. Discipleship of the believers is a part of (major part) of doing healthy mission." This finding suggests that the term "vocation" may need clearer definition for some QB pastors.

While this was the only statement where more pastors disagreed or strongly disagreed than those who agreed or strongly agreed, there were several statements where more respondents were neutral or disagreed with the statement than agreed with it. One such statement which brought a breadth of responses was "There is no more sacred place than the workplace where God calls his people to serve the common good." Although 47.5 percent still agreed or strongly agreed with statement, 25 percent were neutral and 27.6 percent either disagreed or strongly disagreed. However, the issue was not so much the truth of the concept, but that it overstated the case. As one participant said, "All of life is sacred." Another, "No place is more sacred than another. I agree our vacation is holy, not secular, in that we serve the Lord and be his image bearers at the jobsite, but equally the home is sacred space too."

A similarly contentious statement was, "The primary way we love our neighbor is in and through our work." Although 30.0 percent of participants agreed or strongly agreed with the statement, 41.3 percent were neutral and 28.8 percent disagreed or strongly disagreed with the statement. Again, although respondents identified that work was important, they thought it was an overstatement. "Surely there are other ways as well." "Not sure I would use 'primary' as the descriptive."

The statement with the highest level of ambivalence was, "A robust eschatology demonstrates that there will be continuity between the new creation and our present work" (30 percent neutral). Although 58.8 percent of respondents affirmed the statement, clearly many were uncomfortable with it for a variety of reasons. This idea emerges as one that clearly needs greater explanation and justification in the QB context.

The adaption of the quote from Dorothy L. Sayers was also met with some ambivalence. Although 61.3 percent agreed with the notion that the church should be telling a tradesman that the very first demand that his religion makes upon him is that he should make good tables, 20.0 percent disagreed, and 18.8 percent were neutral. "Important, but by no means the first demand," said one, although another who agreed with the statement said "Caveat: from sustainable wood and paying suppliers on time."

The language of "economic flourishing" and "wealth creation" was probably the cause of the ambivalence towards the statement that "The gospel speaks to wealth creation, wise financial management, and economic flourishing." Again, the majority agreed or strongly agreed with the statement (51.3 percent), but 25 percent disagreed or strongly disagreed and 23.8 percent were neutral. As one said, "I struggle with the term 'wealth creation.' Too similar in my mind to prosperity theology." Another said, "Financial prosperity is not the focus of the gospel." Queensland Baptists, on the whole, react negatively to what they label the "prosperity gospel." It could be that more pastors would agree to the notion laying behind this statement if it was worded differently.

The final statement that met with some ambivalence was "We work to live, we don't live to work." In some senses this is a negatively framed statement: advocates of the "WholeLife Discipleship" and "Faith and Work Integration" movements would normally disagree with this statement whereas they would have agreed with most of the statements in the survey. This reversal may have caused some respondent error. However, its relatively high neutral response (22.5 percent) would suggest that "we live to work" is still a debatable assertion in the QB context.

## *The Promotion of WLD and FWI in Queensland Baptist Churches*

Pastors were asked to indicate how these ideas were fostered in their church. Although it was not possible to measure how widely these activities are occurring in QB churches the responses could be grouped into six categories:

1. segments in church services dedicated to testimonies about work

2. careful/revised use of language to break down the sacred/secular divide

3. use of integrated sermon/small group courses like "Fruitfulness on the Frontline"

4. prayer for work during church services
5. gatherings to encourage and pray for businesspeople
6. teaching about workplace ministry in sermons and other contexts.

## Discussion of Findings

The following discussion concludes with recommendations as reflective practitioners specifically for our context at Malyon Theological College. However, cross-referenced with a 2018 Australian College of Theology (ACT) report,[14] there are strong grounds for believing that these implications may be transferrable to other denominationally based colleges. They at least provide a basis for reflection. We begin, however, by considering an encouraging and yet confusing finding.

### How Did the Pastors Discover the Integrated and Holistic Gospel?

Although some of the statements in the survey were questioned or drew ambivalent responses, supporters of the "Whole-Life Discipleship" and "Faith and Work Integration" movements can be encouraged by the response of Queensland Baptist pastors. Only one of the eighteen statements attracted more disagreement than agreement. The vast majority of the statements attracted strong levels of support. Further, it appears the ambivalence towards some of the statements was more a matter of language than the underlying concept itself.

QB pastors resonated with both Nelson and the Protestant Reformers in affirming a vision of a big gospel that impacts all of life, under the sovereignty of Christ. Their construal even avoids the triumphalism often associated with this movement—for instance, "claiming the seven mountains for Christ"[15]—by recognizing how seriously sin has warped all work.

However, an irony presents in this data, namely: from whence comes this positive vision, evolving from perceived QB conservatism that is typically suspicious of conversion's social implications? For QB pastors, we are wondering how they *found* this integrated and holistic gospel. As reported earlier about the respondents, there was no perceived difference in their

---

14. Benson, *State of the Faith–Work Movement*. Hereafter SFWM.
15. See http://7culturalmountains.org/; cf. Hunter, *Change the World*, 123–31.

attitude as a result of when or how long ago they completed theological study, primarily through Malyon Theological College.

The data does not give sufficient detail to interrogate this further. Perhaps QB pastors always held these beliefs, even prior to training? Perhaps they have an inbuilt ambivalence towards, or even resistance to, the clerical paradigm, and that the survey allowed them to express that in particular ways? Alternatively, perhaps theological education has always and equally formed them in these views? Having intentionally integrated WLD and FWI themes into the Malyon curriculum since 2010—the time frame within which 41.3 percent of students completed their studies—it is disappointing to concede that this has not made a noticeable difference compared to older cohorts formed through an evidently more clerical paradigm.

It is significant, however, that across the ACT, most lecturers teaching within this space—broadly categorized as "practical theology"—complained that their subjects were merely electives, taken by less than a third of the student body. This low uptake was only exacerbated for the pastoral track, where its cohort were offered fewer electives and subjects about "work" and "vocation" were perceived to be irrelevant to their "ministry" calling.[16] Denominational colleges, like ours, face added pressures to give primary attention in training ordinands to preparation for church life, with broader vocational themes given low billing.

While most colleges, including Malyon, expressed general support for WLD and FWI, it was unclear what this meant with an over-defined and content-driven curriculum to complete—compressing the time for integratory dialogue—and a growing number of distance/online students who rarely are inculcated into this ethos by reading about it without a face-to-face transformative pedagogy. The perceived disciplinary silos persist such that core biblical themes, including the synergy of work and worship, can easily be missed. Additionally, the Oikonomia Network, in its rubric designed to help seminaries assess integration in theological education, suggested that for students to truly be formed in WLD and FWI requires:

- the majority of faculty being active in curricular integration
- almost all administrators and board members making this a priority
- over 33 percent of courses having explicit FWI/WLD objectives, learning activities and assessments
- multiple and ongoing extracurricular events centered on these themes, including chapel, faculty training, internships, mentoring and more

16. Benson, SFWM, 6, 8, 12, 17, 22. See, for instance, http://traverse.org.au/base/integrating-faith-and-work/.

- institutional level partnerships with church and marketplace for seamless formation.[17]

While we offer a number of elective subjects in this space, clearly there is not the matrix of support and commitment to these movements for our college to make a noticeable impact.

And yet, these pastors still affirmed the movement's theology, which is relatively novel in conservative churches with a narrower focus on "salvation of the soul" rather than the "ontological wholeness" which Nelson confessed.[18] Reading through the detailed eighty responses to the Pastor's Survey, the source is soon apparent. The London Institute for Contemporary Christianity (LICC) and their course, "Fruitfulness on the Frontline," were explicitly named four times, with a further dozen responses using language central to these courses such as "frontline," "sacred–secular divide," "clergy-laity," "scattered–gathered church," and even particular practices on Sundays such as a congregant sharing a TTT ("This Time Tomorrow") to explain what she will be doing on Monday (typically work-wise), opportunities and challenges she will face, and how the fellowship can pray for her.[19] Much of this influence has come through the Malyon Workplace Centre and its various conferences, with word of mouth and social media spreading the difference it has made, thus arguably becoming normalized as a theology among QB pastors.[20] And this is encouraging. In light of this finding, we now make recommendations for pastors and for educators.

## *Recommendations for Pastors*

One word best captures Tom Nelson's article, and even more so his video interview with CT Pastors: *dissonance*.[21] In short, he largely knew the right answer since seminary—that Christ is Lord over all, including one's working life beyond the Sunday gathering. However, he seemingly "stumbled" upon its significance for the scattered church, and his pastoral leadership,

---

17. Sherman and Forster, *How Are You Doing?*

18. See also, concerning the conservative American church context, Sherman, *Kingdom Calling*, 64–76.

19. Hudson, *Imagine Church*, 100–101.

20. See http://malyonworkplace.org.au/host-your-own-transforming-work-conference-resource/, http://malyonworkplace.org.au/fruitfulness-on-the-frontline-a-six-week-course-for-equipping-whole-life-disciples, http://malyonworkplace.org.au/life-on-the-frontline-a-six-week-course-for-equipping-whole-life-disciples/, and https://vimeo.com/179105606.

21. Nelson, "Who's Serving Whom?"

only when the disparity was too great to ignore. Nelson put it down to "stunted theology" and inattention to the "biblical bookends" of Genesis and Revelation—God's original and final purposes for all of life. Apparently, he preached himself out of this inconsistency, gradually allowing right beliefs to descend to his heart and hands, a linear process finally reforming malpractice. In short, he could not "see."

Nelson's prevalence of cognitive terms and intellectualist explanations betrays an anthropological problem common to the QB pastor's *aspirational statements*. In their case, they claim to see the gospel's implications—in terms of needing more embracing language where all are "ministers," centrifugal pastoral care taking visitation and prayer to the workplace, and more inclusive services "bringing Monday into Sunday"—and yet several respondents confessed to still falling short of challenging their largely clerical and ecclesial paradigm. While sympathetic to their perceived failure, we do well to confront this implicit enlightenment anthropology which assumes right belief automatically flows into right action, as though a more gospel-centered worldview will solve the problem. Granted, change will only happen "by God's grace." However, we have a part to play.

In recent years there has been a growing recognition across diverse fields—including habit formation, memory encoding, neuropsychology, pedagogy, as well as philosophical and theological anthropology—that human beings are far more than "thinking things" and "brains-on-a-stick," simply needing to get their doctrinal ideas right so the rest will follow. Instead, as Jamie Smith captures memorably,

> You need to worship well. Because you are what you love. And you worship what you love. And you might not love what you think. Which raises an important question. . . . What do you *want*?[22]

We must reinforce a baptized imagination with bodily practices that align with what our better selves *want*—a form of tangible workplace worship.[23] Were our pastors, for instance, reminded by daily practices such as specific workplace images of congregants and prayers set to a track from Porter's Gate "Work Songs," as the morning alarm goes off, it would be far easier to prioritize a workplace visit than if it simply remained at the level of a good but disembodied idea.[24] We must leverage bodily habits and accountabil-

---

22. Smith, *You Are What You Love*, xi–1, 142 and chap. 1 inter alia.

23. See Benson, "A Litany of Practices"; see also https://christspieces.org/practices/a-litany-of-practices/ and https://christspieces.org/2017/01/04/open-book-on-kingdom-calling/.

24. See https://www.portersgateworship.com/music-vol1.

ity in a community of practice to align orthodoxy, orthopathy, and orthopraxy—head, heart, and hands working as one.

## *Recommendations for Educators*

Four broad foci largely capture the implications for Malyon Theological College's efforts to form QB pastors in WLD and FWI.

### BE CAREFUL OF OVERSTATEMENT

Overstating the case undermines one's cause. As we have seen, Luther's polemic was intended to redress an imbalance, levelling the vocational playing field by deconstructing the "Catholic Distortion" that only clergy have a calling. Leaning too heavily on a single passage (1 Corinthians 7:20), however—and that with poor exegesis—ultimately led to unintended consequences. For detractors invested in upholding the ecclesial status quo, it gave them cause to dismiss Luther's whole argument. However, for radicals joining the cause, it ultimately incited the equal but opposite error, treating one's vocational track as equivalent to fate, and thereby falling into idolatry.[25]

In Guinness's telling, the "Protestant Distortion" is no less dualistic; it privileges "the secular at the expense of the spiritual."[26] We simply baptize our particular line of work—our secondary call, that is—as God's *entire* call on our life. Busy with business, and blind to our other vocational spheres where we are equally called to serve, we conflate our boss's demands and our own drivenness to succeed with God's commandment, thereby swallowing up our primary call to listen to the God who speaks. Over time, the rich and multifaceted notion of *vocation*—where all in our lives is "by him, to him, for him"—is reduced to simply being a job that we have chosen, a type of work like "vocational training," irrespective of a divine call from beyond the mundane.

Granted, some of the contention expressed by QB pastoral respondents was because "vocation" language is so enshrined in our secular culture that they ignored or misunderstood the holistic definition we provided above the survey's first question, which centered on God's call which we follow *through* "domestic, economic, political and cultural relational spheres and

---

25. See Preece, "Vocation," 192–215.
26. Guinness, *Call*, 38–42, at 38.

responsibilities."[27] For them, vocation was equivalent to "work." And "work," in turn, was simply paid employment.

Even so, they sensed in Nelson's apologia for faith–work integration the same kind of unhelpful overstatement that caused Luther's contemporaries problems. Even correcting for their misinterpretation, they are right to challenge the secularizing and immanentizing of the church's "work" as primarily about supporting congregants in their calling, rather than grounded in the body of Christ joining in the heavenly tapestry of worship, and thereby becoming a sign to the world of the reign of God.[28]

Advocates for the FWI movement, in particular, do themselves no favor when they overstate their case to see the "workplace," for instance, as "*the most sacred place . . . to serve the common good.*" This particular avenue as a secondary calling threatens to consume family, neighborhood, sporting teams, and also leisure, recreation, and rest, as equally significant spheres through which we express our primary vocation of following Christ.

In part, this explains LICC's shift from FWI to the more embracing and less contentious language of whole-life *discipleship*, obeying Christ on our various frontlines. In this frame, and following Miroslav Volf, *work* is not about paid employment—which ostracizes children, retirees, the redundant, and many people with disabilities or who simply can't find a stable job—but rather, what he calls *Work in the Spirit* entails "cooperation with God in the transformation of the world."[29] Everyone can participate.

Similarly, the almost total emphasis on "*continuity* between the new creation and our present work"—with no acknowledgement of *discontinuity* even simply by virtue of our fallen state between Christ's coming and consummation—is overreaching, and prone to cause a backlash or easy dismissal. As one respondent added, "This assertion seems very unclear and not solidly argued in Scripture—despite what N. T. Wright argues." While we may find Wright's argument, built especially around 1 Corinthians 15:58, persuasive,[30] it is more theologically warranted speculation than a compelling argument.[31] Does our work only have value if it lasts forever? Surely a cartoon sketched for one's child can hold real meaning precisely in its transience, without being preserved in perpetuity.

27. Schuurman, *Vocation*, 4.

28. Boersma, *Heavenly Participation*.

29. Volf, *Work in the Spirit*, 101.

30. That is, the logic of the resurrection means we can confidently give our all to work in the here and now, for by the Spirit's power it may be brought through the refining flames and used as building blocks for the new creation. See Wright, *Surprised by Hope*, 208–9, 16.

31. See, for instance, Martin, *Workship*, 60.

Following Darrell Cosden, we can avoid unnecessary overstatement by recognizing that our Spirit-empowered work in the present is a proleptic sign anticipating the regeneration of all things, whether or not the particular artefacts persevere.[32] One could easily dismiss further objection as latent dispensationalism, mapping onto the ambivalent and oppositional survey respondent a crass "it will all burn up in the end, so why bother with work now? Besides which, our hope is eternal souls headed to heaven, not a regenerate earth."[33] And yet, this would only inflame the situation, compounding what may be a simple misunderstanding and caution against eisegesis. Great mystery accompanies eschatology. A *first recommendation* for Malyon, therefore, is that we are wise to stick to the central points undergirding the movement, using the most inclusive rhetoric and holistic frame of *discipleship* that pastors may find their own way of turning their church outwards to bless the world. Overstatement may win short-term gains, but ultimately costs the unity of the church.

## Tell the Larger Story

We make sense of the world through larger narratives, and grapple with the pastoral vocation through metaphor.[34] If we exclusively picture pastors as shepherds feeding their sheep (Psalm 23), not balanced by the equally biblical metaphor of a coach helping Christ's team "discipline their bodies" and "work out their salvation" like a gym session (1 Corinthians 9:27; Philippians 2:12–13), then against our holistic picture of the gospel, we may well reinforce a consumeristic church where people drop by for a bite but never shape up to represent Jesus in a competitive workplace.

"Fruitfulness on the Frontline," for instance, draws participants into a picture of holistic flourishing that feeds the world. The new language simply fleshes out this tasty metaphor, as pastors train and equip their fellowship for the six M's: "Modelling godly character; Making good work; Ministering grace and love; Molding culture; Being a Mouthpiece for truth and justice; and Being a Messenger of the gospel."[35] Similarly, through Malyon Workplace, we have painted a picture of joining in God's work across the

---

32. Cosden, *Heavenly Good*, 98–100.

33. Responding to this misuse of 2 Pet 3:10, see Bouma-Prediger, *Beauty of the Earth*, 76–80. On the neoPlatonic heresy of disembodied souls versus resurrection being our final hope, see Marshall and Gilbert, *Not My Hope*; also, Middleton, *New Heaven*.

34. See, for instance MacIntyre, *After Virtue*, also Lakoff and Johnson, *Metaphors*.

35. Greene, *Fruitfulness*, 11.

six legs of the biblical journey, via salvation and toward shalom: ground work—building foundations for life (creation); truth work—welcoming honesty and wisdom (fall); justice work—standing for a fair go (Israel); restoring work—loving people into freedom (Jesus); healing work—caring and restoring community (church); and creative work—crafting a new world (new creation).[36] Grounded in such imagery, pastors and parishioners alike discover deep meaning in their mundane labor, even "seeing the Savior of the world by [their] side, hammering in nails."[37]

A lack of clarity in the metaphorical picture we paint invites unnecessary opposition, whilst a coherent biblical narrative brings peace. This was particularly seen in the case of ambivalence about language of "economic flourishing" and "wealth creation." Against the backdrop of money still being reflexively identified as "the root of all evil" (1 Corinthians 6:10) and thus associated with "odious waste (thus he is "filthy" or "stinking" rich)," it is easy in sometimes fiscally averse circles like Queensland Baptists to "deprecate businesspeople" and distance ourselves from any talk of economics as some form of "prosperity gospel."[38] And to be sure, this false gospel has ravaged much of the world, where godliness is seen as a formulaic path to individual health, wealth, and prosperity (1 Timothy 6:5). Unfortunately for many, this knee-jerk reaction is as far as their theologizing goes.

As such, a second recommendation for Malyon Theological College in this context is to tell a larger story, centered in the mission of God, where the election of Abraham as a channel of blessing to the world is tied to the fulfillment in Christ and sending of his disciples as a sign of the kingdom.[39] Prosperity is better reframed as *shalom*—holistic flourishing in right relationship with God, neighbor, self and creation—which acknowledges both a cultural mandate and a liberative dimension calling for generous justice, given endemic sin.[40] In the words of the Lausanne Covenant,

> We affirm that there is a biblical vision of human prospering, and that the Bible includes material welfare (both health and wealth) within its teaching about the blessing of God. However, we deny as unbiblical the teaching that spiritual welfare can be measured in terms of material welfare, or that wealth is always a

---

36. See Benson, "One Caller." In turn, this language was modified for the Malyon workplace hubs, drawing diverse people and professions into the story of God's labor toward shalom and salvation, transforming the world. See Benson, "Deep Purpose," http://malyonworkplace.org.au/, also https://vimeo.com/malyonworkplace.
37. Benson, "Deep Purpose," 12.
38. Stackhouse, "Complicated Matter."
39. See Stackhouse, "View of Mission."
40. Wright, *Mission of God*, 17, 189–90, 95, 213, 43–52, 313, 527–30.

sign of God's blessing. The Bible shows that wealth can often be obtained by oppression, deceit or corruption. We also deny that poverty, illness or early death are always a sign of God's curse, or evidence of lack of faith, or the result of human curses, since the Bible rejects such simplistic explanations.[41]

Lacking this clarity, and dislocated from a larger story of our purpose wrapped up in *shalom* and *salvation*, QB pastors will likely be unable to grow a mature theology of wealth, which is desperately needed in order that we will be a conduit to bless our neighbors in every way, which is the path of love. On this point, in particular, Tom Nelson has led the way; he shares out of his weakness and family's poverty as a child, alerting all followers of Christ to serve God's mission between creation and consummation, thereby embracing the call to neighborly love like the Good Samaritan.[42]

## Reform Our Language

Queensland Baptist pastors could well do with new language, normalized throughout their college experience. This could unite those in *paid church work* primarily serving the gathered ecclesia, with those working as the *church scattered* on their diverse *frontlines*, as one community under Christ dedicated to "full-life Christian service." We see through our words—not seeing that which lies beyond our linguistic limitations—and this in turn closely ties to our imagination and thus our desires. However, more than a new dictionary, we require fresh metaphors through which we see our service, and potent bodily practices that grab our hearts and direct them toward WLD and FWI.[43]

It would also help if the faculty agreed together on what language we will use across every subject, defining key terms to avoid reinforcing problematic dualisms with offhanded remarks about "leaving work to join the ministry," or treating "church" as a building or one-day-a-week program, or prizing sacred Sundays over secular Mondays. Perhaps we could adopt a coherent metaphor and story, such as presently carried alone by the Malyon Workplace Centre, so that pastors in formation begin to locate themselves in this larger story of God at work?

Further, and lest we produce pastors like Nelson who after four years of study only "stumble" onto the truth that amplifies their dissonance, we

41. Lausanne Movement, "Cape Town Commitment."
42. Nelson, *Neighborly Love*.
43. See, for instance, Lakoff and Johnson, *Philosophy in the Flesh*.

must embed a common reflective process such as see–judge–act, which unites every aspect of a student's theological education and compels faithful integration.[44] This must begin with their naive present practice such that they cannot hide behind unlived dogmatic affirmations, only then engaging in rich theological reflection sensitive to the biblical story of God's labor in the world. They must learn to return to more truthful action for which they are held accountable as part of a community of practice that disciplines not just their thinking, but equally their desiring and doing in a dynamic, multi-directional process. Guided spiritual formation and supervision of pastoral practicums are the ideal place to begin this alignment.

## Keep Persevering

In light of this discussion regarding how pastors came to embrace the ideas of WLD and FWI, two final exhortations are pertinent for Malyon Theological College, united in a fourth recommendation that we persevere in this cause for the sake of the kingdom.

First, we need to continue to champion this movement persistently with administrators, council and denominational leaders, and also with the principal and fellow lecturers, such that it cannot be missed, with success stories freely shared and motivating interest. We may advocate for at least one of these specific WLD/FWI subjects to be compulsory for every pastoral track student. Through professional development stressing pedagogical approaches to bring disparate disciplines into a theological unity associated with holistic flourishing,[45] and unpacking the educational implications of our meaningful vision and purpose statement, we may see a culture progressively formed that is capable of significantly impacting future students to further embed this movement.

Second, while funding is limited, we have good cause to continue our efforts through the Malyon Workplace Centre, partnering with LICC and the Oikonomia Network, and popularizing a range of programs that are easily usable by churches. It is easy for pastors to run "Fruitfulness on the Frontline" once, and then assume this need is permanently met. Additional initiatives progressively moving from the narrower faith–work focus to the more embracing whole-life discipleship—such as "Life on the

---

44. See http://traverse.org.au/base/everyday-theology/, especially module 2, for a curricular model.

45. See Amy Sherman, https://oikonomianetwork.org/2017/09/amy-sherman-on-karam-forum-classroom-applications/.

Frontline," "Whole-Life Preaching," and "Whole-Life Worship"[46]—warrant equal promotion, offering workshops hosted by our college to help churches continue on this positive trajectory. By the grace of God, these humble efforts are bearing fruit.

## Conclusion

In this chapter, we sought to place Tom Nelson's "apology" and confession of pastoral malpractice in the broader context of the "Faith and Work Integration" (FWI) and "Whole-Life Discipleship" (WLD) movements. Subsequently, we surveyed a representative sample of Queensland Baptist (QB) pastors to discern their beliefs, attitudes, and strategies in response to these movements, as captured in the language of Nelson's article. Reflecting on these findings, we made a series of recommendations to pastors, subsequently guiding our calling through Malyon Theological College to form emerging QB pastors.

Based upon this research, we celebrate how supportive our pastors are of a whole-life gospel under the sovereignty of Christ. However, in response to aspirational statements and conflicted present actions by QB churches in this space, we challenge the intellectualist anthropology that explains away dissonance between what we say (in theologically agreeing with WLD) and what we do (largely reinforcing a clerical paradigm) purely on the basis of orthodoxy. Instead, we recommend that pastors be trained to leverage embodied practices—uniting head, heart, and hands as one—toward more truthful action. This is bolstered by adopting a college-wide reflective process moving from our actual actions, through rich theological insight exposing the gap between word and deed, culminating in real changes for which students are graciously held accountable in a community of practice. As our college develops workshops and resources toward this end, the pastors—in turn—will be equipped to help their whole-of-life ministers form integrative practices for their frontlines.

And yet, we confess "academic malpractice" in that our provision of theological education—more intentionally oriented to FWI and WLD in recent years—has apparently made no significant difference to QB pastoral attitudes among graduates. Upon deeper analysis, we recommend a concerted effort by faculty "champions" of these movements to promote the cause and bring institutional alignment at all levels, advocating for a compulsory WLD/FWI subject for pastoral track students. Additionally, we affirm and advance the efforts of Malyon Workplace Centre to partner

46. See https://www.licc.org.uk/ourresources/.

with parachurch ministries such as LICC and the Oikonomia Network, to normalize this movement and raise awareness of key resources usable by the church that may change their culture. We recommend the adoption of consistent language across the college that addresses the sacred–secular divide, located in a larger metaphor and narrative of flourishing where we join God's work in the world.

Finally, we caution against cheap rhetorical wins built upon a slight scriptural base, and challenge an unhelpful "Protestant Distortion of Vocation" in the FWI movement that overstates the importance of work relative to other spheres through which we live our primary call to follow Christ. Instead, we recommend adoption of the more inclusive whole-life *discipleship* frame. This necessitates expansive frameworks centered on the mission of God and the journey toward *shalom*, capable of accommodating a number of theologies coexisting in QB circles. And yet, we must proffer clarity in defining terms such as *vocation*, *work*, and *flourishing*, to address confusion and concerns over aberrations such as the "prosperity gospel." In so doing, QB pastors may each, in their own way, train their congregations, turning them outward as a channel of blessing for the world God loves.

# Appendix 1 | Pastor's Survey

This brief anonymous survey is part of a research project by Dave Benson and Ian Hussey that seeks to measure the attitude of Queensland Baptist Pastors to the "Whole-Life Discipleship" and "Faith and Work Integration" movements. Please complete the survey as honestly as possible.

For the purposes of this research, vocation is defined as all the divinely given avenues through which people respond obediently to the call of God including domestic, economic, political, and cultural relational spheres and responsibilities. Work is defined as one's primary employment, where people consistently invest energy for diverse rewards, typically including income/finance.

---

How many years since you completed your primary theological education (i.e. not including postgraduate studies)?:

☐ 0–9     ☐ 10–19     ☐ 20–29     ☐ 30–39     ☐ 40+

How old are you?

☐ 20–29     ☐ 30–39     ☐ 40–49     ☐ 50–59     ☐ 60+

---

How strongly do you agree or disagree with these statements (please explain why you agree or disagree with the statement in the space under each statement if you would like):

---

I see, from Genesis to Revelation, the high importance of work and the vital connections between faith, work, and economics.

Strongly agree     Agree     Neutral     Disagree     Strongly Disagree

Reason (Optional):

| | | | | |
|---|---|---|---|---|
| The gospel speaks into every nook and cranny of life, connecting Sunday worship with Monday work in a seamless fabric of Holy Spirit-empowered faithfulness. | | | | |
| Strongly agree | Agree | Neutral | Disagree | Strongly Disagree |
| Reason (Optional): | | | | |
| Cultivating an integrated theology of vocation is at the heart of our church's gospel mission. | | | | |
| Strongly agree | Agree | Neutral | Disagree | Strongly Disagree |
| Reason (Optional): | | | | |
| I restrict the language of "full-time ministry" to describe pastoral or missionary work. | | | | |
| Strongly agree | Agree | Neutral | Disagree | Strongly Disagree |
| Reason (Optional): | | | | |
| I regularly visit members of my congregation in their workplaces. | | | | |
| Strongly agree | Agree | Neutral | Disagree | Strongly Disagree |
| Reason (Optional): | | | | |
| Our congregants' vocation is the primary work of the church. | | | | |
| Strongly agree | Agree | Neutral | Disagree | Strongly Disagree |
| Reason (Optional): | | | | |
| We work to live, we don't live to work. | | | | |
| Strongly agree | Agree | Neutral | Disagree | Strongly Disagree |
| Reason (Optional): | | | | |
| Our Sunday worship services seek not only to connect Sunday to Monday, but to bring Monday into Sunday. | | | | |
| Strongly agree | Agree | Neutral | Disagree | Strongly Disagree |
| Reason (Optional): | | | | |

| The gospel speaks to wealth creation, wise financial management, and economic flourishing. |
|---|
| Strongly agree   Agree   Neutral   Disagree   Strongly Disagree |
| Reason (Optional): |

| I almost always make applications to the workplace in my preaching. |
|---|
| Strongly agree   Agree   Neutral   Disagree   Strongly Disagree |
| Reason (Optional): |

| As image-bearers of God we are designed to image a working God. |
|---|
| Strongly agree   Agree   Neutral   Disagree   Strongly Disagree |
| Reason (Optional): |

| A robust eschatology demonstrates that there will be continuity between the new creation and our present work. |
|---|
| Strongly agree   Agree   Neutral   Disagree   Strongly Disagree |
| Reason (Optional): |

| Work is a gift from God, but we are also gifted by God for our work. |
|---|
| Strongly agree   Agree   Neutral   Disagree   Strongly Disagree |
| Reason (Optional): |

| The church should be telling a tradesman that the very first demand that his religion makes upon him is that he should make good tables. (Dorothy L. Sayers) |
|---|
| Strongly agree   Agree   Neutral   Disagree   Strongly Disagree |
| Reason (Optional): |

| There is no more sacred space than the workplace where God calls his people to serve the common good. |
|---|
| Strongly agree   Agree   Neutral   Disagree   Strongly Disagree |
| Reason (Optional): |

| |
|---|
| Much of our accounting before God will be answering for the stewardship of the work we have been called to do. <br><br> Strongly agree      Agree      Neutral      Disagree      Strongly Disagree <br><br> Reason (Optional): |
| The primary way we love our neighbor is in and through our work. <br><br> Strongly agree      Agree      Neutral      Disagree      Strongly Disagree <br><br> Reason (Optional): |
| Our church regularly recognizes and celebrates the diversity of vocations. <br><br> Strongly agree      Agree      Neutral      Disagree      Strongly Disagree <br><br> Reason (Optional): |
| In what ways (if any) does your church foster the ideals of "Whole-Life Discipleship" and "Faith and Work Integration"? |

# Bibliography

Benson, David. "Deep Purpose: Words That Work." *Malyon Workplace Newsletter* (August 2018) 8–12. http://malyonworkplace.org.au/wp-content/uploads/August-MalyonWorkplace.pdf.

———. "A Litany of Practices." *Practical Theology* 12, no. 3 (2019) 253–56.

———. "One Caller, Many Callings: Locating Your Work in God's Labour." In *Malyon College Transforming Work Conference*. Brisbane, June 18, 2016. https://vimeo.com/178460381.

———. *State of the Faith–Work Movement in Australian Theological Education*. Report for the Australian College of Theology 2018. http://bit.ly/ACTFaithWorkReport.

Boersma, Hans. *Heavenly Participation: The Weaving of a Sacramental Tapestry*. Grand Rapids: Wm. B. Eerdmans, 2011.

Bouma-Prediger, Steven. *For the Beauty of the Earth: A Christian Vision for Creation Care*. Engaging Culture. Grand Rapids: Baker Academic, 2001.

Cosden, Darrell. *The Heavenly Good of Earthly Work*. Milton Keynes: Paternoster, 2006.

Greene, Mark. *Fruitfulness on the Frontline: Making a Difference Where You Are*. Nottingham: IVP, 2014.

———. "One More Wall to Go." *Eg Magazine* 28 (March 2011) 2–3.

Guinness, Os. *The Call*. Nashville: Word, 1998.

Hudson, Neil. *Imagine Church: Releasing Whole-Life Disciples*. Nottingham: IVP, 2012.

Hunter, James Davison. *To Change the World: The Irony, Tragedy, and Possibility of Christianity in the Late Modern World*. New York: Oxford University Press, 2010.

Lakoff, George, and Mark Johnson. *Metaphors We Live By*. Chicago: University of Chicago Press, 2003.

———. *Philosophy in the Flesh*. New York: Basic, 1999.

Lausanne Movement. "The Cape Town Commitment." IIE.5 (2010). https://www.lausanne.org/content/ctc/ctcommitment#p2-5-5.

Luther, Martin. *The Babylonian Captivity of the Church*. 1520. http://www.lutherdansk.dk/Web-babylonian%20Captivitate/Martin%20Luther.html.

MacIntyre, Alasdair C. *After Virtue: A Study in Moral Theory*. 2nd ed. Notre Dame, IN: University of Notre Dame Press, 1984.

Marshall, Paul, and Lela Gilbert. *Heaven Is Not My Hope: Living in the Now of God's Creation*. Nashville: Thomas Nelson, 1998.

Martin, Kara. *Workship: How to Use Your Work to Worship God*. Singapore: Graceworks, 2017.

McMillan, Lindsay, and Michelle Koh. *Faith + Work in Australia Survey Results*. Reventure, 2019. https://www.canva.com/michellekoh.

Middleton, J. Richard. *A New Heaven and a New Earth: Reclaiming Biblical Eschatology*. Grand Rapids: Baker Academic, 2014.

Miller, David W. *God at Work: The History and Promise of the Faith at Work Movement*. Oxford: Oxford University Press, 2007.

Nelson, Tom. *The Economics of Neighborly Love: Investing in Your Community's Compassion and Capacity*. Downers Grove: IVP, 2017.

———. "Who's Serving Whom?" *Christianity Today, Pastor* 35 (Spring 2014) 68–71.

Preece, Gordon. "Vocation in a Post-Vocational World: Meaning, De-Meaning and Remeaning of Work." In *The Bible and the Business of Life: Essays in Honor of Robert J. Banks's Sixty-Fifth Birthday*, edited by Simon Holt and Gordon Preece, 192–215. Hindmarsh: ATF, 2004.

Schuurman, Douglas J. *Vocation: Discerning Our Callings in Life*. Grand Rapids: Wm. B. Eerdmans, 2004.

Sherman, Amy L. *Kingdom Calling: Vocational Stewardship for the Common Good*. Downers Grove: IVP, 2011.

Sherman, Amy, and Greg Forster. *How Are You Doing? A Rubric for Schools*. Oikonomia Network, 2018. https://oikonomianetwork.org/2018/04/how-are-you-doing-a-rubric-for-schools/.

Smith, James K. A. *You Are What You Love: The Spiritual Power of Habit*. Grand Rapids: Brazos, 2016.

Stackhouse, John G. Jr. "A Bigger—and Smaller—View of Mission." *Books and Culture: A Christian Review* 13, no. 3 (May/June 2007). https://www.booksandculture.com/articles/2007/mayjun/11.26.html.

———. "A Complicated Matter: Money and Theology in North American Evangelicalism." In *Evangelical Landscapes: Facing Critical Issues of the Day*, edited by John G. Stackhouse, 75–88. Grand Rapids: Baker Academic, 2002.

Volf, Miroslav. *Work in the Spirit: Toward a Theology of Work*. Eugene: Wipf and Stock, 2001.

Wright, Christopher J. H. *The Mission of God: Unlocking the Bible's Grand Narrative*. Downers Grove: IVP Academic, 2006.

Wright, N. T. *Surprised by Hope: Rethinking Heaven, the Resurrection, and the Mission of the Church*. Grand Rapids: Zondervan, 2008.

# PART 3

# Theology of Work

# 10

# Exploring Sabbath as a Response to the Liturgy of the Workplace in Light of the Work of James K. A. Smith

COLIN NOBLE

*Morling College, an affiliated institution
of the Australian College of Theology*

## Abstract

JAMES K. A. SMITH's Cultural Liturgies project, since gaining public attention following publication of *Desiring the Kingdom* in 2009, has rekindled awareness of the significance of liturgy—formative, habitual practices—in shaping desires. This chapter extends Smith's thinking in two areas that receive negligible attention in his work: the workplace as a context in which liturgical practices occur, and Sabbath keeping as a genuine form of Christian counter-liturgy.

The chapter argues that extension of Smith's broad definition of liturgy might reasonably incorporate consideration of Sabbath keeping as a Christian liturgical practice with formative potential to respond to the secular, cultural liturgies of high-pressured, twenty-first-century working life. The argument demonstrates that neglect of Sabbath keeping as a liturgical practice is unjustifiable, by both Smith's own criteria for liturgy and in light of salient biblical passages. To the contrary, Sabbath keeping is presented as having liberating potential. It can reshape anthropology by repositioning us as created and redeemed beings, challenge expectations of 24/7 availability, boost the formative efficacy of other Christian liturgies, and speak powerfully and prophetically in the context of workplaces in which time management is a ubiquitous and perennially unresolved issue.

## Introduction

James K. A. Smith's Cultural Liturgies project has garnered widespread interest since publication of *Desiring the Kingdom*, the first in his Cultural Liturgies trilogy, in 2009. In particular, his work on anthropology and liturgy has rekindled awareness of the significance of liturgy in shaping desires. Smith argues that liturgies—practices that shape desires—are more widespread in society than is generally acknowledged, and that Christians need to be intentionally practicing counter-liturgies in order to have desires rightly ordered. This chapter extends Smith's thinking in two areas that receive negligible attention in his work: workplace practices as liturgy and Sabbath keeping as counter-liturgy.

Although Smith's consideration of liturgy does not address the workplace specifically, his generally inclusive definition of liturgy as deliberate cultural practice does allow room for recognition that routines in the workplace function as liturgical practices. Workplace practices are often intentional, repeated, and teleological. Recognition of such practices as liturgies in turn invites consideration of an important question: What kind of Christian liturgies might counter the formative weight of workplace practices?

This chapter argues that extension of Smith's broad definition of liturgy might reasonably incorporate consideration of Sabbath keeping as a Christian liturgical practice with formative potential to respond to the secular, cultural liturgies of high-pressured, twenty-first-century working life. Despite his generally inclusive definition of liturgy, Smith marginalizes Sabbath keeping as a Christian liturgical practice. The foundation for the argument for its inclusion is a demonstration that, measured by Smith's own definition, his failure to recognize Sabbath observance as a liturgical practice is not warranted. The argument begins with an outline of Smith's view of humanity as worshipping beings.

## Smith's Anthropology

Smith lays the groundwork for his cultural liturgies project by critiquing *prevailing Western anthropologies as reductionist*. His first assertion is that the dominant way of perceiving the human person in modern thought as a "thinking thing"—*homo rationale*—is inadequate, because it invariably leads to functional disembodiment and denial of the material reality of being human.[1] He argues that the "stunted, rationalist picture of the human person" such anthropologies invariably present *has distorted our understanding of what it means to be a Christian. He then* sets out to present in contrast "a retooling of our understanding of the human person in order to push us . . . to consider the central, formative role of worship."[2]

What anthropology does Smith offer instead of the narrow, static models of the rationalist "thinking thing" or even the faith-based but quasi-rationalist "believing thing"?[3] Smith's argument about widespread liturgies rests on the notion of humans as primarily not thinking beings but worshipping beings—*homo liturgicus*. He moves on from his critique of reductionist anthropologies to unpack his preferred understanding of humans as "the kind of animals we are, first and foremost: loving, desiring, affective, liturgical animals who, for the most part, don't inhabit the world as thinkers or cognitive machines."[4] In asserting that humans are loving, liturgical animals, Smith stands on the shoulders of at least one giant: Augustine and the famous opening of his *Confessions* that we are made for God, and our hearts are restless until they find their rest in him.

Smith presents three key elements of the core human identity as lovers rather than thinkers or believers. Simply put, human beings—desiring, loving, worshipping beings—are characterized as beings who direct their love, who direct that love at an object of desire, and who develop their capacity to do so through habitual behavior shaped by communal, formative practices that Smith identifies as liturgies. The relationship between the three he depicts in diagrammatic form.[5]

The first element Smith introduces is the idea that we are inherently beings who intentionally interact with the world. In this he claims an affinity with Augustine. "Augustine would argue that the most fundamental

---

1 My thanks to David Starling for pointing out that Smith consistently uses *homo rationale* rather than the expected *homo rationalis*, perhaps under the influence of the Senecan maxim, *rationale . . . animal est homo* (in which *rationale* is neuter, in agreement with *animal*, rather than masculine, in agreement with *homo*). I will stick with Smith's language throughout this chapter.

2. Smith, *Desiring the Kingdom*, 32. Smith foresees and responds to the potential to misinterpret him as being anti-intellectual; see 17, n. 2.

3. Smith uses "thinking thing"; "believing thing" is my own extrapolation of his vocabulary choice. See Smith, *Desiring the Kingdom*, 43.

4. Smith, *Desiring the Kingdom*, 34.

5. Smith, *Desiring the Kingdom*, 48.

way we intend the world is *love*."⁶ Love is externalized; it must be directed toward an object, that which is desired. The question, argues Smith, is not *whether* we love, but *what* we love. He develops this idea in language unmistakably echoing Jesus's warning that where a person's treasure is, there also will be found that person's heart (Matthew 6:21). Smith is not interested in trivial desires, but in

> ultimate loves—that to which we are fundamentally oriented, what ultimately governs our vision of the good life, what shapes and molds our being-in-the-world—in other words, what we desire above all else, the ultimate desire that shapes and positions and makes sense of our penultimate desires and actions. This sort of ultimate love could also be described as that to which we ultimately pledge allegiance; or, to evoke language that is both religious and ancient, our ultimate love is what we *worship*.⁷

The second critical element of Smith's anthropology is the existence of a target for love. The necessary corollary to a life that is directed is that there must be an intended goal, a telos to which love is directed. "Because love is intentional and teleological, our love is always aimed at some particular vision of the good life that has been pictured for us."⁸ Undirected love is inconceivable. Since the stakes are so high when dealing with ultimate loves, selecting and sustaining focus on the right goal is critical.

The third element of Smith's discussion, that of how love is shaped, flows naturally from the assertion that love is directed at an object of desire: How is desire formed, focused, and maintained? Smith's answer—habits—is unoriginal. Here he stands on the shoulders of a line of giants stretching from Aristotle through Aquinas to Macintyre and Hauerwas. Habits, he argues, "constitute the fulcrum of our desire; they are the hinge that turns our heart, our love, such that it is predisposed to be aimed in certain directions."⁹ Humans are part of a story in which they are shaped through habits that are instilled by bodily practices. Such practices direct the desires of a person toward particular goals.

---

6. Smith, *Desiring the Kingdom*, 50; emphasis in original.
7. Smith, *Desiring the Kingdom*, 51; emphasis in original.
8. Smith, *Desiring the Kingdom*, 54–55.
9. Smith, *Desiring the Kingdom*, 56.

## Smith's Liturgy—Essence and Impact

Having depicted humans as loving, worshipping beings, Smith moves on to discuss the nature of liturgy, with a focus on essence and impact. He categorizes as liturgy only practices that are both communal and teleological, and that serve to teach us to be a certain kind of person by shaping our most fundamental desires.

Liturgies, he argues, are a subset of habits that direct our loves. For a practice to qualify as liturgical for Smith, it must fulfill five essential criteria—it is intentional, *telos*-oriented, formative, communal, and embodied. He distinguishes liturgy from practices, and from rituals more broadly. Some rituals are merely routines, repeated actions that fall outside Smith's meaning of liturgy because they are not directed toward an end. An example would be always putting the left sock on before the right. "Practices" are a step closer to liturgy—"we might suggest that practices are a species of the genus ritual"—and "liturgies, then, are a certain species of practice." Liturgies are *"rituals of ultimate concern*: rituals that are formative for identity, that inculcate particular visions of the good life, and do so in a way that is meant to trump other ritual formation."[10]

His view of how habits become ingrained in our dispositions revolves around our nature as embodied lovers who respond to the world both viscerally (with bodily responses driven by an instinctive, emotional reaction to stimuli) and corporeally (with patterns of behavior intentionally conducted on the basis of considered responses to stimuli). Love must be given direction. Although we are by nature creatures who love, or desire—at a more inherent level than we are creatures who think or believe—and who worship that which we ultimately love, we are *not* by nature creatures who rightly discern that which we *ought* to love. Love must be trained in order to be rightly directed. Good liturgical practices direct desire rightly; bad liturgical practices misdirect desire.

Love is directed through the material reality of our bodies: "habits are inscribed in our heart through daily bodily practices and rituals that train the heart, as it were, to desire certain ends."[11] Building on his notion that love must be directed through embodied practice, Smith identifies two essential features of practices that prove effective in instilling desire-shaping, life-transforming habits.

> First, practices are *communal* or social. There are no "private" practices; rather, practices are social products that come to

10   Smith, *Desiring the Kingdom*, 86; emphasis in original.
11.  Smith, *Desiring the Kingdom*, 58.

have an institutional base and expression. Practices don't float in society; rather, they find expression and articulation in concrete sites and institutions—which is also how and why they actually shape embodied persons. There are no practices without institutions. Second, a *telos* is always embedded in these practices and institutions.[12]

Smith's objective is to raise the stakes of Christian worship. "The goal is to get us to appreciate what's at stake . . . nothing less than the formation of radical disciples who desire the kingdom of God."[13] Worship, in other words, is a teleological activity directed at faith formation. Liturgical practices are critical because they are the heart of worship.

But the "core claim" of *Desiring the Kingdom* is about more than simply the communal and teleological essence of liturgies. Liturgies work; they have impact.

> Liturgies—whether "sacred" or "secular"—shape and constitute our identities by forming our most fundamental desires and our most basic attunements to the world. In short, liturgies make us certain kinds of people, and what defines us is what we *love* . . . every liturgy constitutes a pedagogy that teaches us, in all sorts of precognitive ways, to be a certain kind of person.[14]

The underlying premise of *Desiring the Kingdom* is that liturgies are not a peculiarly Christian thing, nor indeed even something associated only with organized, recognized religion. Smith highlights several contexts in which secular liturgies are seen, paying most attention to the shopping mall. In a mall the same patterns of behavior are practiced repeatedly, on weekly visit after weekly visit. Each visit and repetition of an increasingly comfortable routine (park the car in the same area, use the same entrance, go to the same individual shops, purchase the same brand from the same aisle, stop at the same café for coffee, etc.) further entrenches the desire to come back and do it all over again.

The response is visceral—the mind is not necessarily engaged in conversation about the decisions that are made as a result of oft repeated habit. Engagement in discussion about the shopping mall as a place of worship or character formation is almost certainly nonexistent. Yet despite the lack of intellectual engagement and articulation of what is happening as worship,

---

12. Smith, *Desiring the Kingdom*, 62; emphasis in original. Smith introduces the term "communal" practice here as in interchangeable term for "social" practice, to mean an activity undertaken with other people, rather than as an individual.

13. Smith, *Desiring the Kingdom*, 19.

14. Smith, *Desiring the Kingdom*, 25; emphasis in original.

the embodied habits practiced at the mall do inform the characteristics of people who attend regularly. All such formative practices, Smith argues, are liturgies. Recognition by the participant that the activity is teleological is not required for the activity to have desire-shaping impact. Even if the intentionality of the action is known only to the organizing community, or institution, that does not prevent the liturgy being effective in transforming the desires of a participant.

## Workplace Liturgies

Although Smith does not himself dwell on the workplace as a locus of cultural liturgy, applying his thinking in this area is appropriate. Most individuals spend more time in the workplace than the mall. If a mall can work formative influence through perhaps just a weekly visit of an hour or two, how much more so the workplace through five visits a week of six, eight or ten hours each. Workplaces, particularly those of the twenty-first-century developed economy, are unquestionably venues of habitual practice of all sorts, some daily: commute the same route each day at the same time, sit at the same desk, login to see the same image on the same homepage with the same password, explain the same concept to multiple clients using the same predetermined corporate wording, meet with the same team members in the same boardroom, eat lunch in the same location, watch the same clock till knock off time, and so on; potentially two hundred and fifty times each year. The formative nature of such routines is unquestionable, even though the formation might appear to be incidental rather than intentional.

Nevertheless, the fact is that formative practices in the workplace are not merely incidental. That is not to say that they are always explained, and of Smith's five essential criteria for a practice to be considered liturgy—that it is intentional, *telos*-oriented, formative, communal, and embodied—not all apply to every practice. Workplace habits sometimes appear to be acts done to employees, and sometimes done with workers' compliance. Moreover, in some cases the teleological and formative elements might be most easily perceived by an observing academic, rather than articulated by a participant in a practice orchestrated by an employer or organization.

But the liturgy-like aspects of workplaces are well documented. Workplace analysts Trinca and Fox argue in their provocatively titled *Better than Sex*[15] that in twenty-first-century Australian society, a whole generation has become "hooked on work" in ways that foster meaning-creating ritual. They trace the search for "daily meaning as well as daily bread" in work back to

15. Trinca and Fox, *Better than Sex*.

the 1970s, but assert that it was in the 1990s that "work was repositioned as a place where the individual went for meaning."[16] The milieu of fear that arose particularly in the white collar sector during the downsizing of the 1980s led to deliberate corporate efforts at "creating a belief system."[17]

In short, employers set out with intent to shape their employees. They do so by establishing intentional, communal, teleological routines meant to direct desires toward the good life—as defined by the employer—through repeated, embodied practice. The workplace does more than simply provide a way for workers to access the good life as they understand it. The white collar, brainpower workplace in particular is a space, like educational institutions and arguably the shopping mall, where the institution itself seeks to shape the notion of the good life. The routines need not be daily. One-off induction programs, weekly briefings, Friday afternoon or end-of-project drinks, corporate service days, birthday cake rituals, the office Christmas party, the annual review and celebration of successes, regular reminders of employee perks—and even regularly scheduled research seminars—are all examples of orchestrated, formative liturgies designed to strengthen the loyalty and shape the behavior of participants.

## Smith on Christian Liturgy

Smith positions Christian liturgy as an exercise in counter-formation. Worship is polemic, not simply neutral. "The emphasis on *counter*-formation in worship is a fire-meet-fire response to the deformation of our loves that manifests itself as conformity to 'the world.'"[18] The battlefield language leads to the expectation that Smith will come out with all guns blazing aimed at the source of violence done to visions of the good life—the deforming, secular liturgies of institutions such as the mall, the school, and the workplace. Surprisingly, he does not.

Given Smith's understanding of the all-pervasive nature of liturgical behavior in society, it would be reasonable to expect his definition of Christian liturgy to be equally expansive. However, his interest is particularly narrow. The Christian social imaginary is embedded, he argues, in Christian worship. He spends sixty pages—over one quarter of *Desiring the Kingdom*—describing the scope and sequence of worship services, what might be called "the liturgical hour." Although he includes a section on "Practices Beyond Sunday" and rejects as a caricature of his thesis "the supposed adequacy of 'Sunday

---

16. Trinca and Fox, *Better than Sex*, 38–39.
17. Trinca and Fox, *Better than Sex*, 41.
18. Smith, *Awaiting the King*, 169; emphasis in original.

only' participation" in Christian worship, his articulation of Christian liturgy marginalizes practices outside the formal worship service.[19] It is at this point that room for expansion of his thinking begins to become clear. There are multiple questions that arise from his focus, albeit not exclusively, on such a narrow part of the communal interactions of God's people.

The most intractable problem is the ineffectiveness of Christian liturgy in countering prevailing cultural liturgies. This fatal flaw in Smith's thesis has been identified by critics of his work.[20] Smith himself posits the question: "Why doesn't Christian worship seem to create the 'peculiar people' we sometimes claim?"[21] The question might be put even more starkly: If one of the five essential components of liturgy is that it is formative, but Christian worship is in fact *not* formative in the way anticipated, then is it even liturgy as defined by Smith? Smith rejects the suggestion that the ineffectiveness of Christian liturgical efforts to shape desires places in jeopardy his theory of the power of liturgy. Indeed, in the face of overwhelming evidence, it is difficult to argue with his assertion that his "liturgical anthropology" does in fact make sense of "our cultural assimilation to the disordered loves of consumerism, militarism, nationalism and other performative idolatries."[22] Yet the enigma of the ineffectiveness of Christian liturgy remains.

Why, then, the "ecclesial failure," the inability of Christian liturgies to assimilate us to rightly ordered loves? Smith begins by offering two insights. First, he differentiates between "proper habituation" in Christian liturgical practices and merely selective participation in those practices. Dissonance between engagement in Christian liturgy and engagement in Christian life, he says, is because: "more than likely we see someone who participates in only *some* of the practices of the body of Christ."[23]

Second, he argues that catechesis—teaching why certain practices are undertaken—is indispensable.[24] Yet neither proper habituation nor attendant explanation seems critical to the success of secular cultural liturgies. Ikea does not explain to its customers why they are encouraged along a circuitous route through the store, nor shed tears if a customer accepts only some of their offerings, perhaps happily following the arrows on the floor,

---

19. See Smith, *Awaiting the King*, 204, and *Desiring the Kingdom*, 207–14.

20. See, for example, Trevin Wax's critique of *Desiring the Kingdom* in Wax, "Worldview Training," and Smith's response to the question "*How do you explain the fact that many people immerse themselves in Christian worship week to week and are still not formed into the image of Christ?*" in Wax, "Spiritual Formation."

21. Smith, *Awaiting the King*, 201.

22. Smith, *Awaiting the King*, 201.

23. Smith, *Awaiting the King*, 203.

24. Smith, *Awaiting the King*, 204–5.

but not pushing a trolley as they do so, nor visiting the Ikea café. But Ikea items continue to appeal to customers, who keep coming, and keep submitting to the Ikea formative experience.

Smith's next port of call is what he calls "liturgical capture."[25] Borrowing the concept of "regulatory capture"—the phenomenon of a government agency charged with regulating an industry actually becoming beholden to that industry—he suggests "a situation of 'liturgical capture,' in which the liturgies of the church are captured and dominated by the disordered rival liturgies they are meant to counter."[26] The problem is not, he argues, with the narrowness of his definition of Christian worship, but with the fact that Christian worship has been co-opted for some purpose more aligned with the priorities of alternative cultures such as the nation, the market, or the family. Smith points particularly to conflation of Christianity with national or ethnic identity, such as Irish Catholics or Scottish Presbyterians. His analysis at this point appears to stretch beyond his own narrowly confined definition of worship and thus to allow for wider application. Congregations at formal worship services can be functionally atheist social gatherings, denominational annual gatherings can appear to be political manoeuvrings, the family unit can be elevated to a sacrosanct position beyond criticism and above the body of believers, and so on. The suggestion that this kind of mundane conforming to the world renders Christian liturgy impotent comes as no surprise to any reader of Romans 12:1–2.

In addition to his rebuttal of the idea that inefficacy in formation demands reevaluation of his project, Smith even seems, paradoxically, to soften to some extent emphasis on an element critical to his whole project; namely, the formative efficacy itself of liturgies. He cautions, first and not unreasonably, against eschatologically undisciplined expectations of perfect faith formation in this life, appealing to Paul's use of language that suggests not complete formation but rather formative progress. He also argues, despite his persistent focus on the formative nature of liturgy, against having an instrumental view of liturgy that places too much weight on faith formation. He then goes on to redefine liturgy's purpose: "While we believe that [Christian liturgy] engenders formation, it is a normative good apart from its effectiveness precisely because it is the way we meet God. . . . It is the lived performance of the catholic faith that draws us into the story of God in Christ reconciling the world to himself."[27] The instrumental purpose of worship, he would seem to be saying, is not primarily to form us, but

25. Smith, *Awaiting the King*, 179–81; 205.
26. Smith, *Awaiting the King*, 179.
27. Smith, *Desiring the Kingdom*, 207.

to draw us into the story of God. But the suggestion that liturgy's primary purpose is invitational rather than formative merely redirects the question of efficacy. To what end are we to be invited into a story by worship, if not to be participants in the story, formed by its author? The question remains, but with the criteria for assessing efficacy restated.

Moreover, at this point there appears to be a desire to both have and eat the teleological cake. The claim that liturgical acts draw us into a story calls for substantiation as much as does the claim that those acts form faith. One might reasonably expect that liturgical practices that *effectively* draw us into the story of God would also rightly order our desires to align our lives with the author in order to play a role in that story, but Smith has already conceded that liturgy does not necessarily function in this way.

So despite Smith's offerings, the question remains of why it is that Christian liturgies are outgunned by secular alternatives, rather than the other way round. Smith concedes a quantity challenge: "the rhythms and practices of Christian worship take place, in most cases, in about an hour and a half, one day a week . . . not much time to enact counter-measures to the secular liturgies in which we are immersed the rest of the week."[28] His concessive inclusion, discussed below, of practices beyond the formal liturgical hour affords opportunity, within his framework, for consideration of Sabbath and its potentially desire-shaping power as a liturgical practice—intentional, *telos*-oriented, formative, communal, and embodied.

## Smith and Sabbath

In *Desiring the Kingdom* Smith depicts Christian worship as a cathedral in order to distinguish liturgical practices from other kinds of regular activity and to highlight the centrality of those practices he considers liturgical.

> At the heart of the cathedral, at the intersection of the cross, is the altar: this is the focal point of Christian worship that culminates in the celebration of the Eucharist. However, the cathedral is also home to all sorts of nooks and crannies that are devoted to other kinds of regular activity. . . . There will be still other corners and spaces in the cathedral that host all sorts of activities. . . . This provides a visual metaphor for thinking about the relationship between the *liturgical practices* of gathered worship and other Christian practices outside of that.[29]

---

28. Smith, *Desiring the Kingdom*, 207.
29. Smith, *Desiring the Kingdom*, 213; emphasis added.

For Smith, to the extent that practices in the "other-than-liturgy" category have any formative power, it is only derivative.

> The range of Christian practices "beyond Sunday" are best understood as extensions of the liturgical practices of gathered worship; they are important and formative because (and insofar as) they draw on the formative power of specifically liturgical practices. Or, to put it conversely, the formative force of such extra-Sunday practices is diminished if they are unhooked from the liturgical practices of the ecclesial community.[30]

Smith locates Sabbath keeping in this "other" or "beyond Sunday" or "extraliturgical" category. Given this contingent, second tier status to which he consigns Sabbath, it is understandably of marginal interest to his thesis about liturgical practices. He refers to it in *Desiring the Kingdom* only four times. Two references are made in passing, with a third being in a footnote.[31] In the one remaining, more significant mention, though, Smith acknowledges the formative efficacy of Sabbath keeping, thus offering a glimmer of possibility for Sabbath keeping to be considered as a legitimate liturgical practice within his five-point definition of liturgies.

> Christians engage in all kinds of formative practices and spiritual disciplines beyond the specifically liturgical practices of gathered worship. . . . When Christians engage in the practices of hospitality and Sabbath keeping, singing and forgiveness, simplicity and fasting, they are engaging in a way of life that is formative and constitutive of Christian discipleship. These "practices beyond Sunday" are further opportunities to rehearse a way of life, to practice (for) the kingdom.[32]

The case for consideration of Sabbath keeping as a properly liturgical practice is justified not simply because it seems to fit Smith's conceptual framework, but, more importantly, on biblical grounds. The biblical depiction of Sabbath practice has all the hallmarks of a Smithean liturgy. Contrary to Smith's marginalization of Sabbath keeping as adjunct to liturgical practice, in the context of the Old Testament, the Sabbath is intended as an identity-forming, identity-revealing practice with multiple explicit *telos*, and entails a pedagogical purpose intended to shape and reshape desires. In other words, it fits Smith's criteria for inclusion as a liturgical practice in both essence and intended impact.

30. Smith, *Desiring the Kingdom*, 212–13.
31. See Smith, *Desiring the Kingdom*, 117, 157, n. 3, and 226.
32. Smith, *Desiring the Kingdom*, 211–12.

The intention that Sabbath keeping functions as a formative practice, that it "make[s] us certain kinds of people," is apparent from its description as a covenant or sign that marks the people of God (Exodus 31:12–17). The counter-formative potential of Sabbath observance is underlined by its juxtaposition against apostasy. The Sabbath injunctions of Exodus 31:12–17 and 35:1–3 bookend the idol worship and consequences of Exodus 32—34. The narrative structure suggests that the counterblow to the distorting burden of desire for forward movement in the desert might have been the communal Sabbath practice introduced in Exodus 16. The critical importance of Sabbath as something more than just a day of rest is clear from the severity of punishment for breaches: death at the hands of the whole community (Exodus 31:15; 35:2), affirmed with crystal clarity as appropriate even for breaches seemingly far less problematic than wholesale idolatry (Numbers 15:32–36). So important is Sabbath that it is to take priority even over matters of life and death for an agrarian people: "Six days you shall labor, but on the seventh day you shall rest; even during the plowing season and harvest you must rest" (Exodus 34:21).

The liturgical nature of Sabbath practice is as clear as is the intention that it be formative. Smith's narrow focus on the worship service cannot obscure the liturgical intent of Sabbath commandment and practice. Sabbath is to be a daylong, God-oriented activity, "to the Lord" (Exodus 16:23, 25). A Sabbath practice draws attention to the works of God, who both created (Exodus 20:11) and redeemed his people from slavery (Deuteronomy 5:15). It will draw people to the place of worship (Jeremiah 17:19–27). Knowledge of God will ensue (Ezekiel 20:12–20). The Sabbath operates as a mnemonic device, reminding the people that God is holy, and is in the business of making his people holy (Exodus 31:12–17; Ezekiel 20:12).

The formative and liturgical nature of Sabbath is clear from a number of Old Testament descriptive and prescriptive passages. Smith's focus on the formative role of cultural liturgies and the need for counter-formation through Christian practices provides encouragement to consider Sabbath keeping as a counter-formative practice, despite the minimal consideration he gives it. The biblical evidence suggests that it was clearly intended to, and has the potential to, play a role in directing love in the sense in which Smith argues that formal liturgical services do.

## Sabbath Keeping as a Liturgical Response to Workplace Liturgies

We have argued that a biblical perspective suggests that Sabbath keeping warrants consideration as a properly liturgical, formative practice in line with Smith's broadly defined understanding of liturgy. Nothing in his definition of liturgy warrants the marginalization of Sabbath keeping to an "extra-liturgical" category. The remainder of this chapter will therefore consider the question of the potential that Sabbath keeping might have to counter the powerful, formative forces of contemporary dominant culture seen in the workplace.

It is perhaps in the context of working life that Sabbath keeping most directly offers a counter-liturgy to the prevailing culture. It is beyond the scope of this chapter to give detailed treatment of the semantic range of "work," or to discuss at length the range of contexts in which work takes place. But habitual practices with formative potential occur in all situations in which human endeavor is undertaken, whether that be in traditional workplaces or the more fluid settings associated with digital connectedness, working from home and the gig economy, and whether the worker is financially recompensed or not. How might Sabbath function as a counter-formative liturgical practice in response to liturgies in the workplace, adding value to Smith's project of calling believers to take Christian liturgy seriously as a weapon in the counterattack against secular liturgies?

First, Sabbath observance reshapes our anthropology. A full day of rest dedicated to a deliberately God-honoring avoidance of achieving, acquiring or providing for ourselves reminds believers of the great works of God in creation and redemption, the reasons given in Exodus 20 and Deuteronomy 5 respectively for the Sabbath commandment. In other words, it repositions us as created and redeemed beings. That has potential to liberate us from the need to identify primarily as workers in a workplace, the need to create our identity or reputation through the work we do, and the need to save or justify ourselves by our work outcomes. It cuts against distorted liturgies of work that seek to "make us certain kinds of people," people whose love is directed not toward God but toward the employer, the end of financial year bonus-bearing target, or the longer-term organizational strategic plan.

Second, the notion of a 24-hour Sabbath observance is unique amongst Christian liturgies in that it places a demand on time, rather than activity. It is not so much about doing, as not doing. It invites participants into a temporal sanctuary. To the extent that it causes a reevaluation of time use, Sabbath keeping challenges expectation of the 24/7 availability to employers made possible by twenty-first-century technology. It redirects thinking to the notion that the one for whom all work is done is the creator of the universe who demands all our time for the whole of life, not the employer with the pay cheque who cannot legitimately make the same demand. It signals that the clarion calls of the workplace—these days transmitted courtesy of information and communication technology beyond both the place of work and any notional hours of work—are to be intentionally set aside.

Third, a Sabbath practice offers potential to boost the formative efficacy of the formal liturgical hour—on which Smith places such emphasis and the weakness of which he laments—leading to stronger faith formation and hence greater capacity to resist the formative power of workplace liturgies. In Smith's cathedral of spiritual formation, the altar of formal worship services is the focal point from which other activities that occur in "nooks and crannies" and "corners and spaces" draw their formative life.

> The practices of Christian worship function as the altar of Christian formation . . . but the energy and formative power of gathered worship is extended and amplified . . . in the different gatherings and practices of Christian communities and friends who together intentionally pursue a life formed by the Spirit.[33]

Smith locates Sabbath keeping, because he categorizes it as extraliturgical, in a derivative position:

> If, in a certain sense, the altar is not enough—a sense in which *just* liturgical practices are insufficient counter-measures to secular liturgies—there is also a sense in which extraliturgical practices will have diminished formative power (or worse, could themselves become practices aimed at quite a distorted picture of the kingdom) if they are not tethered to and nourished by the practices of Christian worship.[34]

He appears unwilling to concede that any other practices might have the potential to exert formative influence autonomously on a par with what he posits as the core practice. Yet there is room for consideration of the possibility that the sustaining connection he asserts flows from his narrowly defined liturgical center to his "extraliturgical" is at least matched by the countercurrent-formative life given to the central act when it is legitimized and enhanced by virtue of taking place as one aspect of the larger constellation of liturgical acts.[35] Sabbath observance might in fact reinvigorate

---

33. Smith, *Desiring the Kingdom*, 213.

34. Smith, *Desiring the Kingdom*, 213–14; emphasis in original.

35 A biblical perspective would suggest that the central act can also be delegitimized and debased by the absence of other acts of worship. Note, for example, Amos 5:21;

formal worship. It occurs as frequently, but, as a daylong liturgical practice, it addresses to some extent the "quantity challenge" conceded by Smith to be a hindrance to the efficacy of a liturgical hour.

Trevin Wax sums up the situation: liturgy as defined by Smith cannot be the primary solution to the problem that secular liturgies carry such sway.[36] What if the loss of the formative power of worship services were due to the decontextualization of formal worship by the dismissal of Sabbath keeping as a formative, communal, liturgical practice within which the more specific liturgical practice stands? In the context of a bone-weary, time-pressed, work-oriented culture, might the restoration of a communal practice of devoting a whole day to love-driven, intentionally love-driving, time-forgetting, formative practices possibly offer a more potent alternative to the cultural liturgies Smith is keen to counter than an hour-long service? How might the formative impact on worshippers be enriched by an approach to the service that considered it but one component (whether central or not is not the question at this point) of a whole-day multi-component experience of intentional, *telos*-oriented practice? Moreover, how might the whole-day practice add countercultural, missional depth to the central practice of a formalized service?

Fourth, Sabbath observance practiced in and by the community of God's people declares the need to draw a boundary around sacred time. The practice has prophetic potential to speak powerfully in the context of workplaces in which boundaries are placed around time only with difficulty unless it is for the purpose of redirecting energies to an alternative work task, and in which time management is a ubiquitous and perennially unresolved issue.

Our consideration of Sabbath as a liturgical response to workplace liturgies would be incomplete without a word of caution. If we are to appropriate Sabbath keeping as a counter-formative practice for the workplace, we do well finally to heed Smith's warning about "liturgical capture." One increasingly widespread response to the increased freneticism of some work patterns has been a focus on time off as a mental health maintenance mechanism. But when a solution to present or looming mental health difficulties is confused with Sabbath observance, Sabbath has been eviscerated. Neither can Sabbath—God-oriented rest with intent to worship at its heart—be reduced to simply an instrument of refreshment for

---

Jeremiah 7:1–11 and Jesus's reference to it in condemning temple practice (Matt 21:13 and parallels); and Paul's critique of Corinthian eucharistic practice (1 Cor 11:11–34). In such situations Smith's notion of "liturgical capture" would seem to have relevance.

36. Wax, "Worldview Training." Wax is partially arguing for the centrality of Scripture over practice, but that debate is beyond the scope of this chapter.

future work, or a day off for self-indulgence. Each of these fuels the flame of love misdirected toward work as the source of meaning and identity or self as the focus of attention. Indeed, the misappropriation of Sabbath primarily for the purpose of recuperation has been shown to be ineffective.[37] Sabbath that is not God-focused is simply a day off, not a properly liturgical practice. When a practice becomes instrumental for purposes that are neither doxological nor formative of faith, its status as liturgy must be questioned, as must the appellation of Sabbath.

Smith has done a service in his cultural liturgies project in reminding us that we are not merely intellects, but embodied beings in process of formation, whose essence is to love. His focus on the importance of formative practices provides encouragement to consider Sabbath as one such practice, despite the minimal consideration he gives it. Biblical evidence that presents Sabbath observance as fulfilling his five essential criteria for a properly liturgical practice lends support to at least a prima facie case for serious consideration of Sabbath as liturgy.

Sabbath keeping clearly has the potential to play a role in directing love in the sense in which Smith argues that formal liturgical services do. At the very least it ought to be brought out from dark nooks and crannies into the full light of discussion about Christian formation as a countermeasure to the broad liturgies of contemporary dominant culture, including the expectations of the workplace. It has the potential to increase believers' resilience in the face of secular workplace liturgies and to speak prophetically of a God who, unlike the workplace, offers real rest and unassailably secure identity independent of performance.

## Bibliography

Diddams, Margaret, Lisa Klein Surdyk, and Denise Daniels. "Rediscovering Models of Sabbath Keeping: Implications for Psychological Well-Being." *Journal of Psychology and Theology* 32 (2004) 3–11. https://doi.org/10.1177/009164710403200101.
Smith, James K. A. *Awaiting the King: Reforming Public Theology*. Cultural Liturgies 3. Grand Rapids: Baker Academic, 2017.
———. *Desiring the Kingdom: Worship, Worldview, and Cultural Formation*. Cultural Liturgies 1. Grand Rapids: Baker Academic, 2009.
Trinca, Helen, and Catherine Fox. *Better than Sex: How a Whole Generation Got Hooked on Work*. Sydney: Random House, 2004.

37. For a critique of the adoption of Sabbath practice for personal instrumental reasons, see Diddams et al., "Rediscovering Models," 3–11. The authors clarify that a Sabbath undertaken for instrumental reasons, whether grounded in a faith tradition or not, is unlikely to produce the mental health benefits hoped for.

Wax, Trevin. "Spiritual Formation Through Desire: An Interview with James K. A. Smith." *TGC*, January 12, 2010. https://blogs.thegospelcoalition.org/trevinwax/2010/01/12/spiritual-formation-through-desire-an-interview-with-james-k-a-smith/.

———. "Worldview Training Is Not Enough." *TGC*, December 23, 2009. https://blogs.thegospelcoalition.org/trevinwax/2009/12/23/worldview-training-is-not-enough/.

# 11

# A Fine Line Between Pleasure and Pain

*The Perspective of Labor from the Book of Ecclesiastes*

Andrew W. G. Matthews

*PhD Candidate, Christ College, Sydney*

## Abstract

A dominant theme within the book of Ecclesiastes is the treatment of the benefits of human labor. After "the Preacher" (Qoheleth) pronounces the "vanity of vanities" motto, he asks the probing question, "What does a person gain from all the labor at which they labor under the sun?" This question about the worth of a person's work controls much of Qoheleth's discussion about human living. A key issue is whether work is regarded by Qoheleth as an intrinsically painful and futile enterprise. A study of the work terminology of Ecclesiastes paints a picture in which God has imposed upon humanity a work mandate, much of which is painful and futile, but not necessarily so. Much interpretation of Ecclesiastes assumes that the Hebrew term עמל, "to labor, toil," characterizes all work as "painful labor." However, the term is often associated with pleasure from work. As Qoheleth addresses the theme of the worth of work, he employs a "dialectical polemic" that first demolishes the false expectations and folly of human labor, and then replaces it with a wise and affirming perspective on work's benefits. As a person works within the purposes of God, they can attain the outcomes of true value and happiness from their labor.

## Introduction

After "the Preacher" (*Qoheleth*) pronounces his famous "all is vanity" judgment against everything in this world, he asks a probing question: "What does a person gain from all the labor in which they labor under the sun?" (1:3).[1] The question is generally understood to be a rhetorical question that demands the answer of "nothing," but the question is not so easily answered. Human "labor" (*amal*) is assumed to be inherently futile in its aim to achieve "profit" (*yitron*) in life. No doubt Qoheleth is very critical of many of the aims and results of human workers. Yet Qoheleth changes tack often throughout the course of his discourse to give hope for the possibility of real gains from work. The "good life" is one of eating, drinking, *and* working. People are counseled to work with all their might, and wisdom is the tool for success. So, Qoheleth holds an enigmatic perspective on work in that labor is both the source of humanity's greatest pains and pleasures. Given such polar outcomes, the wise reader should heed the Preacher's counsel on all the pitfalls and profits from work. As I investigate the Preacher's theology of vocation, I will look to see if any of the work terms used in Ecclesiastes may provide a clue to the inherent nature of work. Then, I will look at both the negative and positive outcomes common to human vocation, as the Preacher employs a deconstruction and reconstruction approach in his analysis.

## Work Words

An essential task in studying the theme of labor in Ecclesiastes is to examine the three key terms Qoheleth uses to describe human working: "to labor," "to work, do," and "business." All three terms refer to human labors, all have positive and negative connotations, and all can refer to the act of labor or the fruits of labor. When the words are examined in comparison with their companions, unique connotations surface that reveal how they complement and contrast with each other.

---

1. It is argued by de Jong that the value of labor is the main theme of Ecclesiastes, "Book on Labour," 107–16.

## "Labor"

The most crucial work word employed by Qoheleth is the word "to labor, toil" (*amal*) not merely because of the number of its citations (35x), but also due to the rhetorical importance of "labor" within the message of Qoheleth. The first and most prominent use of "labor" is within the initial question of 1:3, "What does it profit a man for all the *labor in which he labors* under the sun?" The use of "labor" in this question, its saturation of usage (15x) in Qoheleth's royal autobiography, and its repeated use in the enjoyment refrains (8x) makes "labor" the primary term that Qoheleth employs to establish the theme of human work.

The overwhelming understanding of "labor" within the lexicons and commentaries is that *amal* refers to grievous, futile work.[2] Many commentators also take a negative stance on the essential nature of "labor." Fox defines Qoheleth's use of "labor" as follows, "It first of all means toil—arduous, wearisome work . . . . When signifying activity, *'amal* always means onerous strained labor, "overdoing" rather than simply "doing."[3] Crenshaw defines "labor" as "burdensome labor and mental anguish."[4] This line of thinking can be indicated simply in the choice of "toil" as the preferred translation of the underlying Hebrew term in the commentaries and English Bible versions.

Given that Ecclesiastes is grounded in the Genesis account of a fallen creation, it is natural to wonder if the use of "labor" is semantically linked with the cursed work judgment of Genesis 3:17–19.[5] It is notable that the particular terminology of "pain" (*itzbon*) in Genesis 3:16–17 is not utilized in the work terminology of Ecclesiastes. If Qoheleth wanted to establish a theology of painful, cursed work for humanity, why did he forego the opportunity to utilize the Genesis term "pain" as his primary labor term? The fact that such a Hebrew term was available, yet not used, indicates that "labor" and the other work terms have not necessarily inherited *all* the pain and futility depicted in Genesis 3:17–19.

The root from "labor" occurs seventy-five times in the OT and thirty-five of these are in Ecclesiastes. The noun form of *amal* in the OT has three

---

2. The *NIDOTTE* defines *amal*, "The vb *'ml*, all q., denotes labor, often with an eye to its difficulty, its burdensome nature, hence toil." Thompson, "Amal," 453.

3. Fox, *Time*, 97–98.

4. Crenshaw, *Ecclesiastes*, 90.

5. Anderson makes the observation, "In fact, I have not come across a single scholar who denies Qoheleth's use of the Genesis account." Anderson, "Curse of Work," 99. Also, Dell has an insightful article on the relationship between Genesis and Ecclesiastes in "Intertextual Links," 3–13.

distinct senses: "trouble/sorrow," "mischief/wickedness," and "labor" and its product. The examination of how *amal* is utilized outside of Ecclesiastes has impacted interpretation of the term in Ecclesiastes. In Ecclesiastes, *amal* only has the sense of work. There are no allusions to "trouble" or "mischief" in the labor mentioned. Yet the negative connotations of *amal* from its wider use often taint its interpretation in Ecclesiastes. When defining *amal* in Ecclesiastes, many commentators allude to its more ominous renderings to paint a dark picture of its meaning which approximates "painful labor."[6] This is not to argue that "labor" does not carry negative connotations in certain contexts, but that the determination of the nature of the labor sense of *amal* needs to be derived from the context and usage of the term within Ecclesiastes and not from the transferal of other sense classes from other contexts. In light of these considerations, the English gloss "labor" should be used to indicate the work associated with *amal* though in some contexts where pain and futility is in view the gloss "toil" would be appropriate.

## "Deeds"

The verbal terms "to do, work" and the nouns "deed, work" belong to one of the other main roots (*asah*) used in Ecclesiastes to refer to work and appear sixty-four times. "Labor" and "work" function as synonyms when they both refer to *human* work.[7] In his reflection upon all his works (2:10), he uses "labor" to refer to all of these works. Then in verse 2:11, he oscillates between "labor" and "work" with both referring to his grand list of accomplishments, "I looked on all *the works* that my hands had *done* and on the *labor* in which I had *labored* in *doing* it." The fact that both words can have the same referent is significant, because it dispels the notion that there is an absolute dichotomy between the two types of work. Attempts to bifurcate the two types of workings may be motivated by the belief that *amal* only refers to wearisome work and *asah* to pleasant work. A key difference exists between "labor" and "deed" in relation to *who* is the subject of the verb: God or humans. In some cases who is doing the work is ambiguous.[8] Notably, the term "labor" is *never* used of God's work, only

---

6. Seow comments on *amal*, "Perhaps the most startling fact about the occurrences of the noun 'amal "toil" in the Bible is its close association with extremely negative terms.... Elsewhere, too, the word means pain, misery, or mischief. The noun 'amal has strongly negative connotations. Thus "toil" is not just "work" or "activity"; it is not "effort."" Seow, *Ecclesiastes*, 104.

7. Ogden and Zogbo, *Handbook*, 62–63.

8. Ingram, *Ambiguity*, 159.

human labor, whereas "deed" is used of both divine and human work. So God is always "working," but never "laboring."

## *"Business"*

The third key work term in Ecclesiastes is "business" (*inyan*, 12x) which refers to the "business," "occupations," or "tasks" which people are engaged in during the course of their life. The word in Ecclesiastes refers to the vast scope of work in which humans are occupied throughout the course of their lives.[9] Fox is correct in his insight that "business" has a sense of the "bustle of events that fill life" whereby "business" becomes "busyness."[10] Another connotation to "business" is that it is often work that has *been given* by God to people. In this sense the work of humans is a "task" that has been assigned for people in their life. In ten of the eleven uses of "business," the word is used in a critical manner to describe either pain or futility in human labors. In three instances the adjective "evil" directly modifies "business" (1:13; 4:8; 5:13). With the one exception in 5:20, every instance of "business" describes a negative and futile labor situation of humanity.

## *Work or Wealth?*

A key interpretive issue in the study of the three work words is the perplexing manner in which the terms refer to both the *act of work* and the *product of work*. All three terms are used within the parallel constructions "labor in which one labors," "deeds that are done," and "the business in which one busies oneself," wherein distinctions can be more easily made between labor and its product. The noun forms are more ambiguous regarding a "work" and "wealth" reference. When Qoheleth says a person should "rejoice in their labor" (5:19) is he referring to the joy of work or the joy derived from the income? Perhaps when the ambiguous usages of the work terms are employed, Qoheleth has the totality of work and its results under consideration. The actual work of people and the results of the work are inextricably joined within Qoheleth's appraisals. This has significance for the overall interpretation of Ecclesiastes due to the close correlation of "labor" to the experiences of pleasure or pain.

---

9. "Qoheleth uses the nom. *'inyan* as a general term for the concerns, affairs, or tasks of human existence." Diamond, "Anah," 452.

10. Fox, *Time*, 106.

## Labor Pains

Qoheleth is acutely critical of the extent of grief and pain associated with many human endeavors. Surprisingly, there are scant references in Ecclesiastes to the labor itself being painful. However, though work in Ecclesiastes is not *intrinsically* painful, it is often *derivatively* painful, that is, pain often accompanies and is derived from human work. The question amounts to: What are the various causes of sorrow and pain in labor that Qoheleth observes in the world?

### *Grievous Toil*

The category of *grief* associations includes any reference to emotional pain caused by the doing of the work and the anxiety over the results of work. The most direct link of pain with work comes from the error of the *quantity of work* people apply themselves to in life. Most prevalent in Ecclesiastes is the sorrow associated with *overworking*. The clearest expression of the criticism of overworking comes in Qoheleth's judgment against "two hands full of labor" (4:6). The striving for more deprived the worker of "quietness." Brown remarks on the worker's relentless laboring for profit, "In the vicious cycle for gain, toil marks a *sabbath*-less existence."[11] The same overworking mindset is critiqued in the passage that follows (4:7–8) where the worker "has no end to his labors," and thus has no pleasure or family in his life.[12] Ironically, the success of a hardworking person can cause more pain for them. In 5:12–13 Qoheleth twice refers to rich people hurt by their riches. Due to anxiety over maintaining riches, the "full stomach of the rich" causes sleeplessness (5:12), in contrast to the satisfied stomach of the laborer.

The preponderance of pain associations with work often comes from *anxiety over the outcomes* of one's labor. The work itself does not cause as much pain as the mental anguish associated with worrying about its success. Qoheleth confessed that he initially felt pleasure from his work. It was only after he considered the prospects of the future of his work that his positive outlook morphed into "hatred" (2:18) and "despair" (2:20). Qoheleth describes the mental anguish of these inward strivings as "days full of sorrow," one's "work is a vexation," and the worker is deprived of sleep, "at night his

---

11. Brown, "Whatever Your Hand," 277.

12. Mitchell notes that often "all" is prefixed to "labor" and holds the negative view that "the Preacher represents labor as a constant factor in human life, the total impression is that to him, so far from being welcome and agreeable, it was a source of dissatisfaction and irritation." Mitchell, "Work," 133.

heart cannot rest" (2:23). A similar mental affliction is experienced by the failed rich man of 5:13–17, who all his days "eats in darkness in much vexation and sickness and wrath." When one considers that the constellation of pain terminology in Ecclesiastes is applied mainly to the anguish and worry about the future of one's work, it indicates that Qoheleth's work polemic stresses the insecurities and vagaries of human living. The uncertainty of outcomes from work, the frustration of failed goals, and the fear of the future cause considerable stress to people.

## *Laboring in Vain*

Despair over the *futility* of work is more frequent than the grief attending the effort of work. The futility of work describes the emotions of Qoheleth and other workers as they consider and bemoan the failure of their efforts. An essential cause of vanity in work is the fleeting nature of human life and accomplishments. Transience, or impermanence, is an important element in *hebel* ("vanity, breath, meaningless, enigma"), perhaps even its essential meaning.[13] Though wisdom and work may achieve many goals in life, those accomplishments will not endure. The quest for permanent accomplishments is called "vanity" and a "chasing after wind." Qoheleth achieved all that he desired, yet he dreaded the future when another person would enjoy and potentially jeopardize his success. The poor youth who became a popular king lost his honor and legacy, since future generations will not remember him. In 5:11 and 6:1–2 a person gains riches and wealth yet someone else "partakes" of what they had earned. The rich man of 5:13–17 earns his wealth and then loses it through a failed investment. The transient nature of human accomplishments introduces an *ultimate futility* "under the sun" to the works of people.

## *No Satisfaction*

Another dimension of futility in work is found in the tragedy that the labors of people are unable to satisfy their desires. It is evident from several scenarios that the end goal of the worker was not to find meaning but to obtain happiness in life, often denoted by the term "satisfaction." When a person's works fail to accomplish happiness, Qoheleth judges the scenario

---

13. See, Fredericks, *Coping with Transience*; Farmer, *Proverbs and Ecclesiastes*, 142–46; Provan, "Fresh Perspectives," 401–16.

as "vanity."[14] This is seen in the passages of 4:7 and 6:7, where people work to gratify their desires, but they are never able to satisfy the eyes (4:17) or the mouth (6:7). Rudman grimly observes, "Qoheleth's philosophy of life is notable in that human attempts to achieve contentment appear from the very beginning to be doomed to failure."[15] The solitary rich man in 4:7–8 is a tragic figure who tirelessly works, yet never experiences any measure of happiness. His focus on work and riches, ostensibly to gain happiness, caused him to be isolated relationally. The mention of no son or brother and the rhetorical question, "For whom am I laboring?" indicate that his loneliness contributed to his unhappiness. Though his labor produced riches, he was "never satisfied" with them.

The failure to be satisfied in life is considered by Qoheleth to be a grievous evil and the ultimate tragedy of human existence. The "love of money" in 5:10 is seen to be intrinsically unsatisfying. In 6:3–9 Qoheleth postulates a hypothetical scenario of a person who had everything (long life, children, riches) yet was not satisfied. Such a person would have been better off being a stillborn (6:3). From this conclusion Qoheleth holds that the value of any work can be measured by its enhancement or erosion of human happiness. Yet, the enigma of Ecclesiastes is that the possibility of experiencing enjoyment from labor is still set forth for humanity.

## *Sovereign Plans*

Essential to Qoheleth's theology is his belief that God sovereignly controls all the deeds that are done on the earth. The usage of such phrases as "the work of God," "the hand of God," "God makes," and "time" are allusions to the reality of a sovereign plan controlling all human works.[16] The *poem of the times* in 3:1–7 chiefly teaches that everything that occurs in a human life happens according to the timing which God has determined. Without ambiguity, Qoheleth adheres to a worldview that maintains God's absolute sway over the affairs of humankind, so humans must take into account God's designs and purposes. Futility occurs whenever God's purposes undermine the purposes of humans, and when humans find themselves unable

---

14. Reines assumes that "happiness" is the point of Qoheleth's experiment: "Koheleth concludes that wealth does not provide the ultimate satisfaction and happiness . . . From the negative result of his 'experiment,' Koheleth proceeds directly to the positive conclusion that true happiness and joy is a gift of God." Reines, "Koheleth," 80–81.

15. Rudman, *Determinism*, 127.

16. Rudman convincingly argues that these phrases as well as "the deeds which are done under the sun" all refer to God's deterministic working in the world. Rudman, *Determinism*, chap 2.

to amend the purposes of God. A repeated area of human futility comes in the arena of discerning the works of God and future events. Though humans may boast of their plans, they have no ability to foresee or fulfill the best outcomes for their lives. The inability of humans to know God's purposes in life is a key reason for the futility of their work.

## Labor Gains

It would be easy to conclude that Qoheleth consistently views work negatively, however he enigmatically changes tack and speaks effusively over the positive benefits of labor. Beginning in the enjoyment refrain of 2:24–26 Qoheleth's tone towards the prospects of good rewards from labor changes, which begins an oscillating pattern of negative observation and positive advice. The unique feature of the enjoyment refrains is that God determines the reward from work. In these enjoyment passages instead of grief, pleasure becomes the norm, and instead of futility people experience success and happiness.

### *God Apportions*

In these positive passages the term "lot, portion" (*heleq*) features prominently, which can be defined in Ecclesiastes as the accrued benefits from labor given by God for a person to enjoy in life. The "portion" of benefits that a person earns in life is always seen as a gift from God.[17] In both enjoyment refrains, the "gift of God" refers to the material proceeds from one's work and the happiness that comes from enjoying those proceeds. The use of "gift" terminology reminds the reader that though they might have earned their income from hard work, it all ultimately comes from the hand of God. Qoheleth seeks to correct the erroneous thinking that assumes that competent work *guarantees* an equitable return. This type of thinking attributes all rewards to the effort of people without taking into account God's role in their disbursement. All the profitability of human labor is contingent upon the favor of God, so autonomous, self-reliant workers are living in a delusion.

---

17. Zimmerli remarks that "Man being quite unprotected must surrender to what is given him. That is the conclusion which the admonition of Ecclesiastes reaches. It is God who gives." Zimmerli, "Place and Limit," 157.

## Pleasurable Labor

Though it has been acknowledged that labor involves pain, it is not so readily observed that labor gives pleasure. Qoheleth's account of his royal accomplishments in 2:1–11 is a testament to the pleasure of work. This passage is often referred to as a hedonism or materialism experiment, but the whole enterprise is a colossal list of work projects. Drinking wine and amassing things and people (servants, singers, concubines) is what one would expect, yet his pleasure list begins with, "I did great works" (2:4). The extensive list of achievements and acquisitions were all aimed for obtaining pleasure, "I kept my heart from no *pleasure*" (2:10). And pleasure he did find, which was his "portion," for all his labor. In this epic enterprise of work no note of negativity is present in his labors.[18]

There is universal recognition by scholars of God's role in the experience of enjoyment in work and life. The primary positive benefit included within the "portion" and "gift" granted to people by God is enjoyment from work. In 2:26 the eating, drinking, and enjoyment from labor is "from the hand of God."[19] Qoheleth further elaborates that "apart from him" who can eat or "who can enjoy?" The enjoyment refrain of 5:18–20 credits God multiple times for the enjoyment experienced. Eating and drinking and finding enjoyment in work is "his lot." God gives a person "wealth and possessions" and he "gives the power" to do three actions: "to eat [partake of] them," "to accept his lot," and "to rejoice in his toil." These three enjoyable outcomes are "the gift of God."[20]

Qoheleth's view of enjoyment encompasses the process of labor and not just the enjoyment of its proceeds. Many commentators only allow for pleasure to be associated with the proceeds of labor, for they consider "labor" to be inherently displeasing.[21] When Qoheleth implores a person to enjoy "all the labor in which one labors" the whole process of work and rewards is in view. If joy is experienced in labor, then one need not infer from Qoheleth's critical observations of labor that *all* labor is inherently grievous.

---

18. See Foresti's comment on 2:4–10: "Note however, that here, in *'amal*, the idea of sorrow, pain is absent." Foresti, "Amal in Koheleth," 427.

19. Bartholomew writes, "Eating, drinking, and enjoying one's labor are furthermore here positively evoked as the gift of God and resonate with the goodness of creation as it is articulated in Gen 1 and 2." Bartholomew, *Ecclesiastes*, 151.

20. Gianto argues that "joy in the heart [is] a gift from God to help humankind face life's predicaments" caused by *hebel*. Gianto, "Theme of Enjoyment," 531.

21. Fox is a chief denier of work's enjoyment: "Qohelet does not preach the 'joy of labor.'" Fox, *Time*, 100.

It is possible, when accompanied by God's blessing, for the act of labor to be redeemed and attended with pleasure.

## Successful Work

It is logical to conclude that labor is profitable when it is not futile. Qoheleth considers work to be valuable when work achieves its purpose, so he applauds every scenario where a worker successfully completes tasks or obtains revenue from their work. Each of the enjoyment refrains and the admonition of 9:7–10 mention either "labor" or "work" as part of the commendable lifestyle given by God. The enjoyment they experience is related to the pleasure of fulfilled objectives. The successful yield from labor is a "good reward for toil" (4:9), as opposed to "toiling for the wind." Wisdom is applauded because it is instrumental in achieving successful results. Qoheleth recognizes that it is good when a person's works accomplish the goals set out before them—a success given by God.

Qoheleth deems the material proceeds of labor to be another key benefit from work. Qoheleth is not anti-materialistic and does not portray God as being anti-materialistic. God gives "wealth and possessions" in 5:19 and gives all that the "sinner" gathers to "the one who pleases him" (2:26). The enjoyment refrains consider the ownership of riches or possessions as part of the "portion" and "gift" from God. In contrast, no longer owning riches is considered a futile outcome. That the possession of wealth is considered a part of the "gift of God" should guard against those interpretations that champion spiritual values over against material values. Qoheleth's polemic is not aimed at material possessions *per se*, but at each scenario in which a person fails to attain the valid pleasures normally associated with the wealth. Qoheleth's affirmation of the value of the possessions of this world is the basis for his advocacy of enjoying them in the admonitions of 9:7–10 and 11:7–10. Within his perspective of blessed living, Qoheleth does not place the fear of God and the enjoyment of material possession in opposition. Rather, the necessary and valid enjoyment of material possessions is contingent upon God's blessing. In Ecclesiastes, vanity occurs every time people rely upon themselves, without the fear of God, in their pursuit of possessions and pleasures. Thus, one need not "hold in tension" fearing God and pursuing earthly gain. Instead, the two aims are held "hand in hand." Such an outlook can be a helpful perspective for the vast majority of people who are employed in "secular" profit-driven enterprises.

### Fear God

The recognition that God has absolute power to determine the course of a person's life and the outcomes of their labors should inspire the fear of him in people. Qoheleth explicitly states that the "fear of God" is the natural corollary to the recognition of his rule, "I perceived that whatever God does endures forever; nothing can be added to it nor anything taken from it. God has done it, *so that people fear before him*" (3:14). The "fear God" injunction refers to human recognition that God is in control of all that occurs in a person's life. This fear calls for the renunciation of self-reliance and hubris in relation to guiding one's life. Many scholars, however, do not interpret Qoheleth's use of the "fear God" phrase in a positive light. The reference to "fear" is often read in the negative sense of "terror" or "fright" before God, instead of reverence and trust.[22] There are good reasons to believe, however, that Qoheleth's descriptions of God's rule are intended to encourage his readers to trust in God. One can reasonably draw the inference from Qoheleth's observations and affirmations that God's rule is propitious toward those who fear him. If God gives wisdom, righteousness, joy, riches, possessions, and the opportunity to enjoy the fruit of one's labor, it is reasonable to trust in such a deity. Given that Qoheleth ends on a positive note about the prospects of labor and living in chapter 11, the reader should conclude that Qoheleth ultimately holds a positive attitude toward the possibilities of living a valuable life within the purposes of God.

## Conclusion

A credible reading of Ecclesiastes needs to equally appreciate Qoheleth's negative and positive perspectives to work. When Qoheleth declares that "all is vanity," he levels a judgment against the totality of this world's corruption as a result of the curses of Genesis 3. The maladies of ambition, overworking, covetousness, laziness, folly, and anxiety taint the whole "business" of work. Qoheleth questions the worth of work for he knows that all accomplishments have a short shelf life. Humans strive for worldly success for they imagine they will automatically derive happiness from it. Qoheleth observes the ironic tragedy that the success of work often does not engender

---

22. Crenshaw writes that Qoheleth's concept of "the fear of God comes close to terror before an unpredictable despot." Crenshaw, *Ecclesiastes*, 100. Longman refers to the fear as the "fright before a powerful and dangerous being, no respect or awe for a mighty and compassionate deity." And commenting on 3:14 he states that "God acts the way that he does to frighten people into submission." Longman, *Book of Ecclesiastes*, 36, 12.

such happiness. A major frustration of human living is that people cannot comprehend the course of events in life and are unable to control their own destiny due to God's sovereign rule.

The recognition of vanity in the world does not, however, rule out the possibility of people attaining true value and joy in life. Within his dialectical approach Qoheleth changes tack to reconstruct value from the debris of this world's vanity. The primary difference between the negative observations and the positive admonitions is that God confers the benefits of labor to individuals. Qoheleth asserts that all rewards from labor depend upon God's sovereign plans and not merely upon the competency of humans. He adjures people to "fear God" because all human purposes will falter apart from God's blessings. When God gives a "portion" of good things in life people experience success in labor, the enjoyment of this world's goods, and real happiness. People can affect their own happiness by embracing the rule of God over their lives, working with wisdom, and accepting all the enjoyable things that God has made available in life. These benefits from our labor form the partial mitigation of vanity of this world.

# Bibliography

Anderson, William H. U. "The Curse of Work in Qoheleth: An Expose of Ecclesiastes 3:17–19 in Ecclesiastes." *Evangelical Quarterly* 70, no. 2 (1998) 99–113.

Bartholomew, Craig G. *Ecclesiastes*. Baker Commentary on the OT Wisdom and Psalms. Grand Rapids: Baker Academic, 2009.

Brown, William P. "Whatever Your Hand Finds to Do: Qoheleth's Work Ethic." *Interpretation* 55 (2001) 271–84.

Crenshaw, James L. *Ecclesiastes*. OTL. Philadelphia: Westminster, 1987.

Dell, Katherine J. "Exploring Intertextual Links Between Ecclesiastes and Genesis 1–11." In *Interpreting Ecclesiastes: Readers Old and New*, edited by Katherine J. Dell, 3–13. Critical Studies in the Hebrew Bible 3. Winona Lake, IN: Eisenbrauns, 2013.

Diamond, A. R. Pete. "Anah." In *New International Dictionary of Old Testament Exegesis*, edited by Willem VanGemeran, 3:452–53. 5 vols. Grand Rapids: Zondervan, 1997.

Farmer, Kathleen A. *Proverbs and Ecclesiastes: Who Knows What Is Good?* ITC. Grand Rapids: Eerdmans, 1991.

Foresti, Fabrizio. "'Amal in Kohelet: 'Toil or Profit.'" *Ephemerides Carmeliticae* 31 (1980) 415–30.

Fox, Michael V. *A Time to Tear Down and a Time to Build Up: A Rereading of Ecclesiastes*. Grand Rapids: Eerdmans, 1999.

Fredericks, Daniel C. *Coping with Transience: Ecclesiastes on Brevity in Life*. The Biblical Seminar 18. Sheffield: JSOT Press, 1993.

Gianto, Agustinus. "The Theme of Enjoyment in Qohelet." *Biblica* 73 (1992) 528–32.

Ingram, Doug. *Ambiguity in Ecclesiastes*. LHBOTS 431. New York: T. & T. Clark, 2006.

Jong, Stephen de. "A Book on Labour: The Structuring Principles and the Main Theme of the Book of Qohelet." *Journal for the Study of the Old Testament* 54 (1992) 107–16.

Longman, Tremper, III. *The Book of Ecclesiastes*. NICOT. Grand Rapids: Eerdmans, 1998.

Mitchell, H. G. "'Work' in Ecclesiastes." *Journal of Biblical Literature* 32 (1913) 123–38.

Ogden, Graham S., and Lynell Zogbo. *A Handbook on Ecclesiastes*. UBS Handbook Series. New York: United Bible Societies, 1997.

Provan, Iain. "Fresh Perspectives on Ecclesiastes: 'Qohelet for Today.'" In *The Words of the Wise Are Like Goads: Engaging Qohelet in the 21st Century*, edited by Mark Boda, Tremper Longman, and Christian Rata, 401–16. Winona Lake, IN: Eisenbrauns, 2013.

Reines, C. W. "Koheleth on Wisdom and Wealth." *Journal of Jewish Studies* 5 (1954) 80–84.

Rudman, Dominic. *Determinism in the Book of Ecclesiastes*. JSOTSup 316. Sheffield: Sheffield Academic Press, 2001.

Seow, Choon-Leong. *Ecclesiastes*. AYB 18c. Yale: Doubleday, 1997.

Thompson, David "Amal." In *New International Dictionary of Old Testament Exegesis*, edited by Willem VanGemeran, 3:435–37. 5 vols. Grand Rapids: Zondervan, 1997.

Zimmerli, Walther. "The Place and Limit of the Wisdom in the Framework of the Old Testament Theology." *Scottish Journal of Theology* 17 (1964) 146–58.

# 12

# Hegel and Vocation

*Beyond a Sacred–Secular Divide*

SARAH BACALLER

*Western Sydney University*

*Stirling Theological College,
University of Divinity*

## Abstract

THIS CHAPTER ASKS WHETHER the use of an oppositional hermeneutic in positing sacred and secular realms is helpful for Christian self-understanding, particularly in the narratives used within contemporary Christian communities. It explores potential dynamics and implications present in making use of such a point of reference through three theological forays, which draw on the work of G. W. F. Hegel. These forays consider first, the role of demarcation and distinction in understanding identity; second, the way in which a christological lens (here considering Christ as both fulfillment and end of law) is able to move Christian thought beyond an oppositional stance toward the secular; and third, the way in which Hegel's understanding of objective right (as part of his tripartite understanding of self-knowing spirit) illuminates the role of secular social structures in human life, thereby highlighting the importance of Christian engagement beyond sacred–secular dualities. By reworking particular conceptual boundaries and by gently addressing tacit anxieties that diminish the secular by contrast to the sacred, this piece seeks to encourage vocational commitment and aspiration as an expression of shared striving toward human flourishing.

## Sketch Lines

Christian identity has the potential to give particular focus and passion to life, as shaped by values inherent within its christological narrative: hope and freedom, grace and veracity, and all their redemptive possibilities. When Christian identity is interpreted and articulated by reference to a sacred–secular divide—that is, when it is understood as underpinned by an implicit opposition between sacred and secular—it is worth reflecting on the tonalities and attitudes present in such narratives. What are their implicit presuppositions and impending consequences? How is Christian self-understanding and experience shaped by this point of reference?

The demarcation of the sacred from the secular has been a dramatic locus of contest in Western history. Augustine's distinction between the *civitas Dei* (City of God) and the *civitas terrena* (or *diabolia*) is significant as an expression of Christian consciousness, prefacing any use of the term "secular" as we know it today.[1] According to Ebeling, this hermeneutic influenced the development of two significant streams in medieval thought.[2] First, it fortified the notion of an unfolding historical-eschatological battle between God (so also, God's people, the church) and God's opponent(s). Second, it involved the class-type distinction between clergy and laity, which suggested a further distinction between religious and non-religious authorities within the wider realm of Christ's kingdom.[3] These distinctions held significant social implications.

Martin Luther offered a dexterous response to various challenges raised within this milieu. Luther argued that religious authorities were accountable to secular authorities, who nevertheless were under God.[4] Of the distinction between clerical vocations as spiritual, and non-clerical vocations as temporal or profane (with the *spiritual–temporal* distinction carrying similar connotations to the later *sacred–secular* terminology), Luther wrote: "It is pure invention that pope, bishops, priests, and monks are to be called the 'spiritual estate'; princes, lords, artisans, and farmers

---

1. Augustine, *City of God*, esp. book 19; Ebeling, *Luther*, 178–79.
2. Ebeling, *Luther*, 175–91, esp. 179.
3. Ebeling, *Luther*, 178–79, 183–85.
4. Luther, "Temporal Authority."

the 'temporal estate.' That is indeed a fine bit of lying and hypocrisy."[5] Luther variously affirms secular (temporal, profane) life for its essential role in human life and society.

As the shockwaves of the Reformation emanated from their various European epicenters, the ongoing tensions between church and state were central to significant world events of the sixteenth to eighteenth centuries—including, for example, the French Revolution, the English civil wars amid the tumultuous English Reformation, the flight of the Pilgrims and the colonization of New England, and the Declaration of Independence. These events represent important attempts to clarify the relationship between sacred and secular structures, in seeking appropriate sources and loci of authority and social cohesion. It was, in some senses, the affirmation of the equality (and necessity) of the two realms before God (as per Luther) that conceptually underpinned their separation.

The genealogy of the terms *secular* and *secularism* are also worth considering. The Latin term *saeculum* initially referred to fixed time periods and was not necessarily understood by reference to religion.[6] The term *secularism*, with its contemporary connotations as a non-religious ethical approach to life, seems first to have been used by Holyoake in the mid-nineteenth century in Britain, in preference to the term *atheism*.[7] In this sense, it holds anti-religious connotations. Holyoake became a staunch proponent of secularism and developed the idea extensively in his periodical *The Reasoner* and in later publications.[8] Definitions of the term "secular" developed in early English dictionaries from the beginnings of the eighteenth century, and include its contrast to the "spiritual," or "eternal" (being grouped with synonyms such as "worldly").[9] Zuckerman notes the broadness of the current concept of the *secular*; the term involves much terminological slippage.[10]

Attitudes, emotions, and ideas regarding the self, faith, and the world affect the daily lived experience of vocation and work. The question this chapter seeks to address is whether a notion of Christian identity, as existing within the *sacred* as resistance to the *secular*, is consistent with Christology. It is not an uncommon attitude to encounter within Protestant language and

---

5. Luther, *Open Letter*; Taylor, *Secular Age*, 55.
6. Weinstock, *Divus Julius*, 191–97; Taylor, *Secular Age*, 54–55.
7. Zuckerman and Shook, "Introduction," 2–4.
8. Holyoake, *Reasoner*; *Principles of Secularism*; see also Zuckerman and Shook, "Introduction," 2–5.
9. Zuckerman and Shook, "Introduction," 5–7.
10. Zuckerman and Shook, "Introduction," 1–21.

worship, even if it is subtle or implicit as an elevation of the religious by devaluation of the secular. It is this oppositionality and mutually exclusive conceptualization, particularly within communities of faith, that is addressed by this discussion. Is the opposition able to bear the weight of self-understanding that lies upon it? Is this an approach to Christian identity that enables human communities and individuals to flourish?[11]

I will explore the possibility that it is not, and why this is so, without eliminating, but rather by attempting to both integrate and overcome, the distinction whereby one is defined by reference to the other. In a sense, the Reformation distinction between sacred and secular authorities, and the historical division between church and state, are wholly affirmed; the goal is not to return to an imagined pre-divided state, but rather, the question is how to enable Christian communities to integrate this distinction and move beyond an oppositional stance.

To do this, I will draw on the work of G. W. F. Hegel to resource three exploratory theological forays. These forays are not an attempt to present doctrinal formulations, but rather are heuristic in exploring the unfolding implications of dualistically structured subjectivity; they attempt to surmount emerging implications by widening the frame. The aim of this is to expand and resource Christian self-understanding for wholehearted engagement toward human flourishing, both individually and collectively, with a particular focus on the implications of this for experiences of work and vocation.

## Identity by Negation

Is Christian identity confirmed by an ability to tick boxes of belief, behavior, and even belonging, within whichever paradigms and Christian narratives happen to be contingently present or idiosyncratically authoritative?[12] This caricature may be denied, but it is fed by linguistic cultures that narrate Christian identity as staunchly opposed to or distinct from secular life.

Identity requires distinction; this is clear.[13] But what makes anything *Christian* in distinction from anything else? Does Christian identity

---

11. Taylor uses "human flourishing" as an organizing conceptual structure in *A Secular Age*. More recently, the concept is significant in Miroslav Volf. See Volf, *Flourishing*; Volf and Croasmun, *Life of the World*.

12. Marshall, "Behavior," 360–80 provides a genealogy of the "belief, belonging and behavior" paradigm as shorthand for the sociological schematization of religious experience, as does Abby Day in *Believing in Belonging*, 3–27. This paradigm has proliferated within literature addressing Christian experience, though not always with reference to its sociological roots.

13. That is, *identity* as per selfhood, not sameness.

boil down to declarative beliefs, cultural traditions and rites, moral high ground, a particular lexicon, a perceived spiritual impartation, or a presumed afterlife trajectory?

Prescriptive and authoritative corralling of Christian thought and behavior (perhaps, for example, by Christian leaders) suggests anxiety as to identity and uncertainty regarding definition. If, christologically, the *law is written on human hearts*, where exactly is this and what is written?[14] Who is *in*, and who isn't? Who can be trusted, and who can't? And who decides? These questions, though crudely posed, express crucial and existential human concerns that underpin relationality and social cohesion.

Tacit and explicit lines of demarcation between sacred and secular may be invoked as useful markers for Christian communities, to define what falls acceptably within the range of "Christian" and what does not—if "Christian" is equated with what is trustworthy or true. Yet such demarcations can perpetuate the anxiety they seek to allay, by supposing that one could fall off the edge of Christian identity, or perhaps not quite be Christian enough (is my job "more Christian" than yours?).[15] It is not difficult, in such circumstances, for perceived transgression to become a source of anxious attention. The question is whether Christian identity by reference to a binary opposition between sacred and secular, easily fueled by angst, is (christo) logically feasible, and whether it contributes to the health and flourishing of communities of faith and individuals—or whether it diminishes these. This question is as ethical as it is philosophical-theological.

What function do Christian behavioral or belief markers fulfill? Significantly, they limit or demarcate. Demarcation (Hegel's negation) is not negative in a diminishing or punitive sense; without demarcation, nothing is what it is.[16] The Gestalt principle of figureground demonstrates this; limit allows us to break up a field of vision into its various elements, even if the relationship between these is not simply black and white.

Hegel's *determinate negation* describes how any *thing* is what it is only by contrast to what it is not, but in particular (so determinately), by contrast

---

14. See Jer 31:33–34; Matt 22:34–40; Rom 2; and Heb 8:10.

15. "For what the law was powerless to do . . ." (Rom 8). See Slavoj Žižek on the "vicious dialectic" of law and sin: *Fragile Absolute*, 136–38; *Trouble in Paradise*, 99–101. My assertion here is also underpinned by a recognition that physiologically, constant threat, anxiety or trauma can inhibit the formation of narratival identity and cohesive self-understanding, as well as the capacity for the human mind (and so, body) to *learn* beyond and within its context.

16. This is a pervasive Hegelian motif, transposed into various keys throughout his works. See specifically Hegel, *Lectures on Logic*, 103–5; *Science of Logic* (regarding demarcation of finite and infinite), 101, 111–12, 114. Also Inwood, *Hegel Dictionary*, 199–202.

to what it *might* be if it were not itself.[17] Any *thing*'s potential negations are therefore differentiations that are related to it but distinct from it. In Hegel's dialectic, negation is in turn negated, as elevation incorporates previous negation—so *aufheben*, often translated as *sublation*, which both cancels and preserves the moment of distinction in expansion.[18] This movement occurs in diverse ways through human engagement with phenomena and is, Hegel argues, central to the development of human consciousness as particularly *human* consciousness, *self-consciousness*.[19] For Hegel, it also represents a deep logical (Trinitarian) structure that is crucial to the generative relation between the infinite and the finite.[20]

What, then, occurs in the differentiation between *sacred* and *secular*? Once this demarcation (or mutual negation) has been made, it cannot simply disappear. Yet to limit Christian identity to a sacred *versus* secular stance is to remain in "one-sided understanding" in our grasp of the relation between the infinite and finite.[21] The challenge is to preserve and transcend the distinction without violence and opposition, yet without sinking into an undifferentiated soup of non-distinction.[22]

## Internal Resources

To think beyond this opposition, the resources for surmounting it perhaps most effectively come from within. The opposition can of course become violently unstable; sacred and secular can negate one another to death—as can competing claims to sanctity within a religious tradition.[23] If Christian

---

17. "As separated, they are just as much essentially *connected* with each other, through the very negation that divides them." Hegel, *Science of Logic*, 111.

18. For expositions, see Inwood, *Hegel Dictionary*, 283–85; Pinkard, *Hegel's Naturalism*; *Legacy of Idealism*.

19. Especially Hegel, *Philosophy of Mind*; *Phenomenology*.

20. Hodgson, "Introduction," esp. 11–12, 14; Williams, *Proofs and Personhood*. Williams argues that Hegel moves beyond binary dogmatism and skepticism by developing both a philosophical and theological Trinitarianism.

21. Hegel, *Science of Logic*, 117, 120; *Philosophy of Religion*, 405, 412, 424 (but also pervasive).

22. On love as unity that presupposes distinction see Hegel, *Philosophy of Religion*, 418.

23. Hegel, *Science of Logic*: "The progress to infinity is therefore only repetitious monotony, the one and the same tedious *alternation* of this finite and infinite," 113; "The spectacle of this alternation, this infinite progression, occurs wherever one remains fixated on the contradiction of the unity of two determinations and of their *opposition*," 120; 101–27 are highly pertinent.

identity is Christocentric, this central idea of Christian faith might provide tools for surmounting the contradiction.

Christ as the central figure of Christian faith is a model of distinction without violence. The following example demonstrates how religious law, as a marker of definition, can be raised from a potentially simplistic opposition or dualism, into a nuanced, relationally flexible ethic. Think specifically in relation to the superseding of the Jewish law, a social and religious structure that Christ claims not to eliminate, but to fulfill; using a Hegelian motif, we can say that Christ sublates (*aufheben*) previous tradition.[24] One expression of this occurs in the Sermon on the Mount, where Jesus repeatedly says, "You have heard it said, but I say unto you . . . ."[25] Particular religious demarcations are demonstrated already to have been *negated*—they are thrown into relief—by Christ as fulfillment and end (*telos*) of law.[26] Such statements do not eliminate previous law (see vv. 17–20), but raise engagement into a wider frame of reference, while sharpening its subjective focus.[27]

Christ's oratory highlights the axiological (value) structures and interpretive space inherent in frameworks of definition, which are never as simplistic as they seem, and which must dance dialectically with relational epistemologies of human existence. This dynamic is present in many gospel scenarios, as for example, the woes to the Pharisees and the enunciation of the Greatest Commandment.[28] Understandings of selfhood and community are both preserved and cancelled as the politics of belonging are raised into a higher frame by which they are newly defined in their christologically altered context.[29] As written on human hearts, christological identity invites responsibility, existing in the social "space of reason," volition, and intentionality.[30] This opens space in perceived divine immutability for ethical reflection and human responsibility; believers throughout the New

---

24. Matt 5:17–20.

25. Matt 5.

26. Jaeschke, "Christianity and Secularity," 133–36.

27. On moving beyond law as externally valid, to its being "rationally valid" and internal: Hegel, *Philosophy of Religion*, 394–95; 404–13, 481–89. Freedom is made actual in human life by the concrete resolution of the opposition between the finite and infinite.

28. Matt 22, 23; Luke 11.

29. Rom 10. *Aufheben* (sublation) is the "negation of negation" pivotal to Hegel's dialectic.

30. Thus, it surpasses "immutable law"; see Hegel, *Philosophy of Religion*, 374–75. On the "space of reason," see Pinkard, *Hegel's Naturalism*.

Testament face precisely this challenge in the wrestle to interpret an altered relation to previous markers of identity.[31]

To extrapolate, a dualistic stance of Christian identity toward the secular must move beyond oppositionality that relies on binary distinctions, to a wider frame of reference—not a mere transposition of *a more absolute version of law's absoluteness*, but a creative reframing that affirms humanity's unique capacity to *think* situationally, develop practical wisdom, and engage in the development of ethical communities.[32] This occurs through dialectical thought that experiences the sublation of the divine and finite into an expanded finitude (and so, an expanded *infinitude* too).[33] For Hegel, ethical positioning is organic in its potentiality, yet must be intentionally developed as ethical nature, "a second nature"—reborn, not of flesh (i.e., nature) but of spirit, preserving and yet raising nature by volitional agency and development of skill and wisdom.[34] "It is in the ethical realm that the reconciliation of religion with worldliness and actuality comes about and is accomplished."[35] Vocation, as an expression of commitment, responsibility, aspiration, and even passion, offers incessant possibilities for complex thinking, discernment of wisdom, and ethical development.

The implications of this for Christian foci, language, and praxis are significant. Forward movement requires interpretative spaces that move beyond binary thinking, and that involve education, skill development, and relational learning. Rethinking Christian language that is anxious or oppositional toward engagement with our world is a significant step which may invoke the reconfiguration of theological constellations, or core values and commitments, that previously structured the self-understanding of communities and individuals. [36] Yet to resist this challenge is to miss a marvelous, if unnerving, adventure.

---

31. Hegel, *Philosophy of Religion*, 374–75. Bubbio posits relinquishment of an absolute perspective as the crux of Christian sacrifice. See Bubbio, *God and the Self; Sacrifice*.

32. Rom 2; Hegel, *Philosophy of Religion*, 373–75, 395–96, 405–6; Pinkard, *Hegel's Naturalism*.

33. Bubbio, *God and the Self*; Hegel, *Philosophy of Religion*, 404–13; Hodgson, "Introduction," 11–14; Hammer, "Theorist of Secularization."

34. Hegel, *Phenomenology*, 466–67; *Philosophy of Mind*, 130–41; *Philosophy of Religion*, 391–489; *Philosophy of Right*, 26–28, 159–60.

35. Hegel, *Philosophy of Religion*, 484. Also Jaeschke, "Christianity and Secularity," 135.

36. Hegel, *Philosophy of Right*, 159.

## Selfhood in Three Parts

The process of self-conscious life's maturation is traced in Hegel's philosophy as the development of *Geist*—that is, *spirit* or *mind* as restless and always moving. This *spirit*, in human expression within individual bodies and collectively, is shaped in three modes.

These are: first, *subjective mind*, in which the movement of existence is traced from immediacy or immediate sensuous experience, through its various stages to self-conscious thought; second, *objective mind* (or *right*), as the social structures, from family through civil society to state, which concretize identity; and third, *absolute mind* (or *spirit*), in which humans seek to understand themselves through art, religion, and self-reflexive, critical thought (philosophy).[37]

Humans strive toward self-conscious interpretation so that what they are in themselves becomes present for them, akin to the process of subconscious thought moving into conscious articulation. This process of *becoming* shapes what it is that is becoming. Hegel's recognition of the role of sociality in shaping the self in this triunity is significant. In the realm of objective mind, freedom is actualized both in and beyond laws, in customs, social practice, and interpersonal interaction.[38] Hegel recognizes the self as shaped by these structures just as, dialectically, these structures are shaped by human life. Particular communities of tradition and custom are not superior by reference to *sacred* status; phenomenologically, human life simply exists as shaped by the communities, customs, and accountabilities to which it belongs. Nothing is immune to critical reflection as sacred or absolute (even critical reflection itself); life must be observed and reflected upon.[39] For Hegel, it is the recognitive processes in these structures that are significant for humanity; these mark the progress of freedom.[40] This invokes responsibility for shaping social structures that affirm human dignity, shifting the focus from self-protective tribalism between purportedly sacred and secular contexts, to cooperatively resourcing human flourishing.[41]

---

37. On 1, 2, and 3: Hegel, *Philosophy of Mind*; on 2: *Philosophy of Right*.

38. Hegel, *Philosophy of Mind*, 217–56; *Philosophy of Right*, 155–323.

39. Hegel, *Philosophy of World History*; *Philosophy of Religion*.

40. Hegel, *Phenomenology*; *Philosophy of Right* (242–56 on church and state); Honneth, *Struggle for Recognition*; Pinkard, *Hegel's Naturalism*.

41. Clive Marsh also argues for human flourishing as the criterion for judging christological narratives. What this flourishing is, is of course shaped by the christological stories themselves; but it is also fluid and contextual and is therefore always being developed and discovered by dialectical movement with christological anchorage. Marsh, *Christ in Focus*, esp. 187–218.

Relational recalibration is always occurring in micro- and macro-movements within families, societies, nations, and global communities, even if the methods for social change lean problematically toward lawful circumscription, while attempts to inaugurate enhanced freedom might miss the mark. Yet self-reflexive Christian discernment within secular involvement, within which work and vocation are a major expression, cannot fully occur without incarnationally affirmed, relaxed engagement in secular life—as a gift, affirmed by a gospel given for the world.[42]

Again to extrapolate: if narratives of Christian selfhood problematize the phenomenological reality of personhood being shaped through the social and secular structures we inhabit, or if these structures are thoughtlessly or intentionally demonized, even subtly or unintentionally, human life can become torn between a very real need to engage in its social contexts and a sense of compromise in doing so. Secular engagement taints a misperceived purity of Christian identity—think for example, of a young medical student who is driven to alleviate human suffering, but who meaningfully belongs to a Christian community where her passion or vocation is subtly narrated as inferior to that of the young minister; where attempts are made to dissect her motives into pure and profane; where there is suspicion of secular frameworks and education systems; where the time poured into training or study is seen as inferior to specially religious practices or activities; or indeed where there is fear to engage critically in the sorts of significant complex moral dilemmas facing those who work in medicine (of course, this becomes the challenge of self-determination).[43] By resenting engagement in these social structures, such narratives undermine the very social fabric that has the capacity to interweave human community (i.e. objective right), fragmenting the impetus toward christological transformation of human social existence.

It is not to say that such structures do not need reform or that these cultures are necessarily healthy, or that such engagement does not require discernment, but rather that progress is less likely to occur through suspicion, anxious withdrawal, or oppositional positioning.[44] These might also inhibit critical reflection, which requires genuine, trusting, and intelligent engagement in secular life, and a willingness to hold in vulnerability various tensions. If secular social structures are an important facet of human identity, dualistic defensiveness misses opportunities to recognize and assimilate the

---

42. For strong textures on this theme, see Ebeling, *Nature of Faith*; *Theological Theory*.

43. On renunciation of purity, see Bonhoeffer, "Nature of the Church," 86–87; *Reflections*, 91, 95–96.

44. Hegel, *Philosophy of Right*, 242–55.

helpful aspects of recognition (whether legal, social, or creative) afforded by social structures. Inversely, this missed opportunity perpetuates an undercurrent of pressure toward Christian "colonization" of the secular.

Human life at every level of social organization is complex. Interpreting problems and striving toward redemptive actualities requires contextual, deft responsiveness, and perpetual learning. In Christ, a new horizon of human dignity and affirmation within finitude is painted; we must therefore both engage with and think beyond the current state of social structures, recognizing their vital role in shaping human self-understanding and their degrees of compromise, working to reshape them for greater human flourishing by ethical, responsible engagement. Gospel, as given for the world, is given to form social worlds that shape human life through recognitive social structures.

## Conclusion

The secular is already a shared space where infinite and finite dialectically exist together; this is the logic of incarnation.[45] Precisely here, Christian identity cannot rely on arbitrary claims of sacredness to affirm its validity, whether dogmatically or subjectively. Understanding what it is to be Christian is an ongoing wrestle, and includes taking responsibility for the norms created within Christian communities. So, while forward movement may include the loss or sacrifice of previously perceived identity markers, bastions of defense, or interpretative tools, this loss becomes gain as those committed to a Christian stance in the world—to the affirmation of human dignity and the coming-to-be of redemptive possibilities—are affirmed in their vocations.[46] Vocation, as an expression of responsibility, commitment, aspiration, and passion, can be celebrated.

A christological ethos works to transform any space to be life-giving, even as the understanding of what is "life-giving" must be constantly reevaluated and weighed. By engagement with various motifs of Hegelian thought, the process of thinking Christian vocation is resourced and expanded to affirm immediate subjective experience, sociality, and civic interaction, and the role of norms in shaping identity in an ethos of distinctively Christian engagement in the world—all of which leads to an expanded ability to interpret, inhabit, and work within something more than a sacred–secular divide.

---

45. Hegel, "Consummate Religion," in *Philosophy of Religion*, 391–489.
46. Hegel, *Philosophy of Religion*, 481–83; *Philosophy of Right*, 244–47.

# Bibliography

Altizer, Thomas J. J. *The Gospel of Christian Atheism*. London: HarperCollins, 1966.
Augustine, Saint. *City of God*. London: Penguin, 2004.
Bubbio, Paolo Diego. *God and the Self in Hegel: Beyond Subjectivism*. Albany, NY: State University of New York Press, 2017.
———. *Sacrifice in the Post-Kantian Tradition: Perspectivism, Intersubjectivity, and Recognition*. Albany, NY: State University of New York Press, 2014.
Bonhoeffer, Dietrich. "The Nature of the Church (Summer 1932)." In *A Testament to Freedom: The Essential Writings of Dietrich Bonhoeffer*, edited by G. B. Kelly and F. Burton Nelson, 82–87. New York: HarperOne, 1995.
———. *Reflections on the Bible: Human Word and Word of God*. Edited by Manfred Weber and translated by M. Eugene Boring. Peabody, MA: Hendrickson, 2004.
Butler Bass, Diana. *Christianity after Religion: The End of the Church and the Birth of a New Spiritual Awakening*. New York: Harper Collins, 2017.
Day, Abby. *Believing in Belonging: Belief and Social Identity in the Modern World*. Oxford: Oxford University Press, 2011.
Ebeling, Gerhard. *Luther: An Introduction to His Thought*. Minneapolis: Fortress, 2007.
———. *Introduction to a Theological Theory of Language*. Translated by R. A. Wilson. London: Collins, 1973.
———. *The Nature of Faith*. Translated by Ronald Gregor Smith. London: Collins, 1961.
Hammer, Espen. "Hegel as a Theorist of Secularization." *Hegel Bulletin* 34, no. 2 (October 2013) 223–44.
Hegel, Georg Wilhelm Friedrich. *Encyclopedia of the Philosophical Sciences in Basic Outline, Part 1: Science of Logic (1817)*. Translated and edited by Klaus Brinkmann and Daniel O. Dahlstrom. Cambridge: Cambridge University Press, 2015.
———. *G. W. F. Lectures on Logic, Berlin 1831*. Transcribed by Karl Hegel. Translated by Clark Butler. Bloomington, IN: Indiana University Press, 2008.
———. *Lectures on the Philosophy of Religion, One Volume Edition: The Lectures of 1827*. Edited by Peter C. Hodgson. Oxford: Oxford University Press, 2007.
———. *Lectures on the Philosophy of World History*. Translated by Hugh Barr Nisbet. Cambridge: Cambridge University Press, 2002.
———. *Outlines of the Philosophy of Right*. Translated by T. M. Knox. Oxford: Oxford University Press 2008.
———. *Phenomenology of Spirit*. Translated by A. V. Miller. Oxford: Oxford University Press, 1977.
———. *Philosophy of Mind: A Revised Version of the Wallace and Miller Translations*. Translated by W. Wallace and A. V. Miller. Oxford: Oxford University Press, 2010.
———. *The Science of Logic*. Translated and edited by George di Giovanni. Cambridge, UK: Cambridge University Press, 2010.
Hodgson, Peter C, ed. "Introduction." In *Lectures on the Philosophy of Religion: One Volume Edition: The Lectures of 1827*, 1–71. Oxford: Oxford University Press, 2007.
Holyoake, G. J. *The Principles of Secularism*. London: Austin & Co., 1871.
———. *The Reasoner*. Vols. XIII and XIV. London: J. Watson, 1852, 1853.
Honneth, Axel. *The Struggle for Recognition: The Moral Grammar of Social Conflicts*. Oxford, UK: Polity, 1996.

Inwood, Michael. *A Hegel Dictionary*. The Blackwell Philosophers Dictionaries. Massachusetts: Blackwell, 1992.

Jaeschke, Walter. "Christianity and Secularity in Hegel's Concept of the State." *Journal of Religion* 61, no. 2 (April 1981) 127–45.

Luther, Martin. "Temporal Authority: To What Extent It Should Be Obeyed." In *Martin Luther's Basic Theological Writings*, edited by William R. Russell, 428–55. 3rd ed. Minneapolis: Fortress, 2012.

———. "To the Christian Nobility of the German Nation Concerning the Improvement of the Christian Estate (1520)". In *The Annotated Luther Vol. 1: The Roots of Reform*, edited by Timothy J. Wengert et al., 376–466. Minneapolis: Fortress, 2015.

Juergensmeyer, Mark. "The Imagined War between Secularism and Religion." In *The Oxford Handbook of Secularism*, edited by Phil Zuckerman and John R. Shook, 71–84. New York: Oxford University Press, 2017.

Marshall, Douglas A. "Behaviour, Belonging and Belief: A Theory of Ritual Practice." *Sociological Theory* 20, no. 3 (November 2002) 360–80.

Marsh, Clive. *Christ in Focus: Radical Christocentrism in Christian Theology*. London, UK: SCM, 2013.

Pinkard, Terry. *Hegel's Naturalism: Mind, Nature, and the Final Ends of Life*. New York: Oxford University Press, 2012.

Volf, Miroslav. *Flourishing: Why We Need Religion in a Globalized World*. New Haven: Yale University Press, 2015.

Volf, Miroslav, and Michael Croasmun. *For the Life of the World: Theology that Makes a Difference*. Grand Rapids: Brazos, 2019.

Weinstock, Stefan. *Divus Julius*. Oxford: Clarendon, 1971.

Williams, Robert. *Hegel on the Proofs and Personhood of God: Studies in Hegel's Logic and Philosophy of Religion*. New York: Oxford University Press, 2017.

Žižek, Slavoj. *The Fragile Absolute or Why is the Christian Legacy Worth Fighting For?* London: Verso, 2000.

———. *Trouble in Paradise: From the End of History to the End of Capitalism*. UK: Penguin, 2015.

Zuckerman, Phil, and John R. Shook. "Introduction: The Study of Secularism." In *The Oxford Handbook of Secularism*, edited by Stephen Bullivant and Michael Ruse, 114. New York: Oxford University Press, 2017.

# 13

# Encountering Subjectivity

*Terry Eagleton and the Tax Collector's Embodied Vocation*

### Sam Curkpatrick

*Stirling Theological College, University of Divinity*

## Abstract

VOCATION CONCERNS SELF-UNDERSTANDING AS individuals and communities addressed by God, called into new possibilities for life lived before God. In contemporary Australian society, work, relationships, aspirations, the use of time, and ethical concerns are commonly negotiated topographies of vocation. Luke's parable of the Pharisee and tax collector (Luke 18:9–14) illustrates contrasting trajectories of vocation through two distinct characterizations: a religious expert and a government lackey are juxtaposed, and one is declared righteous. This parable is ironic, inverting expectations regarding secular and profane occupation, while encouraging humility in discovering God's possibilities for life.

Terry Eagleton's ethics (*Trouble with Strangers*, 2009) provides a useful frame for unpacking the divergent trajectories of the Pharisee and tax collector, through the categories of the *imaginary*, *symbolic*, and *real* (after Lacan). The Pharisee's self-confident understanding of vocation is mediated through imaginary and symbolic concerns, which suggest vocation as intrinsically linked to an occupational role, religious affiliation, and duty. This identity is self-cultivated and differentiated as sacred, buffered from everyday entanglements of human experience. Drawn away from everyday situations (he stood by himself to pray), the Pharisee's vocation is demarcated and sustained through symbolic and imaginary practices (temple, tithing, law, and so forth).

In contrast, vocation for the tax collector begins in an honest acquiesce to human limitations and contradictions, and a *real* encounter with himself as fractured and strange. Here, Christian identity is not substantiated by religious representations. The vocation of the tax collector does not begin in a cultivated identity or negotiated duties, but an encounter with God *in the flesh*. Similarly, for Eagleton, it is our vulnerable, compromised bodies—the characteristic mode of being in the world—which preface tangible expressions of meaning within human experience and love.

Luke's parable is open-ended: that the tax collector *went home justified* suggests the ongoing discovery of vocation within perennial compromises and resistances of work, relationships, time, ethics, and aspiration. As a calling *into* situation and the secular engagements of human bodies, Christian vocation will be relevant to its christological impetus and contemporary expression, where it fosters genuine relationality by veracious testimony to embodied presence.

*He told this parable to some who trusted in themselves.*

## Vocation and Self-Understanding

If there is an implicit link between vocation and subjectivity, what kind of subjectivity is in focus? That is, how do we understand ourselves in relation to our passions and activities in life? Reciprocally, the outworking of vocation is readily shaped by an individual's understanding of self, as they conceive of life lived before God and in relation to others. Questions of subjectivity and vocation are intrinsically linked.

Contemporary understandings of vocation emphasize a concern for life lived authentically, and the expression of self through work and activity, aspirations, and ethical considerations.[1] On this view, vocation becomes a language for exploring and articulating self-understanding. Differing registers of subjectivity might be emphasized: the subject could be imagined through the representations an individual makes of themselves, as in the

---

1. This is a secular view of vocation, extending from the reformation impetus to broaden vocation beyond a professional religious role or office. Dawson, "History of Vocation," 220–31; Stackhouse, "Vocation."

title someone uses, such as Reverend or Doctor, the biography they submit to a conference program, or the hashtags they append to online posts. Or subjectivity could be located within a network of social interactions, expectations, and responsibilities. For example, the expression of a vocation through a career as a police officer or nurse, with a sense of duty or responsibility to the community or to the sick. Even the identification of an individual's unique "gifting" is necessarily manifest through cultural and institutional frameworks, structuring behavior and shaping an individual's trajectory through life. These approaches to vocation concern the positive definition of human identity and purpose.

Subjectivity is often framed by vocation as a project of self-definition. Vocation provides an individual with a certain assuredness, a narrative that frames their identities and behavior. However, vocation is more than these outward forms of representation and interaction and it poses a risk that a person understands themselves and their possibilities in life only through their projects and activities, which are themselves limited by society and culture, expectation, and imagination.

In contemporary understandings of vocation, subjectivity is typified by outward forms, in the way we work and what we do, our aspirations, our use of time, our relationships within communities, and the ethical considerations we make. Exploring these characteristics of vocation, Sara James has undertaken extensive interviews with Melbournians around narratives of self-identity, work, and meaning. James begins with the observation that work has become increasingly fragmented in modernity. Faced with the insecurity of employment and transience of careers, "the contemporary self must be reflexively made amongst a vast array of possibilities."[2] James's approach emphasizes subjectivity defined through outward forms of life such as work as "a vehicle for expressing one's authenticity." "Calling" is the cohesive, long-term narrative that offsets fragmentation and anxiety, substantiating identity and purpose through work and activity. Similarly, sociologist Giuseppe Giordan sees vocation as a means "to go beyond the provisional nature of the present moment," to give "existence a framework of significance," and to provide the subject with purpose against the contingencies of experience.[3]

These views understand vocation as a means of gauging and expressing subjectivity through work and activity. James's observations, that for most participants in her study "a vocation is not seen as duty to which one

---

2. James, *Making a Living*, 36. James's use of "reflexive" suggests an identity that is self-defined, rather than defined by what it comes up against. Cf. James, "Finding your Passion."

3. Giordan, "Introduction," 7.

must submit, but a pursuit that inspires passionate enthusiasm," emphasizes a positive correspondence between expressions of vocation and self. Thus, vocation *is* a sense of fulfillment, fit and purpose in what one does and seeks, and is decidedly *not* what is confronting, difficult or perplexing.[4] In what might be considered a definition of religion as a means of assuaging anxiety, James indicates the benefits of the "vocation myth," which can create hope for those depressed by their circumstances in life, creating meaning and purpose in the face of contingency.[5]

But do self-woven narratives of vocation provide satisfactory or enduring resolution to the anxieties and dislocations of reality? Luke's parable of the Pharisee and tax collector (Luke 18:9–14) seems to suggest otherwise. The parable is told "to some who trusted in themselves," for whom vocation is expressed through seemingly cohesive narratives of religious identity and behavior. The parable challenges the definition of subjectivity through such outward forms, instead showing vocation to be an encounter with compromised subjectivity. In contrast to the Pharisee's cultivated religious identity, the tax collector of the parable recognizes the real limitations and resistances of human context, capacity, and imagination. His encounter with self and God begins in humility and the capitulation of any self-assured vocational narrative. A view to the contrasting registers of vocation in this parable can be further enhanced with reference to Terry Eagleton's work on ethics. Eagleton's focus on the limitations of *imaginary* and *symbolic* approaches to ethics preface a Christian view of vocation, in which subjectivity is encountered through the loss of self-assuredness, and amid the confronting or perplexing contingences of life.

## The Pharisee's Self-Assured Vocation

In Luke's parable (18:9–14), the Pharisee and tax collector live before God and among others in distinct ways. The Pharisee's vocation is self-assured, as a religious expert whose life and actions are defined by expressions of temple, tithing, and Torah. At the end of the parable, he remains in the temple, distanced from others. In contrast, for the tax collector whose occupation seems disreputable, vocation begins in humility, in recognizing the real and conflicted possibilities of self. Luke tells us that it is the tax collector who, recognizing his limitations, is the one that goes home justified. The parable leads

---

4. For example, vocation smooths over the dislocation felt when individuals are forced by circumstance to change jobs. James, *Making a Living*, 81.

5. James, *Making a Living*, 82.

us toward family and neighborhood, where subjectivity might be worked out continually amid the vicissitudes of life.

Terry Eagleton's study *Trouble with Strangers* is useful in providing further definition to this juxtaposition of Pharisee and tax collector, and to the connection between subjectivity and vocation. Eagleton employs Lacan's three psychoanalytic registers, the *imaginary*, *symbolic*, and *real*, to encompass differing approaches to ethics and the "losses and gains" of each.[6] Extending Eagleton's reading of Lacan, differing views of vocation could be suggested: an *imaginary* perspective that is absorbed with fictive representations of self, society, and world; a *symbolic* perspective, with a prominent view of social mores, responsibilities, and law; and a *realistic* view that encounters life without flinching from its real difficulties, distortions, and dramas. Luke's parable can be readily cast across these registers: the Pharisee's religious profile shaped by pious representation (*imaginary*); the Pharisee's ethical profile, or the ritual and legal systems shaping his behavior (*symbolic*); and the tax collector's contrition and humility (*real*).

The Pharisee's self-exaltation in the temple, cultivated through pious image and behavior, is a concern with separation rather than implication: "God, I thank you that I am not like other people: thieves, rogues, adulterers, or even like this tax collector. I fast twice a week; I give a tenth of all my income" (18:11–12). Here, subjectivity is registered through the projected image as an "tangible incarnation" of selfhood, with reference to Eagleton's reading of Lacan's *imaginary* register.[7] The Pharisee stakes out an identity before God and others through a narrative of vocational distinction and purity.[8]

This view of vocation is typical within the social sciences. For example, Wiergart and Blasi understand vocation as a view to "transcendental" meaning beyond the contingencies of everyday life and "in contrast to a job, [vocation] is in essence a call to be a self-as-good . . . putting the self on track toward some kind of self-fulfilment."[9] Through the lens of the imaginary, vocation projects a representation of self-beyond-self. Yet without recognizing the slippage between a broadcast identity of piety and the actuality underneath this image, the Pharisee remains living within an illusion, unable to conceive of an encounter with God whose solidarity begins in humility and brokenness.

6. Eagleton, *Trouble with Strangers*, 322.
7. Eagleton, *Trouble with Strangers*, 5.
8. Cf. Matt 6:5, "And whenever you pray, do not be like the hypocrites; for they love to stand and pray in the synagogues and at the street corners, so that they may be seen by others. Truly I tell you, they have received their reward."
9. Weigert and Blasi, "Vocation," 19.

Eagleton's critique of the imaginary register as a basis for ethics, and therefore vocation as responsibility, might be extended by a contemporary illustration. First, the Pharisee as someone who continually posts on social media. For the Pharisee blogger, a virtual identity is formed and sustained as representative of values, a visible extension or aestheticization of moral concerns. Because of the instantaneous nature of social media, the curated image appears relevant and on-the-pulse, engaged with sentimental immediacy.

In an era of social media and identity politics, there is a risk that online representations also become the definitive language of self-understanding. Posting to Facebook or LinkedIn, the Pharisee projects a representation of him or herself to be read by others. While the world is opened through new technology and access to media, these virtual domains readily become the primary medium through which social and political issues are engaged. While the emotion and concern of the Pharisee blogger might genuinely be provoked by political or social issues—conveyed with visceral anger, indignance, or sympathy—the body of the Pharisee remains inert: decisive action is delegated to virtual representation and human bodies distanced from the real resistances of living interaction.[10] As the blogger remains in the bedroom, the Pharisee remains in the temple. For vocation, the imaginary leaves no room for discovering ethical responsibilities beyond personal cultivation, or through the resistances of having a body and neighbors.

Ethical responses through an imaginary register are sentimental, in that those responses are demonstrated ostensibly, in the display of appropriate sentiments. For example, Facebook profiles give imaginary definition to an individual and their concerns through the causes they associate with and "Like." Here, an ethical response remains inseparable from the curated image. Eagleton's primary critique of an imaginary ethic is that it cannot recognize those outside of the immediacy of our experience, "the nameless hoards languishing in the outer darkness."[11] Sentiment alone cannot generate a code of ethics that encompasses those who we feel no immediate empathy for, let alone those who elicit revulsion rather than endearment. This has significant implications for the poor, marginalized, and vulnerable.

> Morality is too vital a question to be left to the capricious bigheartedness of those who can afford to be affable. The vulnerable

---

10. Philosopher Slavoj Žižek follows a similar argument: "Are we not more and more monadic in this sense, with no direct windows onto reality, interacting alone with the PC screen, encountering only virtual simulacra, and yet immersed more than ever in a global network, synchronously communicating with the entire world?" Žižek, "Theologico-Political Suspension," 35.

11. Eagleton, *Trouble with Strangers*, 57.

need a material bond or code of obligations to cover their back. A rule-bound ethics may seem less agreeable than a genial impulse, but its point is that you should behave humanely to others whatever you happen to be feeling.[12]

Through the imaginary register, vocation is an aestheticized curation. In considering possibilities for life, work, and relationships, this individual is unable to attend beyond the broadcast image, to those strange individuals and approaches to life beyond the orbit of sentimental concerns.

A view beyond the imaginary register can be seen in Eagleton's symbolic ethic, which entails an awareness of our responsibilities toward others, attuned through law, ritual, and custom. A symbolic ethic is expressed linguistically, through the interactions of signs that constitute ethical codes and cultural traditions, providing a reference for human behavior beyond the variable inclinations of individual perspective.

The symbolic world is "mediated through and through by the signifier,"[13] and the subject located within these symbolic interactions. That is, meaning is created by the relationships between different things, just as meaning in language emerges through the distinction of linguistic signs. Within the symbolic register, the differences between individual subjects are framed positively:

> The subject must be weaned from mistaking itself for an autonomous entity and come instead to confess its dependence upon others in the domain of the intersubjective . . . . Only when one ventures upon the intersubjective exchanges of the symbolic order can one become conscious of oneself as an individual.[14]

This symbolic exile from the "spurious immediacy of the imaginary"[15] is mediated through language and "the great stockpile or repository of codes, rules, and signifiers"[16] which we draw on to make meaning, to think, and to communicate. This symbolic world opens possibilities for ethical formulation. Principles of human rights or social contract, for example, are generalized from concrete situations and experiences (for example, the formation of the United Nations and approaches to human rights following World War II) to guide behavior toward those beyond the felt immediacy of empathetic

---

12. Eagleton, *Trouble with Strangers*, 24.
13. Eagleton, *Trouble with Strangers*, 85.
14. Eagleton, *Trouble with Strangers*, 7.
15. Eagleton, *Trouble with Strangers*, 85.
16. Eagleton, *Trouble with Strangers*, 85.

identification, clarifying our relational interdependencies. On this view, subjectivity and vocation are defined through our responsibilities to others.

For the Pharisee, engagement with God and neighbor is structured through religious law. The law prods the Pharisee toward humility and justice, structuring behavior through tithing, fasting, and regular prayer. To read the Pharisee as a character type in this sense is not unusual within Christian tradition or theology. For Bonhoeffer, the Pharisee is anyone who, in any time, lives by their perception of "disunion," in which the fractured self is continually caught between possibilities for good or evil.[17] The law, as a response to our awareness of disunion—given because of transgressions (Galatians 3:19)—goads the Pharisee toward humility and justice. For Eagleton, the symbolic world of law and responsibility engages the subject with a world beyond the naive immediacy of self-concern and cultivation, from which they are exiled by a recognition of the other. This is somewhat akin to Giordan's view of vocation that gives "existence a framework of significance," as a sense of vocational responsibility within society might entail.[18] Similarly, for Weigert and Blasi, "A vocation will be a particular pattern in which individuals are related to the other people around them."[19] For these sociologists, different religions simply fill out these patterns of interaction with "varying traditional content."[20]

Vocation is regularly framed through forms of duty and pattern, and the stratification of roles and responsibilities within society. Yet while competency and discipline are shaped by law and tradition, this view loses something of the creative dimension of a God who *calls to be things that are not* (Romans 4:17), beyond the scope of law and tradition. As religious (or vocational) ritual and law readily circumscribe eventualities and diminish creativity, emphasizing pattern over person, the Pharisee encounters a God of citation and contractual fulfillment. The possibilities of subjectivity through this symbolic register are constrained.

Akin to contemporary understandings of vocation, the Pharisee's vocation is defined by outward forms, typified through imaginary representations and symbolic interactions, piety, and law. Standing by himself to pray, the Pharisee exudes self-cultivated differentiation, buffered from everyday entanglements of human experience.

---

17. Bonhoeffer, *Ethics*, 151.
18. Giordan, "Introduction," 7.
19. Weigert and Blasi, "Vocation," 15.
20. Weigert and Blasi, "Vocation," 15.

## Encountering the Real

> The human body is not just inscribed with meaning; unlike garden gnomes, it is also the source of it.[21]

The tax collector's understanding of himself before God begins in an encounter with his fragile, compromised body. He "would not even look up to heaven but was beating his breast and saying, 'God, be merciful to me, a sinner!'" (Luke 18:13). The tax collector's trajectory in life—his identity, activity, and relationality—are given renewed impetus by this vocative cry. Here, vocation is not conceived as pious self-cultivation or a pattern of behavior, but as an event. In crying to God, the tax collector's desire for integral relationships and meaningful activity are given voice, expressed in his openness to possibilities for life beyond his own innate resources.

With a similar focus on human compromise, Eagleton's writing refocuses toward what is common to all humans: the fragility and limitation of our human bodies, which are not just inscribed with meaning but are also the source of it. For Eagleton, this is significant in an era when "culturalism" is a dominant ideology.[22] Culturalism is a view of culture as the basic force or dynamic defining human life and relationships, shaping everything we do, say, and think, including the way we perceive and understand the world. As cultural, everything is endlessly malleable: bodies, beliefs, and identities are changeable because they are things created by us. Culturalism can also be understood more simply as prioritising the cultural. For example, in discussing ethics, there can be a tendency to talk of gender pronouns and video games, rather than hunger, poverty, and war.[23] Therefore, culturalism could be typified by an obsession with the signifier, the language games that we play and the identities that shape us.

Within this scene, the limitations of the human body could be experienced as disruptive to our projects of self-curation. Our bodies confront us as they impose real resistances and limitations on our aspirations. For Eagleton, this is not finally negative: "The body is the most palpable sign we have of the givenness of human existence."[24] Rather than diminishing human purpose and imagination, our bodies give us our characteristic mode of being in the world, an inherent language of meaning and possibility, and a tangible grounding to our ethical and political projects.

---

21. Eagleton, *Materialism*, 50.
22. See Eagleton, *Illusions*, 71–74.
23. Eagleton, *Illusions*, 71.
24. Eagleton, *After Theory*, 166.

The tax collector's cry to God resembles Eagleton's understanding of Lacan's *real* as a register of human experience, as well as his critique of culturalism. For the human subject, the real is an eventful recognition that "what is most permanently awry with us" is "most truly of our essence." "Consciousness," Eagleton explains, "itself is a structure of misrecognition."[25] Through the lens of the *real*, far from offsetting fragmentation and anxiety, we recognize that the self-woven narratives of those who trust in themselves are illusory.

Luke's parable gives dramatic expression to this ironic short circuit or subjective misrecognition, in the contrast between tax collector and Pharisee. The Pharisee observes religious law and ritual as a language for encountering God, evident in the tangible structures and comportment of Israel, yet he remains aloof from his neighbor, ultimately constrained by the symbolic limits of the law and regressing from responsibility to self-ingratiation. In contrast, the tax collector would not even look up to heaven but experiences a tearing between self and God, a split between religious and ethical pretence, and compromised reality. Presumably, it was neither pious observance nor religious law that led to his passionate moment of self-alienation. God is here encountered in the limitations of the body, and the denial of religious mitigation and comfort. His body is revealed as flesh like every other, a "stain of senseless material contingency which the symbolic order can never fully assimilate."[26]

The tax collector encounters God through his fractured self-understanding; vocation is not a construed identity or narrative myth that creates meaning out of fragmented existence. If vocation is concerned with human purpose and fulfillment, how might a potentially terrifying encounter such as this have redemptive potential? What is to stop an individual sliding into endlessly compounding anxiety, succumbing to the inadequacies of human experience and aspiration? If Christianity is true, supposes Eagleton, then it is precisely in the material word as "the sole locus of redemption"[27] that the love of God might be encountered "as a radical solution to the terrors of the Real" and, by extension, the endless and nihilistic profusion of self-alienation.[28] "It is on this material foundation [of the human body] that the most durable forms of human solidarity can be built," as it is through the risen, transfigured body of Christ that "material stuff is at one with its meaning."[29]

---

25. Eagleton, *Trouble with Strangers*, 10.
26. Eagleton, *Trouble with Strangers*, 146.
27. Eagleton, *Trouble with Strangers*, 292–93.
28. Eagleton, *Trouble with Strangers*, 323–24.
29. Eagleton, *Materialism*, 152; also 24.

Likewise, the tax collector recognizes that the possibility of encountering a God who is real—with real implications for life—begins with our fractured, material bodies, rather than through the construed identities or cultural behaviors, or the outward forms of vocation.

Importantly for biblical witness, the recognition of a common *fault* at the core of human subjectivity is not finally negative. While we are constrained by material limitations, human experience is not simply finite and contingent. For Eagleton, this is the meaning of the traditional Christian formulation *felix culpa* or *happy fault*.[30] Similarly influenced by Lacan, Alenka Zupančič writes of our "failed finitude," a non-correspondence with ourselves which is also the basis of human possibility.[31] These views resonate with Paul, whose passionate pursuit of righteousness begins with the fault line between *the good I would do but do not do* (Romans 7:19).

In his cry for dignity and renewal beyond any innate human capacity, the tax collector's vocative word to God has an obverse aspect: this cry to God also constitutes a call from beyond himself. Subjectivity is encountered in God's address from without, rather than being construed from within—from that word of *krisis* (judgment) which confronts *those who trust in themselves*. For Eagleton, this is a revolutionary meeting with the real, which "throws us out of joint, re-totalises our world and violently recasts the foundations of our existence,"[32] and is nothing short of a dramatic reorientation within life as a new creation.

## Embodied Vocation

While the Pharisee's God is framed by religious identities and behaviors, the God of the tax collector is encountered amid the real difficulties, distortions, and dramas of life. Appropriately, the tax collector does not stay in the temple but goes home, where God's possibilities for life might unfold within concrete community and locality (Luke 18:14). His home is no idealized sphere of imaginary resolution but a place of continued resistance and disruption, in the everyday tensions and joys of human relationality.

The radical possibility of Luke's parable lies in the humility and vulnerability of shared human bodies. In confronting the limitations and compromises of present experience, the parable neither endorses the revolutionary

---

30. Eagleton, *Trouble with Strangers*, 84–86.

31. Zupančič writes, "Our finitude is always-already a *failed finitude*—one could say a finitude with a leak in it . . . . Not only are we not infinite, we are not even finite." Zupančič, *Odd One In*, 52–53.

32. Eagleton, *Trouble with Strangers*, 298.

overthrow of government or tradition, nor the institution of a new symbolic ideal to replace what is already present. The ethical profiles of the imaginary and symbolic, represented by the Pharisee and temple, are not overthrown but implicitly unsettled—identity and law are necessarily interwoven into human life. Rather than tearing the temple to the ground, the tax collector goes home in a state of self-estrangement.

Luke's parable shifts the hearer's horizon from the potentially endless flux of systems, institutions, and ideologies, to the human body as it is enmeshed in its relations to neighbors and community. This is open-ended, as possibilities for human life and dignity are encountered amid the contingencies of life. Self-estrangement is exacerbated in the endless disruptions and tensions of living as a body which is never self-sufficient, and experienced in the resistances of relationships, the indifference of chores, the ceaseless mechanics of daily sustenance and work, conflicts with family and neighbors, and the negotiated aspirations of vocation. The contingences of life continually scuttle our projects of self-definition and those of the cultures and societies we inhabit, and yet it is amid life's vicissitudes that meaning and identity are discovered. This is something that has been all too apparent as I write this chapter at home with a fourteen-week-old baby.

Considering the identity and self-awareness of Paul's new community of Christian believers in the early church, Julia Kristeva suggests that self-estrangement might come to be experienced as transition or transmutation into a "new creation."[33] Kristeva understands Paul's *ecclesia*—which derives from the Greek *kaleo*, "I call," therefore a gathering called in a public place—as "apposed to the community of citizens in the polis a community that was other: a community of those who were different, of foreigners." These foreigners were those outside the Greco-Roman citadel, the nationalism of Jewish communities, and the regionalism of Eastern worship (see Ephesians 2:11–13 and 2:19–20), and included those who were marginalized, like merchants, sailors, and women, whom Paul often praises in his letters.[34]

Citing John 17:5, the reference point for Kristeva's understanding of Paul's community of foreigners is Jesus as "stranger on this earth."[35] This notion might be extended: Jesus is a stranger on this earth because of the common, fragile body he possessed, a stranger like any other. Such a move would avoid the dangers of reducing the difference of the Christian community to one of identity politics and distinctions of culture, ethnicity, gender, and sexuality as the foundation of communities of distinction. Thus,

---

33. Kristeva, *Strangers to Ourselves*, 82.
34. Kristeva, *Strangers to Ourselves*, 78–80.
35. Kristeva, *Strangers to Ourselves*, 83.

Kristeva's description of the early church as foreigners emboldened in their difference to culture and empire might be properly heard through a christological focus on the common body of Christ.

In his common body, the tax collector becomes a stranger to himself, rather than forming an identity of strangeness in relation to others. Instead of locating his identity, purpose, and dignity in postulations of culture, ethnicity, gender, and sexuality, his horizon is opened to the discovery of meaning in tangible expressions such as work, health, education, security, and freedom—things that have to do with the human body in its common needs and aspirations. In the universal body as the foundation of Christian ethics, there is neither Jew or Greek, but the dignifying gift of life that overwrites any tribal or religious boundary.

For sociologists like James, a key question has been "the difficulty of making a life meaningful, in an era when many of the old certainties have faded and traditional constraints are less binding."[36] Where certainties are sought, one temptation is to replace God with individuals who *trust in themselves* and the vocation narratives they conjure.[37] In contrast, Christian faith does not shy away from the real, compromised nature of human subjectivity which belongs to us all.

Both Luke's and Eagleton's concern for meaning within human experience begins with our common, fragile bodies as the characteristic mode of our being. While our bodily existence is limited to situated perspectives and conditioned by finitude and fallibility, these limitations are foundational to relationality, responsibility, and the pursuit of human dignity. Living among neighbors, the demands of others press in to define our understanding of self and vocation.

Because Eagleton understands Christian faith as a materialist practice—beginning with a fleshy, personal God[38]—it is unsurprising that he finds in it an ironic critique of any project of cultural, religious, or political identity.[39] Human meaning is, for Eagleton, something that begins with the sheer givenness of existence. Authentic human experience and relationality are located amid the contingencies of given materiality, and not in moralism, legalism, or idealism. For Luke, authentic human experience begins in the loss of self-assuredness and an honest encounter with God through the confronting or perplexing contingences of life. Without

---

36. James, *Making a Living*, 2.

37. A similar argument is traced throughout Terry Eagleton's *Culture and the Death of God*.

38. Eagleton, *Culture*, 33; *Materialism*, 48.

39. Eagleton, *Culture*, 207.

succumbing to false certainties or comforts, transformed life begins in the gift of our fragile, human bodies. This view of subjectivity and vocation is decidedly christological.

## Bibliography

Bonhoeffer, Dietrich. *Ethics*. Translated by Eberhard Bethge. London and Beccles, Suffolk: William Clowes and Sons, 1955.
Dawson, Jane. "A History of Vocation: Tracing A Keyword of Work, Meaning and Moral Purpose." *Adult Education Quarterly* 55, no. 3 (2005) 220–31.
Eagleton, Terry. *After Theory*. London: Penguin, 2004.
———. *Culture and the Death of God*. New Haven and London: Yale University Press, 2014.
———. *The Illusions of Postmodernism*. Maldan, MA: Blackwell, 1996.
———. *Materialism*. New Haven and London: Yale University Press, 2016.
———. *Trouble with Strangers: A Study of Ethics*. Chichester, UK: Wiley-Blackwell, 2009.
Giordan, Giuseppe, ed. "Introduction." In *Vocation and Social Context*. Leiden and Boston: Brill, 2007.
James, Sara. "Finding Your Passion: Work and the Authentic Self." *M/C Journal* 18, no. 1 (2015). http://journal.media-culture.org.au/index.php/mcjournal/article/view/954.
———. *Making a Living, Making a Life: Work, Meaning and Self-identity*. Abingdon: Routledge, 2018.
Kristeva, Julia. *Strangers to Ourselves*. Translated by Leon S. Roudiez. New York: Colombia University Press, 1991.
Stackhouse, Max L. "Vocation." In *The Oxford Handbook of Theological Ethics*, edited by Gilbert Meilaender and William Werpehowski. Oxford Handbooks Online, 2009. https://dx.doi.org/10.1093/oxfordhb/9780199227228.003.0012.
Weigert, Andrew J., and Anthony J. Blasi. "Vocation." In *Vocation and Social Context*, edited by Giuseppe Giordan, 13–34. Leiden and Boston: Brill, 2007.
Žižek, Slavoj. "For a Theologico-Political Suspension of the Ethical." In *God in Pain: Inversions of Apocalypse*, edited by Slavoj Žižek and Boris Gunjević. Translated by Ellen Elias-Bursac. New York: Seven Stories, 2012.
Zupančič, Alenka. *The Odd One In: On Comedy*. Cambridge, MA: Massachusetts Institute of Technology, 2008.

# 14

## Theology of Work
### *Eschatology, Co-Creativity, and the Pneumatological Impetus*

MARGUERITE KAPPELHOFF

*University of Divinity*

### Abstract

IN HIS 2001 MONOGRAPH *Work in the Spirit: Toward a Theology of Work*, Miroslav Volf helpfully draws together the doctrines of pneumatology and eschatology to reimagine "work" from a fresh perspective. Shedding traditional views with limiting concepts in relation to vocation and the Holy Spirit, Volf reimagines the scope of work set against an eschatological backdrop that allows not only for a lasting significance of human work, but also that "work" is to be understood as "cooperation with God" for the purpose of world preservation and ultimate transformation. Volf provides a solid foundation for the understanding of *transformatio mundi*, but it is the theme of "cooperation with God" or "co-creativity" with which this chapter engages more fully; specifically, how "co-creativity" across an eschatological backdrop is to be considered in light of the dynamic work of the Holy Spirit with the human agent. Drawing from Volf's understanding of Christ as *eschatological*, the Father as *protological*, and the Holy Spirit as *pneumatological*, this chapter will seek to consider how "we" as humans are the "work" as "we work" through our work.

## Introduction

In his 1991 monograph *Work in the Spirit: Toward a Theology of Work*, Miroslav Volf helpfully draws together the doctrines of pneumatology and eschatology to reimagine "work" from a fresh perspective.[1] Shedding traditional views with limiting concepts in relation to vocation and the Holy Spirit, Volf reimagines the scope of work set against an eschatological backdrop that allows not only for the lasting significance of human work, but an understanding of work as "cooperation with God" for the purpose of world preservation and ultimate transformation. It is a fresh perspective with a clear view that the current work of humanity, as influenced by the Holy Spirit and set against the eschatological backdrop, highlights the possibilities of co-creativity (or "cooperation with God") in the "new creation." This is *transformatio mundi*. It is this theme of "cooperation with God" or "co-creativity" with which this chapter will engage, paying particular attention to the dynamic work of the Holy Spirit with the human agent. Drawing from Volf's understanding of the Father as *protological*, the Holy Spirit as *pneumatological*, and Christ as *eschatological*, this chapter will more fully consider how "we" are the "work" as "we work"—specifically, how to understand "co-creativity" across an eschatological backdrop.

In what follows, I will offer a discussion on *transformatio mundi* as understood in light of the new creation, highlighting Volf's premise of the importance of human work and its inherent value. This places Volf's discussion on protological/pneumatological/eschatological as the foundation for discussing how human work, as co-creativity, can be understood not simply as an "end product" within the here and now, but as a "work that remains" as part of the new creation. It is from this point that the discussion branches off from Volf's work, extending the conversation to consider the role of charisms as part of the co-creativity that contains both a here and now perspective and eschatological significance. To be sure, Volf does base his theology of work on a solid understanding of charisms as integral to the scope of human work; the key departure in this chapter is in understanding the eschatological significance in the development of the charisms themselves. Essentially, I ask how the cultivation of the "gifts" of the Spirit by the human agent in and through their work can be understood within a

---

1. Volf, *Work in the Spirit*, 9–10.

protological/pneumatological/eschatological framework as co-creativity.² I conclude that there exists a *plēroma* through which the "gifts" of the Spirit can be developed as the human agent engages as co-creator and that this expanse should be explored as a biblical imperative for present outworking implications and eschatological significance.

## Father as Protological, Holy Spirit as Pneumatological, and Christ as Eschatological

Volf lays a foundation for a theology of work in part by drawing on the concepts of the Father as *protological*, the Holy Spirit as *pneumatological*, and Christ as *eschatological*.

In this way the "ultimate significance of work" can be discussed by questioning the "continuity or discontinuity between the present and the eschatological orders" and by "arguing in favour of understanding work as cooperation with God."³ The understanding within this framework is that it is the protological Father who initiates/creates, the pneumatological Spirit who empowers/leads/gifts, and the eschatological Christ who reveals redemption as the exemplar of new things.⁴ As with the initiation of creation, the final consummation of the new heavens and the new earth is always retained as a work solely attributed to God. To that end, Volf argues that "through the Spirit God is already working in history, using human actions to create provisional states of affairs that anticipate the new creation in a real way."⁵ That being said, the work of the human can only ever be understood as one of "co-creator" who builds on what has already been initiated. Larive explains,

> The cocreator's job can be divided into two aspects: *maintenance* of the cultural stock that has gone before, and *creativity* acting on the cutting edge of that stock. These aspects harmonize with the *protological* and *eschatological* aspects of the Trinity. The third aspect, the *pneumatological*, is concerned with how the created cocreator is equipped for the role he or she plays in creation.⁶

---

2. "Gifts" are here understood in line with 1 Corinthians 12, Ephesians 4, Romans 12, etc. For more on this see Preece, *Vocation Tradition*.

3. Volf, *Work in the* Spirit, 74.

4. I have borrowed this phrase "exemplar of new things" from Larive, *After Sunday*, 85, in which he apart from this phrase also refers to Christ as the "eschatological exemplar and promise of new things."

5. Volf, *Work in the Spirit*, 100.

6. Larive, *After Sunday*, 74. Emphasis retained.

In Volf's theology, the equipping for the role comes via the Holy Spirit given that any discussion about the new creation must include the "spirit of God" who is the "firstfruits" of the "future salvation," and the "present power of eschatological transformation," and the only mediator "through which the future new creation is anticipated in the present."[7] Therefore, not only does the work of the human agent have intrinsic value within the here and now context, it can further be understood as being a work that remains as part of the new creation.

## *Transformatio Mundi* and the New Creation

Foundational in Volf's theology of work is understanding the opposing eschatological models of *annihilatio mundi* and *transformatio mundi*. The former suggests that the current world will be completely annihilated before the coming of the new creation, which will happen *ex nihilo*. In contrast to this, the second model suggests that this present world will not end but will be transformed into the new creation via *creatio continua*. Volf has a distinct preference for *transformatio mundi*, as it is the only eschatological model that supports his conviction of the inherent value of human work and of its ability to serve as contributing in the new creation. In his thinking, annihilation is "theologically inconsistent" because "the expectation of the eschatological destruction of the world is not consonant with the belief in the goodness of creation" in which "what God will annihilate must be either so bad that it is not possible to be redeemed or so insignificant that it is not worth being redeemed."[8] Therefore, *transformatio mundi* is the logically consistent concept that does not have the world ending in "apocalyptic destruction but in eschatological transformation."[9] In this way, "the cumulative work of human beings have intrinsic value and gain ultimate significance, for they are related to the eschatological new creation."[10] Via *creatio continua*, a continuity can be guaranteed that ensures "that no noble effort will be wasted" but "rather, after being purified in the eschatological *transformatio mundi*, they will be integrated by an act of divine transformation into the new heaven and the new earth."[11] Therefore, according to Volf,

---

7. Volf, *Work in the Spirit*, 102.
8. Volf, *Work in the Spirit*, 90.
9. Volf, *Work in the Spirit*, 91.
10. Volf, *Work in the Spirit*, 91.
11. Volf, *Work in the Spirit*, 92.

The first and most basic feature of a theology of work based on the concept of new creation is that it is a *Christian* theology of work. It is developed on the basis of a specifically Christian soteriology and eschatology, essential to which is the anticipatory experience of God's new creation and a hope of its future consummation.[12]

It is within this new creation that all of God's purposes will come to an end, and therefore "a theological interpretation of work is valid only if it facilitates transformation of work toward ever-greater correspondence with the coming new creation."[13] As such, in light of this eschatological continuity, "the new creation is not simply a negation of the first creation but is also its reaffirmation" in which human co-creativity has been engaged, specifically through a pneumatological impetus.[14] This aspect of Volf's premise, that human work is done through life in the Spirit anticipating the new creation, offers a dynamic perspective on the continuing creative activity of the Triune God and God's desire to engage with the human agent towards this end. It is a distinctive pneumatological theology of work set within an eschatological framework that stresses the role of *charisma*. Further, it understands that it is through the Holy Spirit that the human agent can engage with their unique gifts,[15] along with skills, talents, and abilities, to produce work that will ultimately contribute to the new creation.[16]

## Charisms and Their Expanse

For Volf, cooperation with God through the presence and activity of the Spirit should encapsulate every aspect of a Christian's life. In relation to work particularly, he suggests that as Christians perform their "mundane work," it is the Spirit who empowers them to "cooperate with God in a manner that completes creation and renews heaven and earth."[17] The emphasis is not simply on an obedience to the call of God or in the service to others here on earth, but rather that human work itself has inherent value and can

---

12. Volf, *Work in the Spirit*, 79. Emphasis retained.
13. Volf, *Work in the Spirit*, 83.
14. Volf, *Work in the Spirit*, 101.
15. Going forward, each time the word "gifts" is used in this manner, "skills, talents, and abilities" are also implied.
16. Volf emphatically states that the main point of his book is "to call for a pneumatological theology of work based on the concept of charisma." Volf, *Work in the Spirit*, viii.
17. Volf, *Work in the Spirit*, 115.

be identified as a cocreative cooperation with God in the anticipated *transformatio mundi*. This work that "remains" is not done by human effort alone but rather through additional cooperation with the Holy Spirit by engaging in unique charisms. Volf outlines,

> When God calls people to become children of God, the Spirit gives them callings, talents, and "enablings" (charisms) so that they can do God's will in the Christian fellowship and in the world in anticipation of God's eschatological new creation.[18]

Volf makes a distinction between the "fruit" and "gifts" of the Spirit, indicating that the fruit of the Spirit "designates the general character of Christian existence" whereas the gifts of the Spirit "are related to the specific tasks or functions to which God calls and fits each Christian."[19]

To be sure, Volf's view supports Scripture and understands that the Holy Spirit gives gifts to each individual as he wills (1 Corinthians 12:11) and that the giving of these gifts is "mediated through each person's social interrelations and psychosomatic constitution."[20] That being said, these mediated gifts are not limited by any human or social construct constraints since it is the Spirit of the "crucified and resurrected Christ, the firstfruits of the new creation" who is giving them.[21] In other words, the gifts themselves can be understood as having a dynamic and eschatological structure to them. This reveals a past/present/future understanding through which current human work can be viewed, but further provides a framework through which the "changing" nature of the human agent can be understood.

Any historical development in the theology of work has always contained some level of understanding that the human agent is "changed" through their work (i.e. that there is some form of "sanctification") and that through their work the communities in which they perform this work can also be changed.[22] This understanding of the changing nature of the human agent aligns with an understanding of the doctrine of salvation, which includes justification, sanctification, and ultimately, glorification. Scripture reveals this past/present/future framework referring to Christians as those who are saved, are being saved, and who shall be saved: that Christians

---

18. Volf, *Work in the Spirit*, 124. Volf advocates the work of the Holy Spirit as work in the new creation by citing briefly three Scripture passages: Romans 8:23, 2 Corinthians 1:22, and Matthew 12:28.

19. Volf, *Work in the Spirit*, 111.

20. Volf, *Work in the Spirit*, 115.

21. Volf, *Work in the Spirit*, 115.

22. For more on the historical development of the theology of work see Griesinger, "Theology of Work," 291–304; or Mackenzie, "Faith and Work," 145–62.

are in a constant state of *being* and *becoming*. For instance, Philippians 1:6 reads: "being confident of this, that he who began a good work in you will carry it on to completion until the day of Christ Jesus."[23] Taking this past/present/future framework alongside Volf's understanding of the Triune God within a protological/pneumatological/eschatological framework presents a lens through which the appropriation by the persons of the Trinity can further be identified and considered. Within this framework it is understood that as initiated by the protological Father, humanity is created in the image of God, designed for an eschatological future, redeemed and reconciled via the Son, and conformed to the image of Christ via empowerment by the Holy Spirit. Going further and in relation to the development of the charisms, there presents a dual-framework in operation outlining the Christian journey: who a Christian is within the here and now compared to who they will become in the future must solicit a change in behavior, thought, and deed. Held together in tension, this eschatological reality embraces the here and now perspective. It allows for the dynamic relationship between the Holy Spirit and the human agent to be further revealed and identifies a Christian's engagement with the dynamic Holy Spirit who will empower, lead, guide, and open up a breadth of possibilities in the development of any of the charisms/gifts. Larive writes,

> New creation's requirement to emerge from what was already there presupposes two pre-existing theological conditions: an original creation *ex nihilo*, requiring nothing precedes it except the Uncreated Creator, and, once that is done, a continuing maintenance of a creation that is in flux. It requires also some discarding of what becomes obsolete, undesirable or harmful. This function depends on God as the original Creator and continuing Maintainer, the acts of *ex nihilo* and *creatio continua* respectively, whose functions are foundational and protological but intertwined with the doing of new things . . . .[24]

Creation (whether *ex nihilo* or *continua*) must be "protological because it sets the boundary conditions for creativity," and ensures that any engagement as co-creative agents can never surpass the limits of what God has already envisioned.[25] This understanding is presented in Ephesians 2:10 where it states that "we are God's handiwork, created in Christ Jesus to do good works, which God prepared in advance for us to do."[26] Consideration of

23. *The Holy Bible, New International Version.*
24. Larive, *After Sunday*, 88.
25. Larive, *After Sunday*, 100–101.
26. *The Holy Bible, New International Version.*

this verse in light of the present discussion immediately raises the question: What has God, the protological Creator, already "envisioned" to be included in those "good works"? Remembering that the protological action of Creator God carries within it an "unlimited" possibility of those works as understood and viewed through the concept of *plēroma*.[27]

Larive, in his work *After Sunday*, theologically engages the concept of *plēroma* by understanding God as the "householder" who in caring for his *oikos* (household) does so from a position of fullness that is understood in contradistinction to scarcity.[28] Larive determines that scarcity is a social construct driven by a capitalist system and a market economy whereby success is to consume and maximize.[29] By distinction, *plēroma* is a "timeless truth" set outside such constraints.[30] The act of creation and creation itself testifies to the *plēroma* of God who has created in vastness and abundance rather than in scarcity. Further, that it is within this *plēroma* that the dynamic interaction between the Triune God and the human agent can additionally be understood. Most specifically for the purposes of this chapter, a *plēroma* can be evidenced in the relationship between the pneumatological Holy Spirit and the human agent, with whom the Holy Spirit engages dynamically throughout the Christian journey as they are drawn towards the *eschaton* of the new creation. I argue that this engagement is not simply for the purposes of sanctification, nor for the purposes—as understood in Volf's theology—of work of *transformatio mundi*, but also in relation to the development of the charisms as undertaken by the human agent in and through their everyday work and that this carries an eschatological significance.

Circling back to the foundational starting point of a theology of work, Larive further develops the concept of *plēroma* in light of "good and godly work" by asking this question: What is it that others have that one can also have that is not subject to laws of scarcity?[31] He suggests that the answer is found in considering the "skills and virtues" that are required and developed within daily life and work and that they are "internally related to the results they produce such that means and ends cannot be disconnected."[32] In other words, *how* a person works and *who* a person is while working

---

27. *Plēroma* is defined as "fullness," "filling," "fulfillment," "completion." "Pleroma," *Strong's Concordance*, 4138.

28. Larive, *After Sunday*, 140.

29. Larive, *After Sunday*, 140, 141.

30. Larive, *After Sunday*, 140.

31. Larive, *After Sunday*, 141. Larive understands "good and godly work" to be work that is done based upon skills and the virtues that have been infused with an "overarching power for moral goodness" (142).

32. Larive, *After Sunday*, 141.

directly impacts the end result of their work. He further argues that because skills and virtues are "internally related," they are therefore "not subject to scarcity" as understood within a capitalist system and that "to possess a virtue or a skill does not mean that there is one less on the market."[33] He concludes that good and godly work will be "ennobled by a divine *plēroma* that breaks through ordinary barter and exchange," and therefore any further development of virtues and skills towards "promoting goodness" is to be advocated.[34]

Christians are not simply given gifts (along with skills, talents, and abilities) so that they can do God's will in and through their daily work for the purposes of the "new creation," as Volf suggests, but so that they can fulfill the promise of Ephesians 2:10 as they push towards the *plēroma* of the *eschaton*. In their co-creative cooperation with God and as they are drawn towards the *eschaton*, they are wrapped up in the dual process of sanctification and in the development towards the expanse of the *plēroma* of the gifts that they have been given. In this way, if human work as an end product can be viewed as co-creativity that will be a work that remains as part of the new creation, then it is logically consistent to suggest that the "means" to that end also becomes part of the new creation. Or more specifically, if "work" can be determined to be co-creativity, then the development of one's gifts, skills, and virtues should also be considered as part of the new creation. Drawing from Volf's already established premise, this is not too far a stretch and one that is a naturally intended consequence within his theology of work. Based upon this reasoning and logic, further implications and biblical imperatives can be drawn out.

## Final Comments: Implications and the Biblical Imperative

Any cultivation by the human agent of the Spirit-given "gifts" that take place in and through everyday mundane work should be viewed as co-creativity. While it is the Holy Spirit who gives "gifts" as he determines, there continues to be a dynamic relationship between the Holy Spirit and the human agent in relation to those gifts that goes beyond the purposes of sanctification as deemed necessary for the making of a "holy" life. Instead, as understood against an eschatological backdrop and within the frame of the protological Creator, there exists a *plēroma* through which the "gifts" of the Spirit can be developed as the human agent engages as co-creator. Drawing from the

---

33. Larive, *After Sunday*, 141.
34. Larive, *After Sunday*, 141, 142, 164.

concept of *plēroma*, and especially via the engagement of the human agent with the Holy Spirit, there remains the understanding that the potential development of those gifts is extensive. Further, and as understood within the context of work, the cultivation of those gifts has a direct influence on the type of worker/employer that will emerge and develop. Taking Volf's understanding of *transformatio mundi* into consideration ensures that this development of the individual gifts will also be brought into the new creation. This line of thinking suggests that the human agent as co-creator can influence others for both the here and now and future implications through their everyday work. Therefore, "how" a human goes about their work matters; indeed, how the human agent as co-creator uses their gifts and the level to which they develop those gifts carries a lasting significance.

Scriptural engagement suggests as such, entreating the development of one's gifts for the sake of the other. For example, Romans 12 encourages Christians to "offer their bodies as living sacrifices" and to "be transformed" given that "each member belongs to all the others."[35] While this passage exhorts Christians to use their gifts towards their intended purpose, I would further suggest that there is an understanding that these gifts be developed towards the fullness of their expansive properties. For example,

> If your gift is prophesying, then prophesy in accordance with your faith; if it is serving, then serve; if it is teaching, then teach; if it is to encourage, then give encouragement; if it is giving, then give generously; if it is to lead, do it diligently; if it is to show mercy, do it cheerfully.[36]

Along the same lines, and with specific intention towards Christians serving the body of Christ, Ephesians 4 expands:

> So Christ himself gave the apostles, the prophets, the evangelists, the pastors and teachers, to equip his people for works of service, so that the body of Christ may be built up until we all reach unity in the faith and in the knowledge of the Son of God and become mature, attaining to the whole measure of the fullness of Christ.[37]

In this instance, the roles given and opportunities for the development of those roles is set in the context of mutuality. It is an understanding that to meet the "shared needs" of others will require a "maturity" to be reached within the development of the roles listed. The expressed purpose of this is

---

35. Rom 12:1, 2, 5.
36. Rom 12:6–8.
37. Eph 4:11–13.

for the reaching of the "whole measure of the fullness of Christ." In other words, to become mature to the full measure can only be done by meeting the needs of others, which in and of itself offers an expansive *plēroma* to move in and toward, since the meeting of the needs of others is itself an extensive endeavor. Here again, we can identify the concepts of "working" for the "body of Christ" within an understanding of *plēroma* as set against an eschatological backdrop. The reminder of 1 Corinthians 12 is that just as "gifts" are given in diversity; it can be understood that it is the "same God" who distributes these gifts, albeit via the appropriation of the Holy Spirit. This means that the God of creation who has "prepared in advance" a *plēroma* of "good works" has envisioned within this preparation the allowance of the dynamic Holy Spirit to engage with the human agent, offering an expansive possibility and potential for the development of those gifts. Larive supports this thinking by suggesting that it is the "eschatological promise of Christ" that is "beckoning towards the doing of new things (new creation)."[38] Going a step further, he challenges the thinking by stating that

> an eschatological Christ is a *temporal* phenomenon, not restricted to eternity, coming into the context of human history, leading with the exemplification and promise of new things and new creation, things and creations open for humans to accomplish in their work. Jesus did not postpone this fulfilment until the end of time but demonstrated it every day during his life . . . these demonstrations form the basis of the proleptic promise of the Christ-event. They are nothing more than exhibitions of how breakthroughs, large and small, are possible in an evolving creation that can be "stretched" for doing new things.[39]

Therefore, the gifts of the Holy Spirit, such as in 1 Corinthians 12, Romans 12, and Ephesians 4, are not simply for a here and now engagement for the current community operating as the body of Christ but are also set against an eschatological backdrop. The gifts are not simply given for the purposes of human "work" that will lead to the new creation but can be further understood in terms of the Christian themselves as "being the work" that is continually renewed in the co-creation for the purposes of *transformatio mundi* and as the work that remains. As co-creators, humans do not create in isolation but in cooperation with God, understanding that human "creativity" is set in the context and bounds of God's creativity and not outside of it—and that what "might" be possible is only possible because the protological Father and Creator God has already conceived of it.

38. Larive, *After Sunday*, 76.
39. Larive, *After Sunday*, 76. Emphasis retained.

This co-creation is only possible through the empowerment and gifting of the dynamic Holy Spirit, who leads the human agent towards the eschatological promise of Christ in which all things will be made new. It is within this context that the human agent can engage in co-creativity through the use and development of the gifts that they have been given. In addition, there is rich potential as the human agent, set against an eschatological backdrop and in dynamic relationship with the pneumological Holy Spirit, exercises their gifts: in and through their everyday work, a person can discover more of who they are via those gifts and who they will have the potential of becoming. Finally, it is only through their use that any person can discover the *plēroma* of the gifts for the here and now alongside the eschatological reality. As individual Christians work toward developing the gifts they have been given, within and for the purposes of their daily work, they will further discover and develop the Christian worker/leader they can become as part and parcel of their cooperation with God as co-creator. In this way, cocreativity set against an eschatological backdrop reveals that "we" become the "work" as "we work."

## Bibliography

Griesinger, Donald W. "The Theology of Work and the Work of Christian Scholars." *Christian Scholar's Review* 39, no. 3 (Spring 2010) 291–304.
*The Holy Bible, New International Version*. Grand Rapids: Zondervan, 1984.
Larive, Armand. *After Sunday: A Theology of Work*. New York: Continuum, 2014.
Mackenzie, Alistair. "Faith and Work: From Jesus to the Reformation." In *Faith at Work*, edited by Don Mathieson, 145–62. Auckland: Castle, 2001.
Preece, Gordon. *The Viability of the Vocation Tradition in Trinitarian, Credal and Reformed Perspective: The Threefold Call*. New York: Edwin Mellen, 1998.
*Strong's Exhaustive Bible Concordance Online*. NAS Exhaustive Concordance of the Bible with Hebrew-Aramaic and Greek Dictionaries. La Habra, CA: Lockman Foundation, 1998. https://biblehub.com/strongs.htm.
Volf, Miroslav. *Work in the Spirit: Toward a Theology of Work*. Eugene, OR: Wipf and Stock, 2001.

# 15

## Conclusion

*Where to From Here?*

### Kara Martin

*Mary Andrews College and Alphacrucis College*

We anticipate that this volume is the beginning of a deeper conversation about all aspects of our work as Christians, and how we are equipped for that work.

It is a conversation that will necessarily incorporate the wider issues we are seeing in society—climate change, growing violence, mental health issues, mass migration and the refugee crisis, pandemics and escalating poverty, urbanization, unethical consumption, sexual abuse, identity confusion, religious liberty, and mistrust of anyone in authority—because these issues come up through our work and in our workplaces.

In the midst of this maelstrom is tremendous opportunity for the church to be more active and involved, through its members, representing Jesus in every vocation. A 2018 report by Barna Group[1] concluded that Christians who integrate their faith and work are more active in their church community and report better physical, emotional, mental, and social outcomes. They also enjoy their work more, and are less stressed.

So, what can we imagine for the future, in each domain and at their intersection?

1. Barna Group, "Christians at Work."

## Workplace

- Individual workplace Christians feeling equipped, affirmed, and supported by their churches as they look to bring a taste of the kingdom to their workplaces and transform their vocations

- The breakdown in dualistic thinking—the now infamous sacred–secular divide (SSD) —so that workplace Christians can clearly see how their work serves God, they find purpose and meaning in what they do, they look to make a difference through their work, and they can see that their faith enables them to mold the culture of their workplace[2]

- A proliferation of supportive resources: workday devotional emails, prayer cells in business hubs, access to ideas and books

- Principles of redemptive design understood, enabling entrepreneurs and small business operators to function with an understanding of how their working aligns with God's purposes.[3]

## Christian Organizations

- Christian organizations and Christian-owned businesses modelling the seven markers of Christian businesses:

    1. a sense of calling and purpose

    2. promoting personal intimacy with God

    3. reflecting God's character

    4. using their time and money to foster a life-giving culture

    5. wisely stewarding God's resources

    6. meeting the physical and spiritual needs of those around them (customers, clients, suppliers, and so on)

    7. measurable impact and disciplemaking.[4]

---

2. Barna Group, *Christians at Work*, 49. These are the dimensions they identify in the "Integrators" among workplace Christians.

3. Seed, " Make a Difference." This is the process Seed promotes through their incubator program and purpose discovery course. Seed is a Christian organization in Sydney, Australia. There are similar organizations and movements throughout the world, such as https://home.praxislabs.org/.

4. Mills, "7 Markers." This blog delineates the different elements needed for organizations to integrate faith and business in a practical way.

## Churches

- Churches proactive with the vocational power within their congregations, utilizing the expertise, platforms, networks, influence, positions, skills, and reputation of members of multiple congregations within local areas to bring about gospel renewal: fighting poverty, promoting creation care, creating opportunities for hospitality and community building, and inviting questions of meaning and purpose[5]

- Churches with a broader focus of mission, seeing themselves embedded in an area and cooperating with other churches to engage creatively with the particular needs and concerns in their area: refugees, places of poverty, vertical villages in the city, and alleviating drought stress in regional areas[6]

- Vocations in churches identified and the possibility of vocational mentoring across denominations. Perhaps there could be interest groups formed with a goal of deeply engaging the challenges and opportunities within particular vocations

- The popularity of networking between pastors who are expert in breaking down dualistic thinking and equipping workplace Christians[7]

- A central repository of sermons, program ideas, and resources[8]

- A move to intervene where there needs to be advocacy: on behalf of precarious workers, against unethical workplace practices, revealing the impact of business on the environment, highlighting bullying and harassment, modelling servant leadership, and so forth.

## Theology

- Theological colleges which both model and promote whole-life disciple making, having broken down the sacred–secular divide, and

---

5. Sherman, *Kingdom Calling*. Amy Sherman has identified these different elements of vocational discipleship which can be used as collateral by churches in reaching out to their communities.

6. An example would be Movement Day (https://movementday.com/). This organization catalyzes churches in geographical areas to make a united and coordinated response toward transforming their city/place.

7. An example resourcing the church is Made to Flourish, "a pastor's network for the common good," which operates in the US, and was founded by Pastor Tom Nelson.

8. A model is Faith Driven Entrepreneur, "Get Provisioned," collating books, podcasts, videos, and material for further learning.

encouraging every student to both discover and be affirmed in their calling
- An opportunity for vocational mentoring of every student in their final year, and an exploration of the difference the gospel makes to every vocation
- Each course unit considering vocational and workplace applications of material being learnt both in particular seminars and assessment tasks; and the opportunity for deeper consideration through field experience
- The colleges celebrating their workplace alumni alongside their denominational alumni as equally called and fulfilling the *missio Dei*
- Better linkages between college staff and lecturers so that the organization models the breakdown of dualistic and siloed thinking. There is an equal valuing of every role
- Deeper theological reflection on the nature of work, the nature of rest, the contribution of individual books of the Bible to an understanding of work, a theological overview, practical application, ethical issues, future trends, and so much more!

## Integration

For this to be happen, there needs to be a better understanding of the flows between these domains, lest we merely repeat today's dualism and silos at a macro level. In simplest terms, theological colleges educate pastors who run churches which equip workplace Christians to impact our society as they are fruitful on their frontlines. So, colleges which understand how to equip workplace Christians will be better able to prepare pastors for that role.

We also need better networking and resource exchange between churches, theological colleges, individual workplace Christians, and the different organizations active in the space:

- *Professional Christian organizations* such as the Christian Medical and Dental Fellowship of Australia, Nurses Christian Fellowship, and Lawyers Christian Fellowship
- *Parachurch workplace organizations* such as City Bible Forum, Kingdom Business, and Business as Mission
- *University Christian groups* preparing graduates for the workplace, such as International Fellowship of Evangelical Students, Cru/Power to Change, and Navigators

- *Christian vocational higher education providers* seeking to help their students integrate their faith into their other studies.

The most significant development would be a joyous recognition that we have done ourselves out of a job. Transforming Vocation Conferences and books will become redundant, as individuals, churches, and colleges live and breathe whole-life discipleship, and cannot imagine a different way to be and do life together. Now that's a vision for vocations transformed by God's Spirit in line with God's kingdom.

# Bibliography

Barna Group. "Christians at Work: Examining the Intersection of Calling and Career." Venture: Barna Group with Abilene Christian University, 2018. https://shop.barna.com/products/christians-at-work.

Faith Driven Entrepreneur. "Get Provisioned for the Journey." https://www.faithdrivenentrepreneur.org.

Made to Flourish. "Made to Flourish. A Pastors' Network for the Common Good." https://www.madetoflourish.org/.

Mills, Courtney Rountree. "7 Markers for a Kingdom Business: A Framework for Entrepreneurs." *Business as Mission*, January 23, 2020. https://businessasmission.com/7-markers-for-a-kingdom-business-a-framework-for-entrepreneurs-top-5/.

Movement Day. https://movementday.com/.

Seed. "Want to Make a Difference in Your Corner of the World?" https://www.seed.org.au/individual.

Sherman, Amy L., Reggie McNeal, and Steven Garber. *Kingdom Calling: Vocational Stewardship for the Common Good*. Downers Grove: IVP Books, 2011.

www.ingramcontent.com/pod-product-compliance
Lightning Source LLC
Chambersburg PA
CBHW050342230426
43663CB00010B/1961